Being Vegetarian For Dummies®

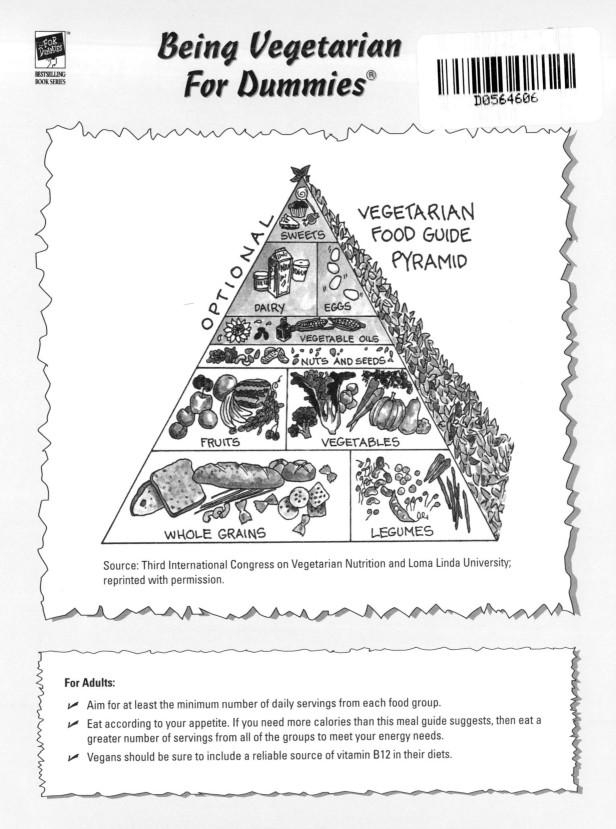

VEGETARIAN FOOD GUIDE PYRAMID

OPTIONAL

SWEETS

DAIRY — EGGS

VEGETABLE OILS

NUTS AND SEEDS

FRUITS — VEGETABLES

WHOLE GRAINS — LEGUMES

Source: Third International Congress on Vegetarian Nutrition and Loma Linda University; reprinted with permission.

For Adults:

- ✔ Aim for at least the minimum number of daily servings from each food group.
- ✔ Eat according to your appetite. If you need more calories than this meal guide suggests, then eat a greater number of servings from all of the groups to meet your energy needs.
- ✔ Vegans should be sure to include a reliable source of vitamin B12 in their diets.

For Dummies: Bestselling Book Series for Beginners

Being Vegetarian For Dummies®

Cheat Sheet

Description of Food Groups and Recommendations for Food Selection

Food Group	Examples of Food Items	Recommendations
Whole grains	Grains: wheat, corn, oats, rice, millet, etc. Grain products: bread, pasta, tortillas.	Select whole-wheat and whole-grain products.
Legumes	Beans and peas: soy, pinto, kidney, navy, limas, peas, lentils, garbanzos. Soy and soy products: tofu, soy drinks, texturized protein foods.	Select soy-based milk alternatives fortified with calcium, vitamin D, and vitamin B12.
Vegetables	All vegetables	Emphasize leafy, green and yellow vegetables. Eat both cooked and raw.
Fruits	All fruits	Emphasize whole fruits rather than juice.
Nuts and seeds	Nuts: almonds, walnuts, peanuts, etc. Seeds: pumpkin, squash, sunflower, etc. Butters: peanut, almond, sesame (tahini).	Eat raw, dry-roasted, or in foods rather than deep fried.
Vegetable oils	Plant oils: canola, corn, olive, etc.	Emphasize those high in monounsaturates such as olive, sesame, and canola. Limit tropical oils (coconut, palm kernel, palm oil). Avoid hydrogenated fats.
Milk and dairy	Milk, yogurt, cheese	Emphasize nonfat and low-fat products. If dairy is avoided, must ensure adequate, reliable sources of calcium and vitamin D.
Eggs		Limit eggs or use egg whites only.
Sweets	Honey, syrup (molasses, maple, carob), sugar, sweeteners, jams, jellies, etc.	Eat in moderation.
Vitamin B12	Dietary supplement of fortified foods	A reliable source of vitamin B12 should be included if dairy and eggs are avoided.

For Dummies: Bestselling Book Series for Beginners

Praise For Being Vegetarian For Dummies

"Informative, entertaining, and right on target, *Being Vegetarian For Dummies* is a superb guide to eating healthfully. This is an outstanding book. Vegetarian nutrition can sometimes seem complicated and confusing, but Suzanne Havala makes it all simple and clear. If you're interested in learning about how to be good to your body, this book is excellent. I can't recommend it highly enough."

> — John Robbins, author of *Diet for a New America* and *The Food Revolution*

"*Being Vegetarian For Dummies* is one of the smartest books you'll find for turning your daily menu into powerfully good medicine. From shopping, to reading labels, to pleasing a family with varying tastes, this guide makes going vegetarian or vegan incredibly easy. Most importantly, it will put you on the road to life-long good health. This is the diet that has proven its ability to lower blood pressure, protect the heart and bones, trim the waistline, and even inhibit certain cancers. Wellness begins with what's on your plate — let this book show you the way."

> — Neal Barnard, M.D., President, Physicians Committee for Responsible Medicine

"If you're thinking of becoming a vegetarian, there's no better place to start than with *Being Vegetarian For Dummies*. If you're already a vegetarian, this book still has a lot to teach you."

> — Marion Nestle, Ph.D., MPH, Professor and Chair, Department of Nutrition and Food Studies, New York University

"Suzanne Havala's commonsense approach to healthy eating makes her a leader in nutrition for the 21st century. *Being Vegetarian For Dummies* removes another huge barrier keeping people from the health and appearance they deserve."

> — John McDougall, M.D., Medical Director of the McDougall Program, St. Helena Hospital, Napa Valley, CA and author of *The McDougall Program for Women* and *The McDougall Program: Twelve Days to Dynamic Health*

More Praise for Suzanne Havala's Work

"In *Good Foods, Bad Foods*, Suzanne Havala achieves two opposing goals at the same time better than any other book of its kind. It's a gutsy, clear-eyed tour of optimal nutrition that you might expect from a hard-nosed scientist and it offers the sympathetic advice about the challenges and practical compromises necessary to turn the vegetables-are-good-for-you message into a rewarding habit. This book is a must."

— Robert Pritikin, Director, Pritikin Longevity Center

"[*Good Foods, Bad Foods* provides] . . . a commonsense message that presents not only the commonly asked questions about food and health but does it in a way that faithfully represents the scientific evidence."

— T. Colin Campbell, Ph.D., Jacob Gould Schurman Professor of Nutritional Biochemistry and Director, China Diet and Health Project, Cornell University

"[In *The Natural Kitchen,*] Sue Havala is providing a true service to all of us who want to integrate wholesome foods into our daily lives. I am grateful to her for making the wonderful (but sometimes confusing) world of natural foods stores so clear and accessible."

— Mollie Katzen, author of *Moosewood Cookbook* and *Vegetable Heaven* and host of *Mollie Katzen's Cooking Show*

"This terrific little book [*The Natural Kitchen*] provides a right-on commonsense guide for anyone trying to find the jewels at the heart of the natural food maze. Reliable information sits right where you need it alongside mouthwatering suggestions for simple, quick ways to make the very best use of the most nutritious and economical selections on every aisle of the natural foods store. With this in hand, you can tell the wheat from the chaff, and the tempeh from the baloney."

— Laurel Robertson, author of *Laurel's Kitchen Recipes*

"[*Shopping for Health: A Nutritionist's Aisle-by-Aisle Guide to Smart, Lowfat Choices at the Supermarket* deserves] . . . an A+ for convenience and overall usefulness."

— *The New York Daily News*

Being Vegetarian

FOR

DUMMIES®

Being Vegetarian FOR DUMMIES®

by Suzanne Havala

Wiley Publishing, Inc.

Being Vegetarian For Dummies®

Published by
Wiley Publishing, Inc.
111 River Street
Hoboken, NJ 07030
www.wiley.com

For general information on our other products and services or to obtain technical support, please contact our Customer Care Department within the U.S. at 800-762-2974, outside the U.S. at 317-572-3993, or fax 317-572-4002.

Wiley also publishes its books in a variety of electronic formats. Some content that appears in print may not be available in electronic books.

Library of Congress Cataloging-in-Publication Data:

Library of Congress Control Number: 11-110827

ISBN: 0-7645-6335-1

Manufactured in the United States of America

10 9 8

3B/TR/QT/QU/IN

About the Author

Suzanne Havala, MS, RD, LDN, FADA, is a nationally recognized author and consultant on food, nutrition, and public policy. Suzanne brings reliable, sound guidance to consumers and organizations on diet and its impact on health. Her advice has been quoted in *Parade, SELF Magazine, Shape, Vegetarian Times, The New York Times, Runner's World, New Woman, YM, Omni, Sassy,* and *Harper's Bazaar* and in appearances on *Good Morning America, Weekend Today in New York,* and the *Susan Powter Show.*

Suzanne is the author of *Being Vegetarian For Dummies, Vegetarian Cooking For Dummies, The Natural Kitchen, Good Foods, Bad Foods: What's Left to Eat?, The Vegetarian Food Guide and Nutrition Counter, Shopping for Health: A Nutritionist's Aisle-by-Aisle Guide to Smart, Low-fat Choices at the Supermarket, Being Vegetarian,* and *Simple, Lowfat & Vegetarian.*

Suzanne is a licensed, registered dietitian and Fellow of the American Dietetic Association. She is based in Chapel Hill, North Carolina, where she is a Public Health Leadership Doctoral Candidate in the Department of Health Policy and Administration in the School of Public Health at the University of North Carolina. She has been a full-fledged vegetarian for over 26 years.

For more information, please visit www.suzannehavala.com.

Author's Acknowledgments

My heartfelt thanks to the following people for making this book possible: to Linda Ingroia, Senior Acquisitions Editor at Wiley, with whom I was delighted to have the opportunity to work again; to Marcia Johnson, Project Editor, and Kitty Jarrett, who so expertly guided the book to completion; to the talented design and production crew at Wiley; and to Patti Breitman, my agent. What a pleasure and privilege it is to be part of such an outstanding team.

Publisher's Acknowledgments

We're proud of this book; please send us your comments through our online registration form located at www.dummies.com/register.

Some of the people who helped bring this book to market include the following:

Acquisitions, Editorial, and Media Development

Project Editor: Marcia L. Johnson

Senior Acquisitions Editor: Linda Ingroia

Acquisitions Coordinator: Erin Connell

Copy Editor: Kitty Jarrett

Technical Editor: Terese Christofferson

Editorial Manager: Pamela Mourouzis

Editorial Assistant: Carol Strickland

Cover Photo: ©David Rosenberg/ Getty Image/Stone

Production

Project Coordinator: Nancee Reeves

Layout and Graphics: Amy Adrian, LeAndra Johnson, Jacque Schneider, Julie Trippetti

Special Art: Elizabeth Kurtzman

Proofreaders: John Bitter, Angel Perez, Nancy Price, York Production Services, Inc.

Indexer: York Production Services, Inc.

Publishing and Editorial for Consumer Dummies

Diane Graves Steele, Vice President and Publisher, Consumer Dummies

Joyce Pepple, Acquisitions Director, Consumer Dummies

Kristin A. Cocks, Product Development Director, Consumer Dummies

Michael Spring, Vice President and Publisher, Travel

Brice Gosnell, Associate Publisher, Travel

Suzanne Jannetta, Editorial Director, Travel

Publishing for Technology Dummies

Richard Swadley, Vice President and Executive Group Publisher

Andy Cummings, Vice President and Publisher

Composition Services

Gerry Fahey, Vice President of Production Services

Debbie Stailey, Director of Composition Services

Contents at a Glance

Cartoons at a Glance

By Rich Tennant

"This isn't some sort of fad diet, is it?"

page 47

"Do I like arugula? I _love_ arugula!! Some of the best beaches in the world are there."

page 145

"Gordon's always had trouble controlling his appetite at restaurants. I had to explain to him that you're not supposed to pull your chair up to the salad bar."

page 195

page 283

"For the last time— pregnant vegetarians do _NOT_ give birth to Cabbage Patch Dolls."

page 227

"Of course you're better off eating grains and vegetables, but for St. Valentine's Day, we've never been very successful with, 'Say it with Legumes'."

page 7

"Relax— another helping of vermicelli, and I'll be done with your precious shredder."

page 97

Cartoon Information:
Fax: 978-546-7747
E-Mail: richtennant@the5thwave.com
World Wide Web: www.the5thwave.com

Table of Contents

Introduction

*W*hen I was a mere sprout — not yet a fully actualized, deviant, non-meat-eater — I wore a button that said, "Real People Wear Fake Furs," which I had picked up at the Ann Arbor street fair when my older sister was in school at the University of Michigan. It was the late '60s, and it was at about that same time that my mother announced to the family that from then on she would be a vegetarian. She never said why, but for the next several years, the former Wisconsinite ate cheese omelets or cheddar-cheese-on-whole-wheat-toast-and-pickle sandwiches for dinner while the rest of us ate the meat that she prepared for us. That is, of course, until one by one, we kids followed her lead and, without fanfare, went vegetarian ourselves.

My dad worried that we'd miss vital nutrients. He chided my mother for planting the idea. Mom, a registered nurse, was pegged as "unusual" at the hospital where she worked. By now, it was the early '70s, and vegetarians either lived on communes or wore Birkies and long hair on college campuses. They weren't kids and middle-aged working moms.

I was a high school athlete — a competitive swimmer — and I hoped that a vegetarian diet would boost my endurance and athletic performance, as it had for record-holder Murray Rose. It didn't help enough, but it did pique my interest in nutrition and set me on the path to a career in dietetics. It would be many years, however, before the scientific community would come around to the idea that a diet based on grains, fruits, vegetables, legumes, seeds, and nuts could be adequate — never mind superior to one based on animal products.

In college, I learned about vegetarianism in a unit on fad diets. At that time, a blood cholesterol level of 300 mg/dl was considered normal, and patients in the coronary care unit in the hospital got bacon and eggs and white toast for breakfast.

My grandmother worried that I wouldn't get enough iron without eating red meat, and she thought that my slender body wasn't "healthy" enough in size to meet her old-world Eastern European standards. Such were the trials and tribulations of being a vegetarian, until today. What's changed? Just about everything!

The American Dietetic Association — generally the conservative hold-out on such matters — has gone from cautious at first, later tentative at best, to now clearly stating in its position paper that vegetarian diets confer health advantages. The U.S. government has given the thumbs-up to vegetarian diets and now recommends that Americans should start basing their meals on fruits, vegetables, grains, and legumes — a thinly-veiled way of saying, "Okay, we give. Plant-based diets are healthier," without stepping on the toes of the meat and dairy industries, whose interests the government is charged with protecting and promoting.

The trend toward vegetarianism is strong, and with the volume of research confirming the advantages of a vegetarian-style diet, there's no going back. Now the task is to help U.S. society make the transition to an eating style that is outside the cultural norm.

Vegetarian diets are no longer an oddity — they're converging with mainstream dietary recommendations. This book, then, is for everyone who wants to peek into the future of preventive nutrition and to get a leg up on making the switch.

About This Book

This book is for vegetarians and prospective veg-heads, too — for anyone who would finally like to know what a "vegan" is, who still has questions about where vegetarians get their protein, for moms and dads who are wringing their hands because Junior has "gone vegetarian," and for Junior to give to Mom and Dad so that they won't worry.

This book is for vegetarians and nonvegetarians alike. Whether you want to enhance your athletic performance, control or prevent the onset of disease, manage your weight (or your pocketbook), help keep the planet healthy and the animals happy, or you just want to look and feel your best, this book's got what you need.

That's because the secret to living well is eating well, and to eat well, you have to get into the veg-head frame of mind. It's the simple truth. Your mantra is three words: Eat. Your. Veggies. (You heard it from Mom first.) Or more accurately: Eat Your Vegetation. Because the foundation of a health supporting diet is foods that come from the soil — fruits, vegetables, grains, legumes, seeds, and nuts.

You don't have to read the chapters in order from cover to cover — but you can. Throughout the text, you'll find cross-references to point you to other parts of the book to find related information.

How This Book Is Organized

This book is divided into seven parts. Each part focuses on a different aspect of vegetarianism, from the basic who, what, and why to the nutritional under-pinnings of a diet without meat, how to make the transition, and how to maintain the changes after you've made them. Together, the seven parts of this book lay the foundation for understanding the vegetarian lifestyle and building the skills necessary to successfully adapt.

Part I: Vegetarianism for Beginners: Getting Started

This part peels away the first layer of mystery around issues of vegetarianism. It gets to the bottom of the various definitions of vegetarian diets, revealing once and for all what the word *vegan* means and how to pronounce it. It looks at what vegetarians *do* eat, including vegetarian traditions around the world, rather than stopping at what they *don't* eat. This part also discusses the reasons that motivate people to adopt a vegetarian diet. And it guides you with good-sense advice and strategies for making the transition to a more plant-based diet.

Part II: Vegetarian NutriSense

If I don't eat meat, where do I get my protein? If I don't drink milk, will I get enough calcium? This part answers these questions and more about where vegetarians get nutrients such as protein, calcium, iron, and vitamin B12. The chapters in this part contain helpful tables that show how much of certain foods you should eat to get the nutrients you need. This section also covers the issue of whether you should take vitamin and mineral supplements.

Part III: Surviving among the Carnivores

This part gets down to the practical stuff, which is what people seem to need help with the most. How can I manage this if I'm the only one in my household who eats this way? What staples should I start out with, and do I have to shop at a health food store? Part III answers these questions and more.

Part IV: Meals Made Easy

This part continues to help you with the practical matters by discussing how to plan tasty, nutritious, satisfying vegetarian meals with a minimum of fuss. A daily food guide and directions for choosing foods are presented in these chapters. You'll get sample menus and ideas for quick and easy meals and snacks. There are great fix 'n' freeze ideas and make-ahead meals for the once-a-week cook, as well as advice for dealing with holidays and entertaining. My favorite part of this section is a chapter on recipe substitutions. These go beyond the ordinary. You'll amaze your friends with some of the versatile and practical ideas that are presented here.

Part V: Movin' on Out!

This part discusses how to do the vegetarian thing while you're away from home — at restaurants and dinner parties, while on the road, or at school or the office. We'll look at the social side and how not to lose your nonvegetarian friends, as well as veggie etiquette, so that you'll know how to handle eating away from home with grace and charm. This part helps you combat the most common situations you'll run into when you're not in the comfort of your own kitchen.

Part VI: Vegetarianism for Special Needs

This part takes you on a stroll through the stages of life and describes how you can adapt a vegetarian diet to meet nutritional needs at all ages and how to deal with some of the special challenges that accompany each stage. We'll start with vegetarian diets in pregnancy, through birth and infancy. Then we'll walk through toddlerhood and beyond, discussing vegetarian diets for older children as well as the challenges of teenage vegetarians. We'll look at vegetarian diets for athletes of all ages, and we'll also discuss the merits of a vegetarian diet for older adults.

Part VII: The Part of Tens

This last part is a final shot of gumption for aspiring vegetarians. Before you start on your merry way, this chapter provides yet more smart ideas for honing your new skills and challenging your increasingly sophisticated taste buds. Simply stated, this chapter is about getting support for your lifestyle choice.

Appendixes

At the end of book, you'll also find a list of helpful vegetarian resources and a glossary of terms.

Icons Used in This Book

You'll definitely want to read these words to the wise. They'll help you avoid pitfalls or mistakes that you might otherwise stumble into.

The information in these paragraphs offers hints and bits of advice to smooth your transition to a vegetarian lifestyle.

These paragraphs contain some interesting facts and other information that, although not vital to your understanding of the subject, might be fun to know.

These paragraphs serve as gentle reminders of the information you should really hold on to.

Throughout this book you can find information that is specifically applicable to a vegan lifestyle or diet. We've marked the text with this icon to make this information easier to find.

This icon points to information throughout the book that stresses the health benefits of eating a vegetarian diet.

Where to Go from Here

The science of nutrition is complicated, but being well nourished is a relatively simple matter. Unfortunately, putting today's dietary recommendations into practice can be a challenge. That's because we live in a culture hooked on quarter-pounders, with skimpy servings of vegetables relegated to the side of the plate. We're besieged by pictures of milk mustaches at every flip of the page or glance to the side of the highway, and fat free foods and fakes are leaving many of us gnawing on our knuckles. Most of us have a hard time visualizing what lies on the other side. That's where this book comes in. Read it and learn about a much better way.

Whether you go vegetarian all of the way or part of the way, you'll be on your way to a happier and healthier you.

Best wishes to you as you take the first step!

Author's Note

The information contained in this book is general and not meant as medical advice for an individual's specific health problems. If you are seriously ill or on medication, please check with your health care provider before changing your diet.

Part I
Vegetarianism for Beginners: Getting Started

The 5th Wave   By Rich Tennant

"Of course you're better off eating grains and vegetables, but for St. Valentine's Day, we've never been very successful with, 'Say it with Legumes'."

In this part . . .

*I*f you are going to get to where you want to be, then there's no getting around it — you have to have a plan. And when it comes to making diet and lifestyle changes, this is especially true. In order to change the way you eat, you not only have to develop and practice new skills and a new mindset, but you have to replace old traditions with new ones. That's the fun of it, and that's the challenge of it as well.

What better place to start than understanding the basics? The chapters that follow present a variety of approaches to vegetarianism as well as sound reasons for making the switch.

Chapter 1

Vegetarianism Defined

Are vegetarians members of a secret club? Seems like it. To gain admission, you have to shop at natural foods stores and eat strange foods such as tempeh and nutritional yeast. It helps if you're a celebrity. Maybe a rock star or an actor. They're into weird lifestyle alternatives. The rules are complicated and somewhat mysterious. Some people are lacto, some are lacto ovo, and some are vegan. What the heck do these terms mean? Not to worry. Sit back, relax, and read on.

Most people who visualize a vegetarian diet see a gaping hole in the center of their dinner plate. Vegetarians, they presume, must eat an awful lot of lettuce and carrot sticks. Just contemplating it leaves them gnawing on their knuckles. Nothing could be further from the truth, however. Still, it's difficult for many nonvegetarians to understand the diversity and abundance of a meat-free eating style. Vegetarian diets are common in some parts of the world, but are outside the culture and personal experience of many people. Table 1-1 shows a sampling of some of the rich variety of vegetarian dishes from around the world.

Table 1-1	Vegetarian Dishes around the World
Food	*Country of Origin*
Spanakopita (spinach pie)	Greece
Beans with cassava	Rwanda
Black-eyed pea stew	Ghana
Lentil stew	Ethiopia
Corn meal with pumpkin	Zimbabwe

(continued)

Table 1-1 *(continued)*

Food	Country of Origin
Couscous	Morocco
Spiced beans in coconut milk	East Africa
Yogurt and spinach soup	Egypt
Fried plantains	West Africa
Garbanzo bean dip (hummus)	Middle East
Yogurt and tomato soup	Afghanistan
Lentil soup	Syria
Apple beanpot	Saudi Arabia
Red kidney beans in sauce	Pakistan
Lentils and curried vegetables	Nepal
Stir-fry with noodles	Cambodia
Stir-fried tempeh	Indonesia
Vegetables stir-fried with spices	Bangladesh
Stuffed eggplant	Haiti
Pigeon peas and rice	Bahamas
Cream of watercress soup	Dominican Republic
Pumpkin soup	Brazil
Bean soup	El Salvador
Corn soup	Guatemala
Squash or pumpkin stew	Bolivia
Bean and pumpkin stew	Chile
Coconut rice and beans	Colombia
Potato cakes with peanut sauce	Ecuador
Lima bean casserole	Peru

Reality is, vegetarians thrive on a wide range of foods, with meals that are colorful, nutritious, delicious, and easy to fix. Figure 1-1 shows some examples. They're often far less expensive than meat-based meals as well. Break out of the meat-and-potatoes rut, and you'll discover that your meals are more interesting, more healthful, and more diverse. You'll find that eating the vegetarian way opens windows to the world as you learn about healthy meal traditions from far-away places where meatless has been the norm for millennia.

Becoming a vegetarian is an evolutionary process for most people. (See Chapter 4 for information on making the switch gradually or all at once.) As Part II describes, relearning what you thought you knew about nutrition is one step. And as Part IV presents, seeing the possibilities for meal planning ("What can I make for dinner tonight?") is another. You'll part with old traditions and replace them with new ones. Practicing new skills takes time and patience. Going vegetarian means adopting a new mind-set about meals. Along the way, be sure to have fun! You'll get there, and this book is the very best first step you can take.

Figure 1-1: Vegetarianism offers variety.

Vegetarian Variations

Most of us are pretty good at describing the essence of a person in just a few words:

"He's a liberal Democrat."

"They're Yuppie Boomers."

"She's a White, Anglo-Saxon Protestant."

It's like the saying goes: "A picture (or label) paints (or says) a thousand words."

People use labels to describe vegetarians, with different terms corresponding to different sets of eating habits. A lacto ovo vegetarian eats differently than a vegan eats. In some cases, the term used to describe a type of vegetarian refers to a whole range of lifestyle preferences, rather than to the diet alone. In general, though, the specific term used to describe a vegetarian has to do with the extent to which that person avoids foods of animal origin.

Defining the types

In 1992, *Vegetarian Times* magazine sponsored a survey of vegetarianism in the U.S. The results showed that almost 7 percent of Americans considered themselves vegetarians. At that time, that figure equated to about 12.4 million adults.

However, a closer look at the eating habits of those "vegetarians" found that most of them were eating chicken and fish occasionally, and many were eating red meat at least a few times each month. That finding prompted many of the more strident vegetarians — those who never ate meat, fish, or poultry — to pose the question, "Since when do chicken, fish, and cows grow in a garden?"

The fact is that many people today use the term *vegetarian* loosely to mean that they are consciously reducing their intake of animal products. The term has a positive connotation, especially among those who know that vegetarian diets confer health benefits.

What about the "real" vegetarians? Who are they and what do they eat (or not eat)? The definition of a vegetarian most widely accepted by fellow vegetarians is a person who eats no meat, fish, or poultry. Not "I eat turkey for Thanksgiving" or "I eat fish once in a while." A vegetarian consistently avoids all flesh foods as well as byproducts of meat, fish, and poultry. A vegetarian avoids refried beans made with lard, soups made with meat stock, and foods made with gelatin, such as some kinds of candy and most marshmallows.

According to a Roper Poll sponsored by the nonprofit Vegetarian Resource Group in 1994, the actual number of people who never eat meat, fish, or poultry is about 1 percent of the adult population. The poll was repeated in 1997, and the number remained the same.

Of course, vegetarian diets vary in the extent to which they exclude animal products. The three major types are

✔ **Lacto ovo vegetarian:** A *lacto ovo vegetarian* diet excludes meat, fish, and poultry but includes dairy products and eggs. Most vegetarians in the U.S., Canada, and Western Europe fall into this category. Lacto ovo vegetarians eat such foods as cheese, ice cream, yogurt, milk, and eggs, as well as foods made with these ingredients.

> ✔ **Lacto vegetarian:** A *lacto vegetarian* diet excludes meat, fish, and poultry, as well as eggs and any foods containing eggs. So, a lacto vegetarian, for instance, would not eat the pancakes at most restaurants, because they contain eggs. Some veggie burger patties are made with egg whites, and many brands of ice cream contain egg. A lacto vegetarian would not eat these foods. A lacto vegetarian would, however, eat dairy products such as milk, yogurt, and cheese.
>
> ✔ **Vegan:** Technically, the term *vegan* refers to more than just the diet alone. A vegan is a vegetarian who avoids eating or using all animal products, including meat, fish, poultry, eggs, dairy products, any foods containing byproducts of these ingredients, wool, silk, leather, and any nonfood items made with animal byproducts. Some vegans avoid honey.

Are vegans from the planet Vegan? No, but they'll think *you're* from another planet if you don't pronounce the word correctly. It's pronounced VEE´gun within the vegetarian community.

In addition to avoiding foods containing animal products, vegans also avoid animal products in all other areas of their lives. The term *strict vegetarian* is the correct term to use to describe those who avoid all animal products in their diets but who don't carry animal product avoidance into other areas of their lives. In practice, however, the term vegan is usually used by both strict vegetarians and vegans, even among those in the know. Call it a bad habit. Rather than call themselves vegans, though, strict vegetarians often say that they "eat a vegan diet."

So, a vegan, for instance, would not use hand lotion that contains lanolin, a byproduct of wool. A vegan would not use margarine that contains casein, a milk protein, and a vegan would not carry luggage trimmed in leather. Vegans (as well as many other vegetarians) also avoid products that have been tested on animals, such as many cosmetics and personal care products. Many vegans avoid using regular, white granulated sugar because much of it has been processed using char from animal bones (for whitening).

It can be difficult to maintain a vegan lifestyle in modern culture. Most vegans are strongly motivated by ethics, however, and rise to the challenge. It's not impossible once you get the hang of it. A large part of maintaining a vegan lifestyle has to do with being aware of where animal products are used and knowing about alternatives. Vegetarian and animal rights organizations offer information and materials to help people maintain a vegan lifestyle. Sometimes vegans unwittingly use a product or eat a food that contains an animal byproduct. There are times when it's hard to know if a product is free of all animal ingredients. However, the intention is to strive for the vegan ideal.

Lacto ovo vegetarian, lacto vegetarian, and vegan are the three primary types of vegetarian diets, but there are yet more labels for vegetarians.

> ## Where macrobiotic diets fit in
>
> Macrobiotic diets are often lumped into the general category of vegetarian diets, even though they may include seafood. The diet excludes all other animal products, however, as well as refined sugars, tropical fruits, and "nightshade vegetables" (for example, potatoes, eggplant, and peppers). The diet is related to principles of Buddhism and is based on the Chinese principles of yin and yang. Therefore, macrobiotic diets include foods common to the Asian culture, such as sea vegetables (such as kelp, nori, arame), root vegetables (such as daikon), and miso. Many people follow a macrobiotic diet as part of a life philosophy. Others follow the diet because they believe it to be effective in curing cancer and other illnesses, an idea for which there is currently little scientific support.

A *semi-vegetarian* is someone who is cutting back on his intake of meat in general. A *pollo vegetarian* avoids red meat and fish but eats chicken. A *pesco pollo vegetarian* avoids red meat but eats chicken and fish. These terms stretch the true definition of a vegetarian, and only the term *semi-vegetarian* is actually used with much frequency.

The list actually goes even further. One adaptation of a vegetarian diet is a *raw foods diet*, in which adherents eat a diet that consists primarily of uncooked foods. Another adaptation, the *fruitarian diet*, consists only of fruits; vegetables that are botanically classified as fruits, such as tomatoes, eggplant, zucchini, and avocados; and seeds and nuts. Planning a nutritionally adequate fruitarian diet is difficult, and the diet is not recommended for children.

This book focuses on the most common forms of vegetarian diets — lacto ovo vegetarian, lacto vegetarian, and vegan diets. These types of vegetarian diets are nutritionally adequate and are associated with health advantages.

As you can see, there's a variation to suit practically everyone.

Breaking the label boundaries

Now that you know the criteria for the different types of vegetarian diets, which label describes the eating style you wish to have? What would you call a person who avoids all flesh foods and only occasionally eats eggs and dairy products, and then usually as a minor ingredient in a baked good or dish, such as a muffin, cookie, or veggie burger? Technically, the person is a lacto ovo vegetarian, right? But this diet seems as though it's leaning toward the vegan end of the spectrum.

As a nutritionist, I see this kind of variation — even within the same category of vegetarian diet — all the time. One lacto ovo vegetarian may eat heaping helpings of cheese and eggs and have a high intake of saturated fat and cholesterol as a result. In fact, this type of vegetarian may have a nutrient intake similar to the typical American's — not so hot. Another lacto ovo vegetarian may use eggs and dairy products, but only in a very limited fashion — as condiments or minor ingredients in foods. This person's nutrient intake could more closely resemble that of a vegan (assuming, of course, that the vegan isn't a soda and french fries vegetarian).

What am I getting at? That labels are only a starting point, and they have their limitations. Even if you know generally what type of vegetarian a person is, there can be a lot of variation in the degree to which the person uses or avoids animal products.

Many new vegetarians find that their diets evolve over time. At the start, for example, many vegetarians rely heavily on cheese and eggs to replace meat. Over time, they learn to cook with grains and beans and vegetables, and they experiment with cuisines of other cultures. They decrease their reliance on foods of animal origin. Gradually, they consume fewer eggs and dairy products. One day, they might even find themselves eating a mostly vegan (or strict vegetarian) diet.

If you are new to vegetarianism, you might begin to notice a bit of peer pressure from some longtime vegetarians who have moved down the continuum closer to the vegan end of the spectrum and are encouraging you to "move along." You may get this sense from materials you read or from people you meet. Ignore it, and compare yourself to no one but yourself. Adopting a vegetarian or partly vegetarian diet is a highly personal decision. Do what's right for you, and move at a pace that's comfortable for you.

You might say that vegetarian diets are on a continuum, starting from the typical American, meat-centered diet to vegan. (See Figure 1-2.) Most vegetarians fall somewhere in-between. Some may be content staying wherever they begin on the continuum. Others may progress along the spectrum; their diets will continue to evolve as they hone their skills and develop new traditions, moving from semi-vegetarian, or lacto ovo vegetarian, closer and closer to the vegan end of the spectrum.

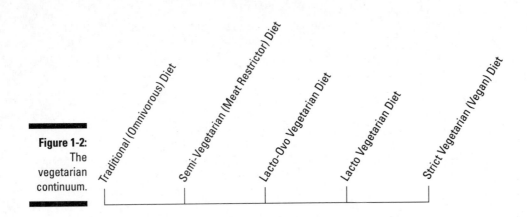

Figure 1-2:
The vegetarian continuum.

What a Vegetarian DOES Eat

Your eating style is a mind-set. For proof, ask your neighbor or coworker what he's having for dinner tonight. The chances are good he's going to say "We're grilling out steaks tonight," or "I'm having fish tonight," or "Chicken." Or he might be going out to eat at a restaurant serving a Western-style, meat-centered meal, such as a 32-ounce steak, for example.

Ever notice how no one mentions the rice, or the potato, or the salad, vegetables, bread, or anything else besides the meat? Those are the incidentals, the "side dishes." They're less important than the "main course." We live in a society in which meals revolve around meat as the focal point of the plate. It's just a habit. Our tradition.

A semi-vegetarian might push the meat to the side of the plate, move the vegetables and grains and legumes to the center, and double their portion sizes. They might eat more meatless meals more often. Other vegetarians push the meat off the plate altogether and build an entirely different kind of meal.

If you are expecting a bona fide vegetarian to come to your house for dinner, you'll want to be sure to leave the chicken stock out of the vegetables or rice and the ground meat or meat flavoring out of the pasta sauce. Worcestershire sauce contains anchovies, and many stir-fry sauces contain oyster sauce. Check the labels. Your guest will appreciate your thoughtfulness.

When people think of vegetarian diets, they often visualize a plate with a gaping bare spot where the meat used to be. They get a little hungry. "What's left to eat?" they wonder. "Rabbit food," they figure, thinking about the stuff that is usually relegated to the side of the plate, or maybe the little bit of fruit garnish teetering on the edge. And they get a little hungrier.

Just the opposite is true, however. The real variety is actually in the plant world — the abundant, colorful, flavorful, fragrant, delicious and nutritious, varied plant world. When you think about it, most people really only eat a few types of meat. They cook it in a bunch of different ways, and they usually doctor it up with spices and condiments to give it some variation in flavor. The lament I hear most often from people trying to improve their diets is, "Chicken and fish, chicken and fish. I know a thousand ways to cook chicken and fish. I'm going to overdose on chicken and fish."

Because an omnivorous diet tends to center on meat (and puts heavy reliance on eggs and dairy products, too), it can be fairly monotonous. Once you make the switch to a vegetarian diet, however, lots of options open up. There are hundreds of different types of fruits, vegetables, grains and grain products, legumes, and other vegetarian foods. (The term legumes refers to dried beans and peas, such as pinto beans, black beans, kidney beans, garbanzo beans, lentils, split peas, azuki beans, black-eyed peas, and navy beans. You can buy them dry, canned, frozen, and sometimes even as flakes and flour.) There is an endless number of ways that you can fix them. Many of those dishes originated in cultures outside the U.S. Some of those may be very familiar to you, and others may open new windows to the world.

The bottom line: There's a tendency to think of vegetarian diets in terms of what they exclude, and that the number of food choices is smaller than in an omnivorous diet. Just the opposite is generally true. Once you adopt a vegetarian diet, more options open up, and your diet is likely to have greater variety than it did before.

Chapter 2

Don't Worry — It's Good for You!

*I*n some aspects of life, what you don't know won't hurt you. On the other hand, there are times when what you *do* know can help you . . . a lot. Vegetarian diets are like that. There are some compelling reasons to go vegetarian. For many people, one of those reasons piques their interest, and then once they learn more, the other reasons reinforce their original reason for being interested. When you think about it from all the various angles, a vegetarian diet makes a whole lot of sense. And one of the most common reasons people consider vegetarianism is their desire to adopt a healthier lifestyle.

In this chapter, we'll take a look at how eating a vegetarian diet helps you achieve overall health, and how many past concerns about vegetarianism are really nothing to worry about.

Making the Connection between Diet and Health

Many people view their health (or lack thereof) as something that just sort of happens to them. Their bad habits "catch up" with them. They've got bad genes. Their doctor had just given them a clean bill of health, and then they had a heart attack out of the blue. (Well, we all have to die of *something*.) Who could have foreseen it? They lived reasonably. Everything in moderation, right? What more could they have done? A lot, most likely. You'd be surprised to learn how much power you wield with your knife and fork. The fact is that vegetarians enjoy better health than nonvegetarians. The fewer animal products vegetarians consume, the better their health.

You are what you eat!

Eating a vegetarian diet doesn't guarantee that you're eating healthfully. After all, cola and fries are vegetarian. A steady diet of junk isn't health-supporting, even if it *is* meat-free. Vegetarian diets are associated with health advantages when meals are comprised of a reasonable variety of foods, including fruits, vegetables, grains, and legumes, and when they provide enough calories to meet your energy needs.

In comparison with nonvegetarians, vegetarians have lower rates of cancer, coronary artery disease, diabetes, high blood pressure, gallstones, and kidney stones. They're less likely to be obese, too. In general, a vegetarian diet is "good for what ails you," and it helps prevent the onset of many ailments in the first place. That's because a diet that is composed primarily of plant matter has protective qualities.

Lowering fat and cholesterol

In general, vegetarians get less total fat in their diets than nonvegetarians. The fewer animal products the diet contains, the less fat it usually contains. Vegan diets, for instance, tend to be lower in fat than lacto vegetarian or lacto-ovo vegetarian diets. Fat is a concentrated source of calories, so diets that are low in fat tend to be lower in calories. No wonder vegetarians tend to be leaner than nonvegetarians.

Vegetarian diets also tend to be lower in *saturated fat* than nonvegetarian diets. Although there are plant sources of saturated fat, saturated fats come primarily from animal products, particularly high-fat dairy foods and meats. In fact, two-thirds of the fat in dairy products is saturated fat. Even so-called low-fat dairy products contain a substantial amount of saturated fat.

Saturated fats are usually firm at room temperature, like a stick of butter. Foods that are high in saturated fat include red meats, the skin on poultry, butter, sour cream, ice cream, cheese, yogurt made with whole milk, 2% milk, and 3.3% whole milk.

Saturated fats stimulate the body to produce more cholesterol. *Cholesterol* is a waxy substance that is found in the plaques on arteries that are diseased. We all need some cholesterol, but our bodies manufacture what we need. We don't need more from outside sources, and for people with a predisposition for heart disease, too much cholesterol can contribute to hardening of the arteries.

Cholesterol is produced in the liver, so it's found only in animal products. Foods of plant origin contain no cholesterol. (Have you ever seen a lima bean with a liver?)

Even though chicken and fish contain less saturated fat than red meat, they contain just as much cholesterol. Vegetarian diets are not only lower in saturated fats than nonvegetarian diets, but they're lower in cholesterol, too. Diets that are low in total fat, saturated fats, and cholesterol are the healthiest. They are associated with a reduced risk of cancer, coronary artery disease, diabetes, high blood pressure, and obesity.

Lacto ovo vegetarian diets have the potential to be high in total fat, saturated fats, and cholesterol if care is not taken to limit the amount of eggs and high-fat dairy products consumed. If you switch to a lacto-ovo vegetarian diet, be careful not to rely too heavily on these foods to replace the meat that you once ate.

Benefiting from fiber

Dietary fiber is the part of a plant that is only partially digested by our bodies or not digested at all. It's our lack of ability to digest fiber that gives us the health benefits. Fiber can bind with environmental contaminants and help them pass out of the body. Fiber also decreases the amount of time that it takes for waste material to pass out of the body so that potentially harmful substances have less time to be in contact with the lining of the intestines.

Foods that are high in fiber are bulky. They have a tendency to fill you up before you can "fill out." In that way, foods that are rich in fiber help to control your weight. When you eat foods that are fiber rich, you tend to get full before you take in too many calories.

Fiber has other benefits, too. People who get plenty of fiber in their diets are less likely than others to have trouble with constipation, hemorrhoids, varicose veins, and diverticulosis. Getting plenty of fiber (and water) in your diet keeps your stools large and soft and easy to pass. You don't have to strain and exert a lot of pressure to have a bowel movement.

Diverticulosis is a painful condition in which there are herniations or small outpouchings in the large intestine. These pouches can become filled with debris and inflamed. Diverticular disease is caused in large part by not having enough fiber in the diet.

Diets that are high in fiber are associated with less obesity and lower rates of cancer and coronary artery disease than are diets that are low in fiber. Also, diabetics can better control their blood sugar levels by eating a diet that's high in fiber.

Most Americans get only 12 grams of fiber in their diets each day. Vegetarians get at least twice that much or more. One cup of oatmeal contains 8 grams of fiber, a medium pear with skin has 4 grams of fiber, a cup of vegetarian chili has 14 grams of fiber, a slice of whole wheat bread contains 2 grams of fiber, and a cup of chopped, steamed broccoli provides 6 grams of fiber.

Current dietary recommendations call for fiber intakes of at least 25 grams per day, but 35 or 40 grams is even better. Vegetarians can easily reach the higher figures. It's also important to drink plenty of fluids when your fiber intake is high, and water is an especially good choice.

There shouldn't be a need for a magazine rack in the bathroom (unless the reading material is for use in the bathtub). If you have enough time to read an article, then you probably aren't getting enough fiber and water in your diet.

Getting the right amount and kind of protein

Most vegetarians get enough protein, but they don't overdo it. There are benefits to that. When you moderate your protein intake, you help to conserve your body's stores of calcium (see Chapters 5 and 6 for more about the protein and calcium connection). Diets that are too high in protein, especially protein from animal sources, cause the kidneys to let more calcium pass into the urine. Meat protein is high in sulfur-containing amino acids which, when metabolized, result in higher acid levels in the body. To neutralize or buffer some of the excessive acid, calcium is leached from the bones and excreted in the urine.

That's part of the reason that standard recommendations for calcium intake for Americans are so high: The recommendations are jacked up to compensate for calcium losses that are caused by Flintstones-sized crown-rib roasts and 16-ounce steaks that cover the plate. Americans love meat, and they pay for it with calcium loss.

Speaking of your kidneys . . . when you moderate your protein intake by eating a vegetarian diet, you also cause less wear and tear on your kidneys. Vegetarians have fewer kidney stones and less kidney disease than nonvegetarians. High intakes of animal protein are also linked with higher blood cholesterol levels and more coronary artery disease, as well as a greater incidence of some types of cancer.

One of the problems that astronauts face upon returning to Earth after a mission in space is an increased incidence of kidney stones. As part of NASA's space station program, preparations are under way to serve a vegetarian diet to astronauts on long missions. There are several practical reasons for this, but NASA hopes that one of the benefits will be a lower incidence of kidney stones due to a lower intake of animal protein.

Eating wonderful whole foods

It wasn't long ago that news of the health benefits of *beta-carotene* got people running to the drugstore for supplements. Then, studies found that supplements of beta-carotene didn't provide the same health benefits as did whole foods that were high in beta-carotene — whole plant foods, that is.

Whole foods are foods that are as close to their natural state as possible, or the least processed as compared to other foods in the same category. For instance, whole wheat flour is a whole food; white flour is not. A baking potato is a whole food; a potato chip is not.

Whole foods contain *phytochemicals*, substances found in foods of plant origin that play a role in our body processes and help protect our health. Certain phytochemicals, for example, are thought to help reduce the risk of coronary artery disease, and others help prevent some forms of cancer. Because it's the consumption of whole foods, rather than individual nutrients, that seems to be associated with good health, it's possible that phytochemicals work in synergy with each other to keep our bodies healthy.

Beta-carotene is one phytochemical found in abundance in deep yellow or deep orange and red fruits and vegetables. Along with other phytochemicals found in whole foods, beta-carotene may help protect against cancer and coronary artery disease.

We know that there are more than 600 different carotenoids, and beta-carotene is only one of them. In fact, we know that there are probably thousands of other phytochemicals such as these at work in our bodies. It's also a sure thing that scientists haven't identified all the beneficial phytochemicals in foods yet. So, taking supplements of individual, isolated nutrients isn't as good as getting these substances directly from the foods you eat. The less processed a food is, the richer it is likely to be in phytochemicals.

Phytochemicals such as beta-carotene, other carotenoids, vitamins E and C, and the mineral selenium are examples of *antioxidant nutrients*. These nutrients are abundant in foods of plant origin. They are thought to help reduce the risk of cancer, coronary artery disease, lung disease, cataracts, and other diseases by their ability to rid the body of *free radicals*.

Free radicals aren't renegades from the '60s. They're molecules that are produced as a by-product of your body's normal metabolism. They are also produced when you are exposed to environmental contaminants such as air pollution and ozone, sunlight and X-rays, and certain dietary components such as fat and the form of iron found in meat. Free radicals speed up the aging process by damaging your cells. They can impair your immune system and cause numerous diseases and illnesses. Meat is high in the oxidants that cause your body to produce free radicals, and meat is low in the antioxidants that help rid your body of free radicals.

The bottom line is that vegetarian diets are rich in the phytochemicals that promote and protect human health. The more animal products you include in your diet, the less room there is in your diet for plant matter. Whether you make the transition to a fully vegetarian diet or not, you could benefit greatly from radically increasing the ratio of plant to animal products in your diet (Figure 2-1 shows a typical American diet and the vegetarian goal).

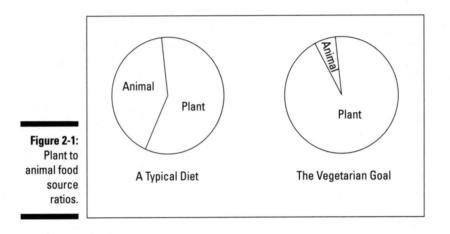

Figure 2-1:
Plant to animal food source ratios.

A Typical Diet   The Vegetarian Goal

Knowing You're Not Alone

Some of the world's greatest thinkers and philosophers have chosen or advocated a vegetarian lifestyle, including Pythagoras, Socrates, Leonardo da Vinci, and Benjamin Franklin.

For some, a vegetarian lifestyle stems from religious or spiritual teachings. Some Christians interpret the passage Genesis 1:29 from the Old Testament to mean that humans should eat a vegetarian diet: "And God said, behold, I have given you every herb-bearing seed, which is upon the face of all the earth, and every tree, in which is the fruit of a tree yielding seed; to you it shall be for meat."

Members of the Seventh-Day Adventist Church are encouraged to follow a vegetarian diet, and about half of its members do so. The Trappist monks, who are Catholic, are also vegetarians, and numerous Eastern religions or philosophies, including Buddhism, Jainism, and Hinduism, also advocate vegetarianism. Many athletes also adopt a vegetarian diet to gain an edge in their athletic performance (see the chapters in Part VI for more on vegetarianism for special needs).

Table 2-1 lists people throughout the centuries who have been advocates of a vegetarian lifestyle.

Table 2-1	**Famous Advocates of a Vegetarian Lifestyle**
Name	*Profession*
Hank Aaron	Professional baseball player
Louisa May Alcott	Author
Susan B. Anthony	Suffragist
David Bowie	Rock musician
Berke Breathed	Cartoonist
Isadora Duncan	Dancer
Thomas Edison	Inventor
Albert Einstein	Physicist
Mahatma Gandhi	Spiritual leader
Jerry Garcia	Musician
Philip Glass	Composer
Dustin Hoffman	Actor
Desmond Howard	Professional football player
Steve Jobs	Founder of Apple Computer
Carl Lewis	Olympic runner
Martina Navratilova	Tennis champion
Sir Isaac Newton	Physicist
Bill Pearl	Bodybuilder and four-time Mr. Universe
Plato	Philosopher
Fred Rogers	Television's "Mister Rogers"
Albert Schweitzer	Physician and Nobel Peace Prize winner
Benjamin Spock	Pediatrician and author

You don't say!

"The average age (life expectancy) of a meat eater is 63. I am on the verge of 85 and still work as hard as ever. I have lived quite long enough and I am trying to die; but I simply cannot do it. A single beefsteak would finish me; but I cannot bring myself to swallow it. I am oppressed with a dread of living forever. That is the only disadvantage of vegetarianism."

—George Bernard Shaw

"Nothing will benefit human health and increase the chances for survival of life on earth as much as the evolution to a vegetarian diet."

—Albert Einstein

Chapter 3

Vegetarianism Benefits All of Us

Some people go vegetarian for the simple reason that they don't like meat. They chew and chew and chew, and still there's a glob of aesthetically unpleasant flesh in their mouth. Some people find meat hard to digest. Some people just like rice, potatoes, and other vegetables better.

Still others adopt a vegetarian lifestyle because they see a link between their food choices and the health of the planet, the health of their own bodies and that of the people they love, the welfare of animals, or the ability of nations to feed hungry people around the world. No matter which issue first grabs their attention, the other advantages soon weigh in and cement their resolve.

Environmental Reasons

Smokey the Bear said, "Only *you* can prevent forest fires." And Woodsy Owl urged us to "Give a Hoot, Don't Pollute." Neither of them were vegetarians, but *you* can go one giant step further toward keeping the planet clean and healthy by adopting a vegetarian diet. "How so?" you ask.

A disproportionate amount of the earth's natural resources is used to produce meat and other animal products. For starters:

✔ It takes about 25 gallons of water to grow 1 pound of wheat, but it takes about 390 gallons of water to produce 1 pound of beef.

✔ A steer has to eat 7 pounds of grain or soybeans to produce 1 pound of beef. With that kind of return on investment, most businesses would be closing up shop for good.

In short, animal agriculture — the production of meat, eggs, and dairy products — places heavy demands on our land, water, and fuel supplies.

Depleting land resources to feed the meat habit

"This land is your land; this land is my land. . . . This land was made for you and me." As it turns out, though, the earth doesn't take kindly to the degree of animal agriculture to which it's being subjected.

Livestock grazing causes *desertification* of the land by causing erosion of the topsoil and drying out the land, preventing it from supporting the growth of plant life. Topsoil is being depleted faster than it can be created. Healthy, abundant supplies of topsoil help ensure that we'll have enough arable land to grow the food that we need to survive. Unfortunately, the amount of land resources needed to raise animals for their meat is exponentially greater than the amount needed to grow enough plant matter to feed the same number of people directly. Satisfying a big collective appetite for meat means paying with our precious land.

The appetite for meat and other animal products also costs us our trees and forests, although these trees may not be the ones in your own backyard or your neighbor's. Much of the deforestation happens in Latin America, Central America, and South America, where the number of acres of tropical rain forest cleared to make way for grazing cattle is so big that most of us would have a hard time comprehending its enormity.

Tropical rain forests are sort of like our planet's lungs. One of the many ways that trees help keep our world healthy is by exchanging the earth's carbon dioxide for fresh oxygen. The trees take our waste and convert it into a product (oxygen) that we need to survive. If we didn't have trees, we'd all be huffing and puffing as though we had reached the summit of Everest; "breathing through a straw" is how mountain climbers describe the feeling of thinning oxygen. Losing a large percentage of the earth's rainforests has repercussions for every corner of the planet.

In the wake of deforestation, many species of plants and animals are also wiped out. These plants and animals hold the keys to many scientific discoveries that may benefit humankind. The plants and animals of the rainforests are on the "front line," but eventually the assault on them will reach all of us.

Wasting water on animal production

When you look at a map of the earth, you sure see a lot of blue. It's hard to believe that we could be short of water anytime soon. There's lots of the salty kind of water, but one of the greatest threats of animal agriculture is to our supplies of *fresh* water. The aquifers that lie deep below the earth's surface hold the kind of water that we need to irrigate our land and to drink. Those giant pools of fresh water are dwindling rapidly because we're sucking up great quantities of the stuff to irrigate the vast amount of land needed to graze the animals from which we get a relatively small amount of food — a very inefficient use of a very precious resource.

Furthermore, whether fresh or salt, all of our water is being polluted, and animal agriculture is a major contributor to that problem. Pesticides, herbicides, and fertilizers used to grow feed for animals — in addition to the nitrogenous fecal waste that is produced by the animals themselves and washed into our streams, rivers, lakes, and bays — are contaminating our water supplies. We have less clean water than we once did, and the creatures that live in water are becoming contaminated or being killed off by the pollution as well.

Filching fossil fuels to keep animal farms running

Webster's defines *filching* as "appropriating furtively or casually," as in snitching a doughnut from a platter. It's synonymous with "stealing." However, "stealing" sounds a little more serious. In this context, I use the term *filching* to say that animal agriculture is ransacking our planet of fossil fuels.

The production of meat, eggs, and dairy products requires the intensive use of fossil fuels, including petroleum, for everything from transporting animal feed and the animals themselves to running farm machinery and operating the factory-homes where the animals are raised.

Vegetarian diets make more efficient use of land, water, and fossil fuel resources than diets that give prominence to meat, eggs, and dairy products.

Meat costs even more than you think!

If the true cost to society of producing animal products for human consumption were passed on to consumers, few of us could afford to put these foods on the dinner table. At least we wouldn't be able to afford them in the amounts we presently consume. Fortunately for those who have a hankering for ham and eggs, the U.S. government subsidizes many of these foods to keep producers in business and consumers satisfied. Of course, the costs don't go away — they are just deferred. We'll have to pay eventually. Sound familiar? It's sort of like the cost of tobacco to society, which has been divvied up among all of us in dollars spent for health care. As someone once said, "You can pay me now, or you can pay me later."

Social Reasons

Of course, choosing a vegetarian diet isn't just about improving our own health and well being. When you adopt a vegetarian diet, you are also helping to diminish the pain and suffering of others less fortunate than yourself.

Sustaining food sources for us all

Hunger for you and me, and for most people in the United States, is a fairly temporary state — often the result of skipping a meal because we were in too much of a rush. When we get the midnight munchies, we pop a bag of popcorn or grab a bowl of cereal. For much of the rest of the world, hunger is a state of slow starvation with no next meal or snack in sight.

World hunger is a problem of epic proportions and is complicated in terms of ethics, politics, and economics. Many people choose a vegetarian lifestyle as a way of making a contribution to the fight against world hunger. In the same sense of knowing that one's lone vote really does count, many people choose to cast their vote in favor of a diet and lifestyle that can sustain the most people.

In the simplest sense, when we eat foods directly from the soil — fruits, vegetables, grains, legumes, nuts, and seeds — we can nourish many more people than could be fed if the plant matter were fed to animals first and we, in turn, ate the animals.

More people can be fed on a vegetarian diet than can be fed on a nonvegetarian diet.

The appetite of affluent nations for meat and other animal products creates a market in poor countries for the resources needed to produce those foods. The result is that in developing nations, those with the power often opt to grow cash crops or feed for livestock for export, rather than grow less profitable crops that might feed the local people.

Another result of the market for meat in affluent nations is the choice of those in power in poor countries to raise animals for export to the wealthy overseas. The losers are again the local people, who might have benefited from less profitable plant foods grown to feed the masses. Another downside to this practice is that in some developing nations, natural resources such as land and forest are depleted and are no longer suitable for growing the crops that could feed the masses.

Protecting animal life

Nobel Peace Prize winner Albert Schweitzer once said, "Until he extends his circle of compassion to all living things, man will not himself find peace." Inhumane treatment of animals leads many people to adopt a vegetarian lifestyle. Many vegetarians, whether vegan or not, consider a meatless diet to be a humane and compassionate choice.

If you share your life with dogs or cats, you know that animals have feelings. You probably also know that cattle, chickens, and pigs don't live in idyllic pastures and barnyards anymore. They live and die in factory farms and slaughterhouses, the likes of which would rival any horror movie. The part we see is the neat and tidy packages of legs and shoulders in little Styrofoam plates wrapped in plastic.

Suffice it to say that some people do allow themselves to think about how animals are treated. They put themselves into the hooves and claws of other creatures, and they take a stand for nonviolence.

> *"I have from an early age abjured the use of meat, and the time will come when men such as I will look on the murder of animals as they now look on the murder of men."*
>
> —Leonardo da Vinci (1452 – 1519)

In addition to avoiding meat, fish, and poultry, many vegetarians avoid the use of all other animal products. In part, that's because many animal by-products, such as leather and wool, subsidize the meat industry. The production of other animal products, such as eggs, milk, and other dairy products, are also seen as exploiting those animals, subjecting them to inhumane conditions and treatment, and supporting the meat industry.

Male calves that are born to dairy cows, for instance, are typically taken from their mothers and raised in less-than-comfortable surroundings for veal. Chickens that are raised for their eggs generally live in factory-farm conditions in which they are routinely subjected to the practice of *debeaking,* Debeaking is the practice of using a machine to cut off the end of a chicken's beak to reduce the pecking damage caused when crowded chickens lash out at each other.

For more information about animal rights, including sources of cruelty-free products, contact People for the Ethical Treatment of Animals (PETA), 501 Front Street, Norfolk, VA 23510; phone 757-622-7382; Web site www. peta-online.org.

Health Reasons

In addition to making the world a better place to live, choosing to adopt a vegetarian lifestyle presents specific health benefits, such as increased energy and reduced rates of disease. In general, people who make a conscious choice to go vegetarian are also more likely to pay closer attention to their health than those who don't consciously choose such a lifestyle.

Staying healthy

The single most important dietary change you can make to improve your health is to reduce the frequency and amount of meat you eat. Meat is a rich source of artery-clogging saturated fat and cholesterol. High intakes of animal protein raise cholesterol levels and are associated with higher rates of coronary artery disease, some forms of cancer, and kidney disease. A high protein, meat-centered diet can increase your risk of kidney stones and cause calcium to be leached out of your bones. And that's just the beginning.

Avoiding disease

Some people are turned off by thoughts of *Listeria, Salmonella,* and mad cow disease. *Listeria* and *Salmonella* are types of bacteria found in meats and in other animal products. A good dose of either can cause severe illness at best and death at worst, though a small dose of *Salmonella* poisoning may be passed off as the "24-hour flu." In fact, a sizable number of cases thought to be 24-hour flu are actually caused by a food-borne pathogen, usually carried in an animal product. Turkey, anyone?

Mad cow disease, also known as *Creutzfeldt-Jakob Disease* (CJD), is a progressive and fatal disease characterized by the brain tissue of a human or an animal becoming spongy and porous; the animal or person literally loses its mind.

Mad cow disease is probably not caused by a bacterium or virus. The best guess at the present time is that it may be caused by an infectious protein. In England, the practice of feeding ground bone meal from dead cows and sheep to cows that were then marketed as food for people is thought to have spread the disease. The practice was fairly commonplace in the U.S. as well, until recently, when recognition of the risks (and the public's disgust at finding this out) forced meat producers to halt the practice.

Speaking out against beef

Despite assurances from U.S. cattle producers that there had never been a case of CJD in the United States, viewers of *The Oprah Winfrey Show* heard Oprah swear off cheeseburgers and then saw her get into major legal trouble with the cattle ranchers in Texas, who wanted her tried for libeling beef. The case against Oprah was thrown out of court.

Vegetarian diets are as important to health for what they *don't* include — excessive amounts of animal protein, saturated fat, and cholesterol — as they are for what they *do* include. Vegetarian diets tend to be rich sources of dietary fiber, antioxidant vitamins and minerals, and phytochemicals, which all help protect the body against such ills as cancer and coronary artery disease, among others.

Chapter 4

Making the Switch to Vegetarianism

"Where are you going?" the cat asked.

"I don't know."

"Well, either road will get you there."

—Lewis Carroll, *Alice in Wonderland*

Don't be like Alice, who doesn't know which route to take to get where she wants to go. When it comes to changing your eating style, *how* you do it isn't as important as having a plan in mind for getting there; without a plan, you're less likely to achieve your goal.

We all have different personalities and styles of doing things. What's important is that you find a method that works for you. There's no right or wrong way of making a lifestyle change, as long as you are successful. So do what's comfortable for you. This chapter covers some of the things you might want to think about in formulating your plan of action as you make the switch to a vegetarian lifestyle.

The Overnight Approach

One day he's chewing on a 10-ounce rib-eye at a local steakhouse, and the next day he's ordering the tempeh burger at his neighborhood natural foods café. Although it's not a likely scenario, some people do make the decision to go vegetarian overnight. They see a video or hear a lecture that inspires them, or they read a book or an article about the horrors of the slaughterhouse. Or even worse, they visit a slaughterhouse in person. Instant vegetarian.

The overnight transition to vegetarianism typically isn't flawless, but these people are motivated to make the change as soon as possible. Some people just prefer to make big changes quickly as opposed to dragging them out over months or years. That's fine.

Benefits of the quick switch

There are some benefits to making the switch to a vegetarian diet in one fell swoop:

✔ **You get to enjoy the benefits sooner.** People who make big changes right away tend to notice the benefits quickly, and they may especially want to if they have health concerns. For example, an overweight person might begin losing weight right away, or a diabetic's blood sugar level may drop immediately.

✔ **You get immediate gratification.** Your personality may be such that you need the satisfaction that comes with taking immediate action and reaching your goal as soon as possible.

✔ **You know you'll get there in this lifetime.** In comparison to people who take the gradual approach, people who make the change all at once jump one big hurdle to arrive at their goal. They don't run the same risk that the others run of getting stuck in a rut along the way and never moving on to the goal.

The overnight approach works best for people who

✔ **Have done some homework:** Even a little bit of reading or talking with another vegetarian about basic nutrition questions and ideas for quick and easy meals can help immensely.

✔ **Are surrounded by support:** The overnight approach is easier for people who live or work with other vegetarians and have someone they can emulate or question about basic nutrition and meal-planning issues than for people who don't have this type of support.

✔ **Are relatively free of other distractions:** It's easier to make a big change overnight if you don't have a new baby, a new job, or an 80-hour workweek.

Some people don't have a choice. They may have witnessed a scene that won't let them ever again look at a package of hamburger the same way. They're going vegetarian, and there's no looking back. No time for planning, no time for reading up on the subject. Move over and make room at the salad bar.

If you make the decision to switch that quickly, then you'll need to do the best you can until you can get your hands on some resources to help you continue successfully on that path.

If you have switched to a vegetarian diet but find yourself tired and hungry or irritable, you may not be eating enough. Some people who switch overnight haven't had time to figure out what they can eat. They end up eating only a few different types of foods, and they often don't get enough calories. Don't fall prey to the "iceberg lettuce syndrome." There are an almost infinite number of foods you can eat. If you can't figure out what to make for meals, see the chapters in Part IV for ideas on what you might eat.

If you are a diabetic and switch to a vegetarian diet, you should pay your health provider a visit. Diabetics who adopt a vegetarian diet frequently need less insulin or oral medication and need to have their dosages adjusted. In some cases, diabetics' blood sugar levels decrease enough to allow them to discontinue their medication altogether. Don't attempt to change your medications without checking with your doctor or other health care provider first, however.

Drawbacks of instant vegetarianism

If you take the instant route to gratification, you'll soon find out you've got no time to develop the necessary new skills and to put supports in place. It takes time to soak up the background information about nutrition and meal planning, as well as to learn how to deal with all sorts of practical issues such as eating out and handling questions from friends and family. These are some of the things that are necessary for a successful transition, and if they're not taken care of before you dive in, your entry can be a bit sloppy, or you can do a big belly flop.

If you opt for the overnight approach, use your wits to do the best you can at the outset, but make it a point to come up with a plan for smoothing the transition as soon as possible. Get yourself educated, get a plan, and get some support as soon as possible. See Parts III, IV, V, and VII for more on vegetarian survival strategies.

The Gradual Approach

Most people fare best by taking the gradual approach to adopting a vegetarian diet, letting their diets evolve at their own pace as they develop new skills and educate themselves about this new eating style. As you master each new skill, you become more secure and comfortable with meal planning and handling a variety of food-related situations. Parts IV and V offer lots of practical information to make the transition to a vegetarian lifestyle as easy as possible.

Benefits of the gradual approach

Two advantages to making a gradual switch to vegetarianism come to mind. Think about them and let them help you strengthen your resolve:

- ✔ **Your new eating habits are more likely to stick.** By making changes gradually as you collect the information and support you need to make it work, you build a strong foundation.

- ✔ **The gradual approach may be less disruptive to your routine.** If you have more time to adapt to each change every small step of the way, you may have a better chance of sticking with it.

Drawbacks of the gradual approach

There are two disadvantages to taking the gradual approach as opposed to making the switch overnight. Keep these in mind and try to avoid them:

- ✔ **You could get stuck in a rut along the way.** You can get stuck anywhere along the line and never make the transition to a full-fledged vegetarian diet. Some people cut out red meat as one step toward following a vegetarian diet, but they never make it any further. They're forever stuck in the chicken-and-fish rut, and before long they're considering jumping off the Empire State Building. Or they get as far as substituting cheese and eggs for meat, but they don't get beyond it. Their blood cholesterol levels are soaring because they're living on cheese omelets, macaroni and cheese, and grilled cheese sandwiches. Don't let this happen to you. Have a plan to keep moving.

- ✔ **You face the possibility of procrastinating and dragging the change out too long.** Some people will grab any opportunity to take it easy. If you take too long to make the change, it may never happen. Don't delude yourself. If you want to adopt a vegetarian diet but it's been a year since you started, it's time to put pen to paper and develop a more structured plan with dated goals for getting there.

Making the Change

When you decide to adopt a vegetarian eating style, you'll need to master skills in a variety of areas, and this book is here to help:

- ✔ **Basic vegetarian nutrition:** See Part II for help in this area.

- ✔ **Grocery shopping and stocking your pantry:** Chapter 10 offers advice on what to buy and where.

✔ **Meal planning and fixing new recipes:** Look to the chapters in Part IV for a variety of food ideas.

✔ **Dealing with social situations surrounding family, friends, and business associates:** Chapters 11, 12, and 18 are guides to making your vegetarian lifestyle fit in with other aspects of your life.

✔ **Eating away from home at the office, restaurants, school, friends' homes, or while traveling:** Part V focuses on sticking to your vegetarian goals when you're not in control of the kitchen.

✔ **Establishing new food traditions for holidays and special occasions:** You don't have to follow the same old holiday traditions when you switch to vegetarianism, and Chapter 17 can help you break the old mold.

Whether you choose to make the switch to a vegetarian diet overnight or gradually, there are a variety of ways in which you can tackle these areas of change. It's just a matter of personal preference. You may be especially interested in nutrition and devour books on the subject, or you may love to cook and find yourself experimenting with recipes long before you get around to thinking about vegetarian meals while traveling. You may like to read, or you may prefer talking to other vegetarians or attending lectures instead.

How you choose to proceed is up to you. The following guide is only one suggestion for planning a reasonably paced transition to a vegetarian eating style.

Focusing on the parts of the project

Have you ever had to write a term paper or thesis? Cringe! Any large project can seem overwhelming when you look at it in its entirety.

To tackle such a project, it's a good idea to break the project up into smaller pieces, and focus on only one piece at a time. Psychologically, this may make it easier for you. It can also get you moving if dwelling on the immense size of the task causes you to become immobilized. Writing down the steps you plan to take and checking them off as you master each one can give you a sense of accomplishment and help keep you motivated along the way.

Draw up a weekly or monthly plan of action outlining the things on which you want to focus each step of the way. For instance, you might want to concentrate on reading several books and other written materials for the first two months. From there, you might pick up a few vegetarian cookbooks and experiment with recipes, adding a few meatless meals per week to your schedule for the next month. You may step it up to five meatless days per week for the next few months, and begin attending a local vegetarian society's meetings.

Your plan should reflect your lifestyle, your personality and preferences for making these changes, and any constraints that may have to be factored in, such as cooking for a family or traveling frequently.

It helps to set time goals in your plan for transitioning to a vegetarian diet. If you can keep these "deadlines" in your head, fine. If not, or if you find yourself dragging your feet about getting to the next step, you may need more structure. Write your plan on paper, and break it down week by week. Give yourself a reasonable amount of time to complete each task, and stick to your plan.

Educating yourself

If you're not a reader, skip to the next step. If you do like to read, you're in luck because there are many, many excellent resources. It's a great idea to spend several weeks to a few months reading everything you can get your hands on that pertains to vegetarianism. There's a lot of material out there to help you. See Appendix A for some suggestions.

Some books and magazines may seem to cover the same subjects, but it's worth reading them all because each author presents the information in his or her own style, and the repetition of the subject matter in different words can help you learn. You'll find materials on all aspects of vegetarianism. Read them, and you'll build a solid foundation for your transition.

Once you begin to tap into books and magazines and other resources on vegetarianism, you'll become aware of videos, lectures, television programs, audiotapes, vegetarian groups, and other sources of information about vegetarianism. Take advantage of them and soak up the information like a sponge. Right now, you're in the information-gathering stage.

Reducing your meat intake

While you're doing the background work, reading and soaking up other forms of information about vegetarian diets, you can start reducing your meat intake in some easy ways:

- ✔ Add two or three meatless main meals to your diet each week. Begin with some easy and familiar entrées, such as spaghetti with tomato sauce, vegetarian pizza, bean burritos, vegetable lasagna, and pasta primavera.

- ✔ Try some vegetarian convenience foods, such as veggie burger patties, veggie breakfast meats, frozen vegetarian dinners, and veggie hotdogs. They're quick and convenient. Many supermarkets now carry most or all of these, and you can also find a large selection at natural foods stores. Substitute these for their meat counterparts.

✔ When you do eat meat, make it a minor part of the meal rather than the focal point of the plate. Use meat as more of a condiment or side dish. Keep portions small, and use it only in dishes in which the meat is extended by mixing it with rice, vegetables, pasta, or other plant products. For instance, rather than eat a chicken breast as an entrée, cut it up and mix it into a big vegetable stir-fry that feeds four to six people.

From there, just keep going. Add a few more meatless meals to your weekly schedule and stick with it for a month or so. Set a date beyond which you'll be eating only vegetarian meals. Mark that date with a big star on your calendar, and then cross off each day that you're meat-free after that.

Maintaining your resolve

Once you've started the switch to vegetarianism, it's all about practicing and continuing to expand your base of knowledge and experience. Expect some bumps in the road, but keep on going. Experiment with recipes, new foods, and vegetarian entrées at restaurants, invite friends and family members over to your place for meals, read some more about nutrition and meal planning, and allow yourself more time to get comfortable with your new lifestyle. Table 4-1 suggests a yearlong time line for reaching your goal.

Table 4-1	Twelve Months to a Vegetarian Eating Style
Time Frame	*What to Do*
Months 1 and 2	*Read about basic nutrition, meal planning, dealing with social situations, and other aspects of vegetarian diets.* Borrow books from the library, buy a few good resources at a bookstore, send away to vegetarian organizations for materials, read all you can online, and subscribe to vegetarian magazines. Attend lectures, listen to audiotapes, or view videos on the subject. Absorb information.
Month 3	*Begin to reduce your meat intake.* Add two or three meatless meals to your repertoire each week, experiment with new products, make a list of all of the vegetarian foods that you already enjoy, and when you do eat meat, make it a minor part of the meal, rather than the focal point of the plate.

(continued)

Table 4-1 *(continued)*

Time Frame	What to Do
Months 4 through 6	*Cut back even more on your meat intake.* Plan five meatless days each week. Limit meat to use as a condiment, a side dish, or a minor ingredient in a dish. Plan a cutoff date after which you'll move on to all vegetarian meals. Mark that date on your calendar. A week or two before that date, stop buying meat and products containing meat, such as soup with ham or bacon and baked beans with pork. Keep a diary or log of everything you eat for several days. You'll refer to it later to gauge your progress. Be specific about the ingredients. For example, if you eat a sandwich, make note of the kind of bread and filling you chose.
Months 6 through 8	*Look into joining a local vegetarian society or attending a national vegetarian conference.* Seek out occasions when you can be surrounded by like-minded individuals from whom you can learn. Continue reading and absorbing information. Continue experimenting with new recipes. Go out to eat and order vegetarian entrées at restaurants.
Months 9 through 12	*Practice.* Continue to seek new information. Socialize and invite friends and family members to your home for vegetarian meals. Look back over the past year and evaluate how you have handled holiday and special occasions, vacations, and breaks in your routine. Are there situations that need attention, such as eating away from home or finding quick and easy meal ideas? Keep a food diary for several days and compare it to your first one.

More Ways to Ease the Transition

You're on your way! This section offers more tips to make the journey a little easier.

Many people are their own worst critics. Although you don't want to delude yourself into thinking that you're making progress when you're not, you also don't want to be too harsh with yourself if you have a setback now and then. Change takes time and patience.

Occasional slips are normal. If you have to eat cereal for dinner for an entire week, or if you have to pick the pepperoni off the pizza rather than refuse it altogether at a friend's house on Super Bowl Sunday, don't let it get you down. If you have a lapse from your plan, pick up where you left off and start again. No one is keeping score but you.

Listing meatless foods you already like

If you are just starting out, make a list of the vegetarian foods that you already enjoy, and fix them often. You probably already eat a number of meatless foods, but you haven't thought of them as being vegetarian until now. Here are some examples:

- Vegetable stir-fry over rice
- Macaroni and cheese
- Vegetarian lasagna
- Pancakes
- Bean burritos and tacos
- Grilled cheese sandwiches
- Spaghetti with tomato sauce
- Pasta primavera
- Lentil soup
- Baked potato topped with broccoli and cheese

If your favorite vegetarian foods happen to contain dairy products such as cheese or milk, gradually reduce the amount of dairy products contained in them and switch to nonfat varieties. Some of your other favorite foods can probably be easily modified to make them vegetarian. Some examples:

- **Chili:** Make it with beans, tempeh, or textured vegetable protein instead of meat.
- **Bean soups:** Leave out the ham or bacon.
- **Sandwiches:** Load up on lettuce, tomatoes, mustard, chopped or shredded vegetables, add a little cheese if you like, and leave out the meat. Use pita pockets, hard rolls, and whole-grain breads to give sandwiches more personality.
- **Burgers:** Buy veggie burger patties instead of meat.
- **Breakfast meats:** Use veggie versions of link sausage, or sausage patties, and bacon. They taste great and can replace meat at breakfast or in a BLT.
- **Hotdogs and luncheon meats:** Buy veggie versions. All natural foods stores carry them, and so do some supermarkets. They look and taste like the real thing but are far better for you.
- **Meatloaf:** Even that all-American food can be made with lentils, chopped nuts, grated vegetables, and other ingredients. Many vegetarian cookbooks include a number of delicious variations.

✔ **Pasta sauces:** Why add meat or meat flavorings when you have basil, oregano, mushrooms, red peppers, sun-dried tomatoes, pimentos, black olives, and scores of other delicious ingredients to give sauces flavor? Great on cannelloni, stuffed shells, manicotti, ravioli, fettuccine, and steamed or roasted vegetables.

✔ **Stuffed cabbage:** Instead of using pork or beef, fill cabbage leaves with a mixture of rice and garbanzo beans and seasonings. It's worth perusing vegetarian cookbooks for gems like this one.

Be aware that interruptions in your routine, such as a vacation, holiday, or sickness, can trigger a lapse in your eating plan. In times of stress or a break in the usual routine, it's common for people to fall back into familiar patterns, including old ways of eating. Give yourself a break, and then start fresh again. With time, you'll learn how to handle these breaks in routine and won't be derailed.

Browsing vegetarian cookbooks

Go to the library and check out all the vegetarian cookbooks you can find. If you have friends who are vegetarians, borrow their cookbooks. Then begin to page through each one. Read the names of the recipes. If you see one that grabs you, look at the list of ingredients. If the recipe inspires you, fix it. When you find a cookbook with lots of recipes that appeal to you, go to a bookstore and buy it, or order it by mail from a vegetarian organization or catalog. Natural foods stores also carry a good selection of popular vegetarian cookbooks.

Do this to orient yourself to the options on a vegetarian diet. You'll be surprised at the variety. You may also notice lots of ethnic foods borrowed from cultures that have vegetarian traditions. There's more variety on a vegetarian diet than on a meat-centered diet, and reviewing cookbooks will help you see that. See Appendix A for some recommended cookbooks.

Touring a natural foods store

Head to your neighborhood natural foods store. Walk up and down all the aisles, including the frozen foods case. You'll find dozens of vegetarian foods. Buy a few on this trip, and then try a few more next time.

Whole foods — products that are as close to their natural state as possible — are healthiest. However, prepared foods and vegetarian specialty products, such as frozen entrées, veggie burger patties, and boxed mixes, can be an acceptable convenience, particularly when you don't have time to cook or are facing unusual circumstances that would otherwise make it difficult to stick with your new vegetarian eating style.

When you sample new products, expect to find a few duds. That comes with the territory and is true of nonvegetarian food as well. Next time, try another brand of the same type of product because there can be a lot of variation from one brand to the next. Once you start experimenting with new foods, you'll discover a long list of great products that will become regulars in your repertoire.

Accentuating the positive

Some people hit the floor happy each morning, and others have to work at it. Likewise, some people see the fun in a challenge, and others just see the challenge.

Many people think of the restrictions when they visualize a vegetarian diet. They focus on the "don'ts" — don't eat hamburger, steak, fish, shrimp, chicken, turkey, sausage, hotdogs, gelatin, beef broth, chicken fat, and so on. They see a big hole in the middle of their plates where the meat used to be.

It's a mindset and an attitude. It doesn't have to be that way.

Any experienced vegetarian will tell you that there is more variety in a vegetarian diet than in a nonvegetarian diet. More choices, more interesting foods, and no bare spots on their plates. That's another mindset, and a positive attitude.

Try to keep all the good choices in mind when you think about meal planning, and don't bother to waste energy thinking about what you used to eat. In time, you won't even have to try. Eventually, you'll reach the point where meat and meat products don't even cross your mind.

Just for comparison

Keeping a food diary can help you chart your progress as you adopt a vegetarian eating style. It can be fun to compare "before" and "after." Keep a log of what you eat each day for several days at the outset of your transition, and then file it away. Six months later, keep another log for several more days. Compare this one to the first one and note the changes. You can do this every so often to help evaluate your progress. A food diary can also help you recognize whether you are stuck in a rut.

Part II
Vegetarian NutriSense

The 5th Wave By Rich Tennant

"This isn't some sort of fad diet, is it?"

In this part . . .

*L*et's face it, every one of us has the basic four food groups branded on our frontal lobes. We will forever conjure up pictures of Swiss and Gouda, rib-eye steaks, 12-ounce glasses of cold, frothy, white milk, hamburger patties, and Elsie the Cow every time someone asks us to name the foods that provide us with protein, calcium, and iron.

Even though you may be savvy enough to know that there are other food sources of key nutrients, it's hard to change your mindset in a culture in which animal products have held center stage for generations.

That's why I'm devoting this whole part of the book to some basic nutrition issues. The chapters that follow should help clear up any questions or concerns you might have about the nutritional adequacy of a diet that limits or excludes foods of animal origin.

Chapter 5

Protein Particulars

. . . .

. . . .

Many vegetarians worry too much about whether they are getting enough protein, and if they aren't worried, then it's a good bet that their mother or their spouse or another family member *is*.

There's rarely a need to worry about the protein intake of vegetarians, but it's not hard to understand why people do. In first grade, their teachers made them cut out pictures of protein-containing foods from magazines and paste them on a cardboard poster of the Basic Four Food Groups. They cut out pictures of hamburgers, hotdogs, pot roasts, and ham-and-cheese sandwiches. They got extra credit if they included peanut butter — a tricky and unexpected choice because it didn't come from an animal.

It's hard to shed ideas that have been wired into your brain, but this chapter is here to help you loosen your grip on some of them and tell you all you need to know about protein in meatless diets.

Protein Facts

The word *protein* comes from a Greek word meaning "of first importance." It was the first material identified as being a vital part of all living organisms. Proteins make up the basic structure of all living cells, and they are a component of hormones, enzymes, and antibodies.

Most of the protein in our bodies is found in our muscles, but there's also protein in our bones, teeth, blood, and other body fluids. The collagen in connective tissue is a protein, and so is the keratin in hair. The casein in milk, albumin in eggs, blood albumin, and hemoglobin are all examples of proteins as well.

You've got good chemistry!

The building blocks of protein are *amino acids*. There are 20 amino acids found in most proteins. Linked together, amino acids form proteins, but individual amino acids have specialized functions in the body as well. The amino acid *tryptophan*, for instance, plays a role in the creation of the vitamin *niacin*. The amino acid *glycine* combines with toxic substances and converts them into harmless forms that are then excreted from the body. *Histidine* is involved in the formation of the vasodilator histamine, a substance that you've probably had experience with if you've ever had a stuffy nose from hay fever or another allergy. Individual amino acids can also combine with other nonprotein substances to perform still other functions in the body.

Your body can manufacture most of the amino acids that it needs to build proteins. It does this by using parts from carbohydrates, fats, and other amino acids. However, there are 9 amino acids that the body cannot manufacture, and these have to come from the food that you eat. These amino acids are called *essential amino acids* or *indispensable amino acids*. The "big nine" are histidine, isoleucine, leucine, lysine, methionine, phenylalanine, threonine, tryptophan, and valine.

Protein is a vital part of all living tissues. Proteins are nitrogen-containing compounds that break down into amino acids during digestion. Amino acids are the building blocks of proteins and have other functions in the body as well. Essential amino acids are amino acids that cannot be manufactured by the body. There are nine of them, and you have to get them from your food.

Protein is a component of every cell in your body. Your body uses protein to manufacture hormones, enzymes, antibodies, and blood. Your body manufactures some of the protein it needs; the rest you have to get from the foods you eat. Most people think that meat is the only — or the best — place to get protein. The fact is that animal products are concentrated sources of protein; actually, diets in which animal products play a prominent role are often *too high* in protein. But plant foods are sources of protein as well. Figure 5-1 shows several vegetarian sources of protein.

Rather than rely on animal products, we can get plenty of protein from plant foods. It's easy to do, and it's healthier, too. Vegetables, grains, legumes, seeds, and nuts all contain protein. The following is a list of some vegetarian foods that are good sources of protein:

- ✔ Bean burritos
- ✔ Tofu lasagna
- ✔ Lentil soup
- ✔ Bean soup
- ✔ Vegetarian chili

- Falafel (garbanzo bean balls)
- Pasta primavera
- Red beans and rice
- Vegetarian pizza
- Oatmeal
- Cereal and soy milk
- Barbecued tempeh
- Vegetable stir-fry
- Veggie burgers

Plants contain all the essential amino acids in varying amounts. Some plants are high in some essential amino acids and low in others. It's easy to get enough of what you need, even if you eat nothing but plant products and your diet contains no meat, eggs, or dairy products at all.

In fact, as long as you get enough calories to meet your energy needs, it's nearly impossible to be deficient in protein. If you ate nothing but potatoes but got enough potatoes to meet your energy needs, you'd get all the essential amino acids you need.

Figure 5-1:
Vegetarian foods rich in protein.

Now, I'd never suggest that you should eat nothing but potatoes. There are other nutrients that you need from foods besides protein, and no one food has them all. That's why it's important to include a reasonable variety of foods in your diet. However, the practical matter about protein and essential amino acids is that if you eat enough vegetables, grains, legumes, nuts, and seeds (or a reasonable variety of most of those foods), you'll be sure to meet or exceed your need for all the essential amino acids.

Protein Fiction: The Combining Myth

Despite what you may have heard or read, you don't have to consciously combine foods (called *complementing proteins*) to make sure you get enough protein in a vegetarian diet. The idea was that since plant foods are limited in one or more of the essential amino acids, we should combine a food that is limited in a particular amino acid with a food that has an abundance of that same amino acid. The concept was to complement one plant food's amino acid profile with another's, fitting two foods together like puzzle pieces. That way, you'd have a "complete protein," with adequate amounts of all the essential amino acids present and available to the body at the same time.

Experts even went so far as to create complex protein complementarity charts that detailed the manner in which foods should be combined, and con-scientious vegetarians were careful to eat their beans with rice or corn and to add milk or cheese to their grains (macaroni and cheese was a big favorite). They ruefully acknowledged that they should have taken better notes in organic chemistry class.

In recent years, however, nutrition scientists have given the issue of protein complementarity a little more thought, and the verdict is that we might have gone a wee bit overboard. Suffice it to say that the practice of combining foods is no longer considered necessary.

Your body can complement its proteins without much help from you. Your job is to do two things:

- ✔ Make sure you get enough calories to meet your energy needs.
- ✔ Eat a reasonable variety of foods over the course of the day.

That's really all there is to it.

Bottom line? The only combination you have to worry about is the one on your locker at the gym.

Historical info

What gave people the idea that vegetarians had to be careful about combining foods in the first place?

In the early 1970s, Frances Moore Lappé wrote a book titled *Diet for a Small Planet*. This classic raised awareness about the relationships between food choices and the efficient use of our natural resources, and it advocated a vegetarian diet. But the book also made generations of vegetarians aware of the concept of protein complementarity. Unfortunately, it was this idea that made it seem as though it may be difficult or risky to eat a vegetarian diet.

Some health professionals and writers who don't realize that the recommendations have changed are actually still perpetuating the idea that vegetarians have to carefully combine foods in a certain way. The next time you read a magazine article that says that vegetarians have to "complement their proteins," you can smile smugly to yourself, knowing that you know better. Write a letter to the editor, too.

When I open the front cover of my dog-eared, 1972 copy of *Diet for a Small Planet* — the one with the crunchy, yellowing pages — the very first thing that appears is the following:

> *"What is protein complementarity? The combination, in the proper proportions, of non-meat foods, that produces high-grade protein nutrition equivalent to — or better than — meat proteins. And that is what this book is all about."*

The idea that proteins had to be complemented was also supported by some very early lab data from studies of protein-deprived rats. The rats were fed diets that were deficient in individual essential amino acids. Without these essential amino acids, the rats couldn't build complete proteins and became protein deficient. Of course, those were laboratory conditions. In real life, we eat whole foods that contain an array of amino acids, including all the essential amino acids. We don't eat specially developed, amino-acid-deficient laboratory rat chow. So these studies had little relevance for free-living human beings.

The Protein Balance

Really, you don't have to worry about your protein intake. Okay, if you live on Twinkies and Dr. Pepper, then maybe you could end up protein deficient. But you'd be lacking in many vitamins and minerals and other phytochemicals, too. Nevertheless, I know that some of you want to know precisely how much protein you need, so here's a simple way to figure it out:

The rule of thumb for determining recommended protein intake is to aim for 0.8 gram of protein for every kilogram of your body weight. One kilogram is equal to 2.2 pounds. That's body weight (in kilograms) × 0.8 = grams of protein needed. This formula has a generous margin of error worked into it. In reality, your body actually requires less than this amount.

So, for example, if you weighed 120 pounds, that would be about 54.5 kilograms (120 pounds divided by 2.2 kilograms). Multiply 54.5 kilograms by 0.8 grams of protein per kilogram of body weight, and you get 43.6 grams of protein, or approximately 44 grams of protein. That's how much protein your body would need, and it isn't very much.

Protein is the least likely nutrient to be deficient in a vegetarian diet, but it's interesting to note that soybeans are a rich source of all the essential amino acids. Soy could actually serve as the sole source of protein in a person's diet if that were necessary for some reason.

Serving it up right

To get an idea of how easy it is to get the protein you need, take a look at the list of foods and their protein contents presented in Table 5-1. Think about what you eat in the course of a day and the size of the portions you take. Calculate your own protein requirement using the formula I gave earlier in this section, and then compare that to the amount of protein you eat in a typical day.

Table 5-1	Protein Values of Common Foods
Food	*Grams of Protein*
Animal Products	
1 ounce any type of meat	7
1 ounce cheese	7
1 egg	7
1 cup milk	8
Quarter-pound hamburger (no bun)	28
4-ounce chicken breast	28
10-ounce rib-eye steak	70
3-egg omelet with 2 ounces of cheese	35

Food	Grams of Protein
Animal Product Alternatives	
1 typical veggie burger	5 – 25
1 typical veggie hotdog (1 link)	8
4 ounces tempeh	20
4 ounces tofu (depending on type)	5 – 9
8 ounces soymilk (plain)	10
Legumes (Dried Beans and Peas)	
½ cup most legumes (depending on type)	5 – 9
½ cup bean burrito filling	6
1 cup black bean soup	16
1 cup vegetarian chili	24
½ cup vegetarian baked beans	6
½ cup garbanzo beans on a salad	6
Nuts and Seeds	
1 ounce nuts (depending on type)	4 – 7
1 ounce seeds (depending on type)	4 – 11
2 tablespoons tahini (sesame seed butter)	6
2 tablespoons cashew, almond, or peanut butter	8
Grains and Grain Products	
1 slice whole wheat bread (dense style)	2 – 3
1 bran muffin	3
½ cup whole-grain flake cereal	2
½ cup cooked oatmeal	3
1 whole bagel	6
½ cup cooked pasta	7
½ cup cooked rice	4
1 flour tortilla	2

(continued)

Table 5-1 *(continued)*	
Food	*Grams of Protein*
Vegetables and Fruits	
1 cup most vegetables (for example, green beans, tomatoes, cabbage, broccoli)	4
Most fruits	trace amounts

Take a look at the sample one-day vegan menu that follows:

Breakfast

    1 cup cooked oatmeal, with cinnamon, raisins, and 1 cup plain soymilk

    1 slice whole wheat toast, with margarine and jelly

    6 ounces fresh orange juice

Lunch

    Mixed green salad with vinaigrette dressing

    1 cup lentil soup

    1 chunk corn bread

    ½ cup fresh fruit salad

    Water

Dinner

    4 ounces bean curd mixed with Chinese vegetables and brown sauce

    1 cup steamed rice

    ½ cup cooked greens with sesame

    Orange wedges

    Herbal tea

Snack

    Bagel with tofu cream cheese

    Herbal iced tea mixed with fruit juice

This menu provides about 1,600 calories and 53 grams of protein. You can see that even if no animal products are included at all, it's easy to get all the protein you need.

To beef up your muscles, you don't need beef

A message to body builders: Listen up! Flooding yourself with protein from powders, egg white shakes, and big steaks doesn't build muscle. *Work* builds muscle, and your body can make those muscles from pasta and vegetables. Eating more meat doesn't help you build more muscle. Any extra calories from meat will just be converted into body fat. Elite athletes do need slightly more protein than the average person, but they easily get that protein in the extra calories they consume due to their high activity levels.

Technically, vegetarians may actually need a smidgen more protein than non-vegetarians. That's because many plant sources of protein are somewhat less digestible than animal sources or processed plant protein products, such as soymilk, tofu, and some veggie burger patties.

Avoiding protein pitfalls

 It bears repeating that, as mentioned in Chapter 1, there really is such a thing as too much protein. Excessively high protein intake — a habit that many people are guilty of — causes you to lose calcium. It increases your blood cholesterol level as well as your risk of heart disease and cancer. Vegetarian diets typically contain enough protein, without providing too much. Avoiding excessive amounts of protein in your diet has definite health advantages.

Chapter 6

The Calcium Connection

Dogs do it. Deer do it. Even chipmunks and raccoons do it. They all produce milk for their babies. Cows do it, too. So do humans.

But dogs don't drink chipmunks' milk. And deer don't drink raccoons' milk because milk is species specific. The milk of each species is tailor-made for its own kind. So how on earth did people start drinking milk from cows? Even adult cows don't drink cows' milk.

Calcium is vital to a healthy body. Too little calcium in your diet can make you a prime candidate for health problems like *osteoporosis,* the condition that results when the bones begin to waste away and become porous and brittle. Bones in this condition are susceptible to fractures. In the most severe cases, the bones can break with the slightest stress, such as a sneeze or a cough. Osteoporosis is a major health problem that affects 15 to 20 million Americans, often with life-threatening consequences.

The countries with the highest intakes of dairy products and animal protein also have the highest rates of hip fracture.

For the record, vegetarians around the world tend to have rates of *osteoporosis* that are the same as, or lower than, those of nonvegetarians. In cultures where a plant-based diet is the norm, data about bone health is fairly widely available. Unfortunately, there isn't enough reliable research data about the bone health of Western vegetarians, particularly vegans. So it's hard to tailor calcium recommendations for vegetarians distinct from those made for the general, nonvegetarian public.

There are too many questions about how such factors as physical activity level and environment may differ from one culture to the next, and how those factors may affect calcium needs. For this reason, scientists can't take calcium intake recommendations from nonwestern populations and apply them to Western vegetarians with confidence. In the U.S. and Canada, now that more people are moving away from a traditional Western eating style, efforts are under way to collect more data about the bone health of vegans and other vegetarians. Until more data is available, nutritionists have to hedge a little bit when asked to make specific recommendations about calcium intakes for Western vegans and other vegetarians.

Calcium and You

We associate calcium intake with the health of our bones and teeth, but actually, bone health isn't only about getting enough calcium. In fact, other important factors relate to bone health besides how much calcium you have in your diet.

U.S. recommendations for calcium intake take several factors into consideration. First, scientists know that a body normally loses a certain amount of calcium every day, through feces, sweat, and urine. Scientists can also estimate the amount of calcium your body typically absorbs from the food that you eat. With these two figures, they can estimate how much calcium you need to take in each day in order to break even. Then they add a little extra — a "fudge factor" — just to be on the safe side.

Factors that influence how much calcium you need

For vegetarians, the amount of calcium that is actually absorbed and retained from food is probably a good deal higher than for most Americans, so recommended intakes could theoretically be lower. How much lower depends on a few factors:

- **The protein factor:** Americans generally have a penchant for meat and other high-protein foods, and they pay for it in calcium loss. The amount of protein in your diet probably has a greater bearing on the health of your bones than does the amount of calcium in your diet. Scientists think that the ideal ratio of calcium to protein is about 16:1.

- **The sodium factor:** Like protein, sodium has a profound calcium-depleting effect on the body. Table salt and processed foods contain lots of sodium, as do canned foods and condiments such as ketchup, mustard, and pickles. We all need sodium, but we can get all we need from what is naturally found in our food supply. We don't have to add sodium to foods. Read the labels on the packaged foods that you buy, and try to limit your sodium intake to not more than about 2,000 milligrams each day — good advice for vegetarians and nonvegetarians alike.

✔ **The phosphorous factor:** Too much phosphorus (found in red meats and soft drinks) causes the body to lose calcium, as does the caffeine found in such things as cola drinks, other soft drinks, coffee, and tea. These have a lesser effect on calcium balance than do protein and sodium, though.

✔ **The phytates and oxalates factor:** Substances such as *phytates* and *oxalates*, found in plant foods, inhibit your body's ability to absorb the calcium in the foods that contain them. Whole grains are high in phytates, and spinach is high in oxalates, making most of the calcium in these foods unavailable to your body. Overall, though, plant foods contain plenty of calcium that can be well absorbed. In fact, some research shows that the calcium in such plant foods as kale, Chinese cabbage, and broccoli is absorbed better than the calcium found in cows' milk. Keep in mind that cooking destroys the oxalates, which makes the calcium easier to absorb.

✔ **The physical activity factor:** The more weight-bearing exercise you include in your daily routine, the more calcium you'll hang on to. People who walk regularly or engage in strength training by using a weight set at home or at the gym have denser bones than people who are couch potatoes.

✔ **The sunshine factor:** Even your exposure to sunshine makes a difference in how much calcium your bones absorb. Your body manufactures vitamin D when you are exposed to sunlight. And vitamin D helps your body absorb calcium. See Chapter 9 for more on vitamin D.

✔ **The absorption factor:** There's one more factor that people often forget. Your body adjusts the absorption of many nutrients, including calcium, according to its needs. In other words, when you need more calcium, your body magically becomes more efficient at absorbing the calcium that is present in your food. When you need less calcium, your body absorbs less, even if you flood yourself with calcium from dairy products or supplements.

Protein from plant sources doesn't have the same effect on the human body as protein from animal sources. That's because proteins from animal sources have more *sulfur-containing amino acids.* Now we're getting a little more technical. When you eat meat and other forms of animal protein, your blood becomes more acidic. In order to neutralize the acid in the blood, your body draws calcium from your bones and sends it into the bloodstream. This calcium is eventually lost through your urine as your kidneys filter your blood. The sulfur also has an effect on the kidneys that causes more calcium to be lost in the urine.

Imagine how much protein and sodium a junk-food junkie gets in his bacon double cheeseburger and fries, sausage biscuit with gravy, and cold cuts such as ham and bologna. Imagine how much more calcium is needed to compensate for what is lost due to foods like these.

It's a good idea for everyone to limit intake of high-sodium foods. Even vegetarians, who typically moderate their protein intakes, need to be aware that too much sodium in the diet can increase calcium loss.

Vegetarians who eat lots of salty snack chips, condiments such as ketchup and soy sauce, and processed foods such as many soups and meat substitutes, may be sacrificing calcium as a result. If this sounds like you, you can improve your diet by limiting foods such as these.

Determining your body's calcium requirements

Do you have to eat a truckload of broccoli to get the calcium your body needs? Probably not. It's most likely that vegetarians need less dietary calcium than nonvegetarians because they absorb and retain calcium better than nonvegetarians. So, intakes of calcium below current recommendations are probably not a problem for most vegetarians. But determining calcium requirements is more complicated than you may realize. The recommendations for calcium intake for Americans vary by age and sex. They are also based on certain assumptions, some of which are relevant to the culture in which we live.

Basically, you should get about 16 milligrams of calcium in your diet for every gram of protein that your diet contains. So, if your protein intake is about 45 grams a day (a typical intake for many vegetarians), your calcium intake should be at least 720 milligrams. If you're a meat-eater getting 90 grams of protein in your diet (and many meat-eaters get more), then you would need 1,440 milligrams of calcium each day.

Making Sure You Get Enough

Generally, it's a good idea for adult vegetarians, particularly vegans, to try to include two or more servings of calcium-rich foods in their diets each day. Teens and young adults should get an extra serving. Figure 6-1 shows some vegetarian foods that will help you meet your calcium needs. It's important for all of us limit our protein intakes to moderate levels (not more than 70 grams per day for most people). Sodium intakes should also be kept in check (not more than 2,000 milligrams per day).

Keep in mind that your calcium requirement depends largely on your protein intake and that the recommended ratio of calcium to protein is 16:1. Although you'll have to determine your own protein intake in order to know how much calcium you need, Table 6-1 can give you some numbers for comparison. (See Chapter 5 for a sampling of protein values.)

Table 6-1	Calcium Found in Vegetarian Foods
Food	*Calcium Content (milligrams)*
Dairy Sources	
1 cup skim milk	350
1 ounce mozzarella cheese (part skim)	183
1 cup nonfat yogurt (plain)	274
Plant Sources	
1 tablespoon almond butter	43
1 tablespoon blackstrap molasses	172
1 cup cooked bok choy	160
1 cup cooked broccoli	70
1 cup cooked collard greens	360
½ cup dried figs	143
1 cup canned garbanzo beans	77
1 cup cooked kale	180
1 cup canned kidney beans	69
1 cup cooked lentils	38
1 cup cooked mustard greens	104
1 cup canned navy beans	123
1 medium orange	61
1 cup canned pinto beans	103
1 cup fortified soymilk	200
1 cup calcium-fortified orange juice	300
½ cup firm tofu (processed with calcium sulfate)	861
1 cup cooked turnip greens	197
2 slices whole wheat bread	40

Figure 6-1:
Vegetarian
foods that
are rich in
calcium.

Vegetarian Sources of Calcium

Good plant sources of calcium include dark green, leafy vegetables, broccoli, legumes, figs, almonds, tofu processed with calcium, fortified soymilk or orange juice, and many others. A sampling of calcium-rich plant foods includes

- Dark green, leafy vegetables such as kale, Swiss chard, collards, and mustard and turnip greens
- Broccoli
- Chinese cabbage
- Tofu processed with calcium
- Legumes such as pinto beans, black beans, and garbanzo beans
- Almonds and sesame seeds
- Dried figs
- Calcium-fortified orange juice or soymilk

There are many others. Don't worry — you don't have to eat sardines with bones. And there are lots of delicious ways to work high-calcium foods into your meals. Here are some examples:

- ✔ Bean chili over rice with steamed broccoli and a chunk of cornbread
- ✔ Stir-fried Chinese vegetables with bean curd (tofu) over rice
- ✔ Falafel (garbanzo bean balls) served in pita pockets and a glass of orange juice
- ✔ Steamed kale with garlic and sesame seeds
- ✔ Fig cookies with a glass of fortified soymilk
- ✔ Green beans with slivered almonds
- ✔ Black bean dip, with broccoli and cauliflower florets and carrot sticks

What about Milk?

Cows' milk is a concentrated source of several nutrients. It's rich in calcium, riboflavin, fat, protein, and calories. It has to be because it has to enable a calf to grow into a several hundred pound cow with a massive skeleton in a matter of months. It's made to meet the special needs of a baby cow. And as with all mammals, including humans, after infancy the cow doesn't need milk anymore. From that point on, the cow gets the calcium and other nutrients it needs from the plants on which it grazes. In other words, you don't need cows' milk to maintain a healthy diet.

Need a replacement for cows' milk? Try soymilk. You can find it in any natural foods store and in most supermarkets. Many brands are calcium fortified. You'll also see rice milks and soy/rice blends, but they aren't as nutritious as soymilk. Soymilks vary in flavor from brand to brand, so experiment to find the one you like the best.

If you don't drink milk, you're not the oddball. In fact, you've got lots of company. You might be surprised to learn that most of the world's people do not drink cows' milk. The reason? Most of them can't digest it.

During infancy, the human body produces an enzyme called *lactase*. Lactase helps the body digest *lactose*, the form of sugar found in milk. As a baby becomes a toddler, it needs less of its mother's milk, so the body's production of lactase also begins to decline. By the time a human child is 3 to 5 years of age, he or she has stopped breast-feeding and doesn't naturally require milk in his or her diet anymore. By this time, the body has stopped or nearly stopped producing lactase. That's natural, too.

The politics of milk promotion

The United States Department of Agriculture is in the business of protecting and promoting agriculture. In large part, that means advocating for the meat and dairy industries. However, the Department of Agriculture is also charged with issuing dietary recommendations for the American public. A conflict of interest? You bet. Even when research into the connections between diet and disease began to implicate dairy products and meats and it became clear that we need to limit our intake of these foods, the Department of Agriculture was reluctant to pointedly say so. Today's guidelines make note of the fact that we need to eat more plant products and that vegetarian diets can be an acceptable alternative, but they are less clear in acknowledging that this means that people also need to reduce their consumption of animal products.

So, for generations we've had the Basic Four Food Groups, a model for meal planning that had meat and dairy products forming two of the four pillars of the diet. Never mind that there was never a human requirement for any of those foods. Fruits and vegetables? Squashed together in one group of their own. Breads and cereals formed the fourth group.

The Basic Four has finally been retired and replaced with a different model — the Food Guide Pyramid. The pyramid has its own set of problems, but it's an improvement on the old Basic Four. In the meantime, the dairy industry continues its marketing efforts to get more people to drink milk.

The dairy industry has historically been aggressive about providing nutrition education for the public. For decades, the industry has produced its own versions of meal planning guides and distributed them free of charge to schools, hospitals, and doctors' offices. For many of us, these were the only nutrition education materials we ever saw while we were in school. I remember the guides showing that good sources of calcium included milk, cheese, and ice cream. If you didn't want these, well . . . there were always the dreaded *sardines with bones.* Or voluminous quantities of broccoli. The choice seemed obvious at the time. After all, how much broccoli can a person eat?

Most adults in the world don't drink milk because they have stopped producing the lactase needed to digest the milk. They don't need human milk anymore, so there's no need for their bodies to produce the lactase, either. They have lost the ability to digest milk from their own species, and they certainly can't digest milk from another species. Because they can't digest milk sugar, the sugar moves into the intestines without having been completely digested. If they tried to drink milk, they'd likely show symptoms of *lactose intolerance,* such as gas, bloating, abdominal cramps, and diarrhea.

Among your friends and family members, those who are of Asian, African, Mediterranean, Native American, or South American descent are probably lactose intolerant to some degree. Most Hispanics and Jews are at least somewhat lactose intolerant. Who's not? People of Northern European descent.

That's thought to be due to a genetic mutation that occurred some time in generations past that allowed those people to continue to produce lactase into adulthood.

So, people of English and Scandinavian descent, for instance, are not as likely to have problems digesting milk. Because people of Northern European descent colonized the United States, Canada, Australia, and New Zealand, dairy products were a cultural tradition brought over to those countries from Northern Europe. Cultural diversity is increasing in the United States as more people from other countries settle in the U.S., and the prevalence of lactose intolerance is also increasing.

If so many people can't tolerate it, why do health professionals promote cow's milk as an important part of a "balanced" diet? The answer is partially as simple as the fact that it was a cultural tradition brought by people for whom it was a staple food for generations. But after that tradition took root, economic and political forces maintained it.

Chapter 7

Iron Intake

"List three good food sources of iron."

***W**hen I ask most people that question, they say, "Red meat," and draw a blank after that. Like protein and calcium, most people associate iron with an animal product, and also like protein and calcium, iron is widely available in foods of plant origin.

You may also associate having enough iron with having enough energy. Do you remember the old Geritol commercials from the late '60s? People with "iron-poor blood" were tired all the time — lethargic and groggy.

Iron is a mineral that forms part of the *hemoglobin* of red blood cells and helps carry oxygen to the body's cells. Iron is also part of the *myoglobin* that provides oxygen to the muscles in your body. When your iron stores are low or depleted, you can't get enough oxygen to the cells of your body. A form of *anemia* results, and you may feel very tired.

Before you begin yawning, you might like to know that vegetarians are not more prone than nonvegetarians to iron deficiency. *Iron-deficiency anemia* happens to be one of the most common nutritional deficiencies around the world, but most of it occurs in developing countries, rather than in affluent countries, and the cause is more likely to be parasites than diet. In developed countries, iron deficiency is most likely to affect children and young people, as well as pregnant and premenopausal women.

Knowing How Much Iron You Need

The recommended dietary allowances for iron vary by age and sex. Generally, the recommendations are higher for premenopausal women than for men and for postmenopausal women because women who menstruate lose more iron than women who do not. So, the recommendations for adult men and postmenopausal women are only 10 milligrams per day, compared to 15 milligrams per day for premenopausal women.

Vegetarians need more iron in their diets than nonvegetarians do because the iron in plant foods is not absorbed as efficiently as the iron in meat. However, you might be surprised to learn that on average, vegetarians tend to get substantially more iron in their diets than nonvegetarians. Vegans get the most because the dairy products that other vegetarians eat contain virtually no iron and tend to displace iron-containing plant foods.

It's not practical, though, for most people to count the milligrams of iron in their diets. Rather than live life with a calculator in the palm of your hand, it's far more enjoyable just to keep a couple of key points in mind:

✔ Be aware of which foods are particularly good sources of iron, and include them in your diet regularly.

✔ Be sure to eat plenty of vitamin C – rich fruits and vegetables.

You can't go wrong with fruits and vegetables. That's a common theme nowadays in discussions about nutrition. One national campaign urges everyone to eat "five a day" — five servings of fruits or vegetables. Of course, they're talking about small, half-cup servings. For most vegetarians, a goal of five half-cup servings would mean cutting *back*! When we're talking "servings" for vegetarians, we're talking heaping helpings. Eating lots of fruits and vegetables is a health-wise goal for anyone — vegetarian or not. Figure 7-1 shows some vegetarian foods that are rich in iron.

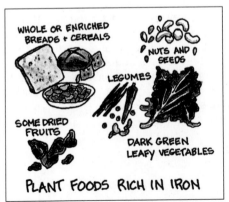

Figure 7-1:
Vegetarian
sources
of iron.

A primary reason that some people don't get the nutrition they need is that they let the junk push the good stuff out of their diets. If you load up on soft drinks, snack chips, and desserts, you'll end up displacing the healthier foods that you need. A small piece of cake or a few pieces of candy can add up to 300 calories or more. For 300 calories, you can eat a lot of broccoli, beans, and rice. Be honest with yourself about how much junk your diet contains, and when you want a snack, reach for a piece of fruit.

Finding Iron in Plant Foods

Iron is available everywhere you look in the plant world. Rich sources include whole or enriched breads and cereals, legumes, nuts and seeds, dark green, leafy vegetables, and some dried fruits. Vegetarians typically don't have trouble getting enough iron. Table 7-1 shows a selection of vegetarian foods and their iron values.

Table 7-1	Vegetarian Sources of Iron
Food	*Iron Content (milligrams)*
Breads and Cereals	
1 cup bran flakes	8.1
1 slice whole wheat bread	0.9
1 cup cooked oatmeal	1.6
1 cup steamed brown rice	1.0
Legumes	
1 cup cooked black beans	3.6
1 cup cooked garbanzo beans	4.7
1 cup lentil soup	2.7
1 cup cooked navy beans	4.5
1 cup cooked pinto beans	4.5
1 cup cooked soybeans	8.8
4 ounces tempeh	1.9
4 ounces firm tofu	1.8
1 cup vegetarian chili	3.5

(continued)

Table 7-1 *(continued)*

Food	Iron Content (milligrams)
Nuts and Seeds	
2 tablespoons peanut butter	0.6
2 tablespoons almond butter	1.2
1 cup sunflower seeds	1.0
Fruits	
1 cup dried apricots	1.5
¼ large cantaloupe	0.4
1 cup prunes	1.1
8 ounces prune juice	3.0
1.5 ounces raisins	0.9
1 cup diced watermelon	0.3
Vegetables	
1 cup cooked bok choy	0.4
1 cup cooked broccoli	1.3
1 cup cooked brussels sprouts	1.9
1 cup cooked collard greens	0.9
1 cup cooked kale	1.2
2 tablespoons kelp (seaweed)	0.3
1 cup cooked mustard greens	1.0
1 cup cooked Swiss chard	4.0
1 cup cooked turnip greens	1.2
Other	
2 tablespoons blackstrap molasses	7.0

Helping Your Body Absorb Iron

Just because you consume a certain amount of iron doesn't mean that that entire amount of iron is available for your body to use. There's actually a little game of tug-of-war over iron going on in your body. That's because there are substances in the foods you eat that enhance iron absorption in your body, as well as those that inhibit it.

Enhancers to remember

Meat is a common iron-absorption enhancer. But vegetarians don't eat meat, so what are they to do? Figure 7-2 suggests some plant foods that enhance your body's ability to absorb iron. The most potent enhancer from a plant source is vitamin C. When vegetarians eat a rich food source of vitamin C with a meal, they can enhance the absorption of the iron present in the meal by as much as 20 times.

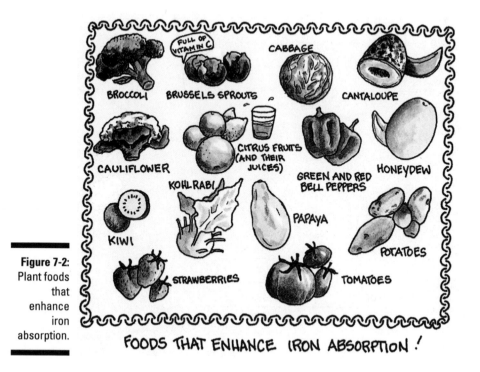

Figure 7-2: Plant foods that enhance iron absorption.

FOODS THAT ENHANCE IRON ABSORPTION !

Many fruits and vegetables are good sources of vitamin C. Here are some to keep in mind:

- ✔ Broccoli
- ✔ Brussels sprouts
- ✔ Cabbage
- ✔ Cantaloupe
- ✔ Cauliflower
- ✔ Citrus fruits (and their juices), such as grapefruits, lemons, and oranges
- ✔ Green and red bell peppers
- ✔ Honeydew
- ✔ Kiwi
- ✔ Kohlrabi
- ✔ Papaya
- ✔ Potatoes
- ✔ Strawberries
- ✔ Tomatoes

You probably eat vitamin C – rich foods with many of your favorite meals and don't even realize it. In each of the following vegetarian meals, a vitamin C – rich food helps the body absorb the iron that is present at that meal:

- ✔ Bowl of cooked oatmeal with fresh strawberry slices and soymilk
- ✔ Pasta tossed with steamed broccoli, cauliflower, carrots, green peppers, and onions, with marinara (tomato) sauce or garlic and olive oil
- ✔ Veggie burger with tomato and lettuce and a side of home fries
- ✔ Tempeh sloppy Joe, with a side of coleslaw
- ✔ Peanut butter and jelly sandwich on whole-wheat bread, with orange quarters
- ✔ Bowl of black bean soup with sourdough roll; a mixed green salad with tomatoes, green peppers, and onions; and a slice of cantaloupe
- ✔ Vegetarian chili over brown rice with steamed broccoli or Brussels sprouts

Other plant components also improve iron absorption, but vitamin C is the most powerful. Using cast iron cookware such as skillets, pots, and pans, can also increase the amount of iron you absorb, especially when you use them to cook acidic foods, such as tomatoes or tomato sauce.

TECHNICAL STUFF

Introducing heme and nonheme iron

You may have heard that the iron in plant foods isn't absorbed as well as the iron that comes from meat. That's true, but it really doesn't matter for most vegetarians.

Iron in food can have two forms: *heme* and *nonheme* iron. It pays to understand the differences between the two types because it will help you understand the issues surrounding iron in the vegetarian diet. You'll be ready with the answers the next time someone asks you, "If you're a vegetarian, where do you get your iron?"

The iron found in meat, poultry, and fish is the *heme* form. The human body easily absorbs heme iron. In fact, when meat is present in the diet, it increases the amount of iron that you absorb from plant foods as well. This characteristic doesn't necessarily make heme iron a better source of iron, and it may even have drawbacks.

Iron is a potent oxidant that changes cholesterol into a form that is more readily absorbed by the arteries, leading to hardening of the arteries, or coronary artery disease. In fact, it's for this very reason that men — most of whom are at a higher risk of developing coronary artery disease than most women — are now advised *not* to take daily multivitamin and mineral supplements containing iron.

The form of iron found in plant foods is called *nonheme* iron. Nonheme iron is absorbed less efficiently than heme iron. However, certain other food components — the enhancers I talk about in this chapter — can radically improve the body's absorption of nonheme iron. These other enhancers of iron absorption in plant foods help vegetarians absorb the iron they need.

Inhibitors to avoid

Other substances in your food can inhibit your body's ability to absorb iron. One of those is the tannic acid in tea. In poor countries where diets are low in vitamin C – rich fruits and vegetables and low in iron, a tradition of tea drinking can tip the scales and cause iron deficiency. That doesn't commonly happen in Western countries, where people generally eat a wider variety of foods and have access to plenty of fruits and vegetables.

Just as many substances enhance iron absorption, many inhibit it as well. Certain spices, the *phytates* found in whole grains, the calcium in dairy products, and coffee all decrease the availability of dietary iron. The reality is, however, that if you eat a reasonable mix of foods, inhibitors and enhancers of iron absorption offset each other.

WARNING!

If you are an avid tea drinker, be careful. More than coffee, tea impairs your body's ability to absorb dietary iron. In some areas of the country, it's commonplace for people to drink half a gallon of iced tea or more each day, and quantities of tannins that large may be problematic for some people. Consider switching to herbal tea because most do not contain tannins.

Your body's adaptability

So, your iron status depends on the mix of foods that you eat. The enhancers and inhibitors of iron absorption that occur naturally in foods usually offset each other, assuming that your diet contains a reasonable amount of variety.

Your body's ability to absorb iron also depends on the degree to which you need the iron in the first place. Never underestimate your body's ability to adapt to varying dietary conditions. When you need more, your body becomes more efficient at absorbing the iron that is present in your food. When you need less, your body absorbs less. Pretty neat, huh?

Getting Enough Iron, but Not Too Much

Recently, nutrition scientists have been speculating that it may be healthier to get the bulk of your iron from plant sources rather than from meat. The fact that iron from meat is so readily absorbed can pose a problem for people with *hemochromatosis*, a condition in which the body stores an excessive amount of iron that is associated with increased rates of coronary artery disease. But there's much more to the picture than that.

Certain dietary factors, such as the fat and iron in meat, can cause the production of free radicals that, in turn, can damage the cells in the body and lead to disease. Iron is a potent oxidant. Scientists believe that when sufficient quantities of heme iron are present, such as in diets that center around meat, cholesterol is oxidized into a form that is more readily absorbed by the arteries. This leads to increased rates of coronary artery disease.

Plant sources of iron, on the other hand, are not absorbed as easily. In the case of nonheme iron, the body absorbs only what it needs. This helps to minimize the body's exposure to oxidants such as iron. The additional antioxidants found in plant foods also help to offset the effects of free radicals. See Chapter 2 for more on free radicals and antioxidants.

Chapter 8

Vitamin B12 Basics

*T*he science of nutrition is in its infancy, and the issues surrounding vitamin B12 in the vegetarian diet are evidence of this fact. For all that we know about the nutrients that are essential to human health, there is often even more that we don't know. In the case of vitamin B12, some mysteries and unanswered questions about sources of the vitamin and how the body utilizes it have created controversy over recommendations for vegetarians, and particularly for vegans.

But we do know that vitamin B12 is necessary for the proper functioning of certain enzymes that play a role in the metabolism of amino acids and fatty acids. Too little vitamin B12 results in a form of anemia as well as the breakdown of nerves in the body's extremities, the spinal cord, and the brain.

The U.S. Recommended Dietary Allowance (RDA) for vitamin B12 is teeny tiny — just 2 micrograms per day. Just a fraction of a pinch would be enough to last your entire life. So what's the big deal about vitamin B12?

The issue is this: Vitamin B12 is found only in animal products. As far as anyone knows, plants contain none. So vegans could theoretically risk a vitamin B12 deficiency if their diets didn't contain a source of it. Strangely enough, however, symptoms of vitamin B12 deficiency are rare among vegans.

Vitamin B12 deficiency can lead to severe and irreversible nerve damage. Despite the need for such a miniscule amount of the vitamin, the stakes are high if you don't get what you need.

We also know that the body hoards and recycles much of the vitamin B12 that it gets. This means that the body conserves vitamin B12 and excretes very little of it, helping to ensure adequate levels. Most of us have at least a three-year supply of vitamin B12 stored in our livers and other tissues, and some people can go without vitamin B12 as long as 20 years before depleting their body stores and developing deficiency symptoms.

In fact, the most common cause of vitamin B12 deficiency isn't a lack of the vitamin in the diet. It's the diminished ability of the body to absorb the vitamin. This problem occurs in the general omnivorous public, and is not strictly a vegetarian issue. It's thought that older adults are at the greatest risk because the body's ability to produce *intrinsic factor*, the substance needed to absorb vitamin B12, diminishes with age. In fact, recommendations for adults over the age of 50 have recently been increased to 2.4 micrograms per day.

Finding Sources of Vitamin B12

Vitamin B12 is being manufactured all around us and inside us, as well. The vitamin is produced by microorganisms — bacteria that exist in the soil, in ponds, in streams and rivers, and in the guts of animals, including humans. Bacteria are busy making vitamin B12 in the guts of all animals, including you. So, if you eat any animal products at all, you're getting vitamin B12 from them. If you are a vegetarian who includes eggs, cheese, yogurt, cows' milk, or other dairy products in your diet, then you have a source of vitamin B12. Nonvegetarians get even more vitamin B12 from meat, poultry, and seafood.

In your own body, vitamin B12 is produced in your intestines, but the current thinking is that it's produced past the site of absorption. In other words, bacteria in your intestines produce vitamin B12, but you can't reliably use what your own body produces.

Some scientists think that humans must be able to use the vitamin B12 that's produced in their own bodies. After all, why would the human body evolve in such a way that an essential substance is produced but can't be utilized? Mother Nature would have weeded that inefficient creature out of the pack — pronto!

Vitamin B12 is also being produced all around us, outside our bodies. For instance, microorganisms living in and around rivers, streams, and ponds produce it. So if you were living in the wild, drinking from a mountain stream, you'd have a natural source of vitamin B12 in the water. These days, it isn't safe for most of us to drink from these sources. Instead, we drink chlorinated tap water and hope there are no microorganisms or other forms of bacteria living in it. Of course, that means that city tap water doesn't contain any vitamin B12.

The other place you'll find vitamin B12 is in the soil. Vitamin B12-producing microorganisms live in the soil in your garden and everywhere outdoors. If you raise vegetables, pick them, and eat them without first thoroughly washing them, it's possible that you might ingest some particles of vitamin B12 – containing soil still clinging to the food.

I have childhood memories of raiding my family's carrot patch like one of the neighborhood rabbits. I'd look at the green tops poking out of the ground and try to guess where the biggest carrot was hiding. Then I'd pull it out of the ground, rinse it off a little with the garden hose (*little* being the operative word here) and munch away. No doubt there was dirt on that carrot, and no doubt I ate it. Voilà! Vitamin B12 the natural way.

These days, most of us don't eat food that we grow in backyard gardens. We eat fruits and vegetables that we "picked" from bins at the grocery store, shiny and clean without a hint of soil — or vitamin B12 — clinging to them. Table 8-1 lists some vegetarian food sources that do contain vitamin B12, even without soil attached.

Table 8-1	Vegetarian Food Sources of Vitamin B12
Food	**Vitamin B12 Content (micrograms)**
Breakfast Cereals	
1 cup Wheat Chex*	2.4
1 cup Fiber-7 Flakes (Health Valley)*	0.6
1 cup Grape Nuts (Post)*	1.5
1 cup Just Right, Fruit and Nut (Kellogg)*	1.4
1 cup Mueslix, Apple and Almond Crunch (Kellogg)*	1.3
¾ cup Nutri-Grain, Wheat (Kellogg)*	1.5
1 cup Product 19 (Kellogg)*	6.0
1 cup Raisin Bran (Kellogg)*	1.6
1 cup Total (General Mills)*	7.7
Meat Substitutes	
1 patty Harvest Burger (Green Giant)*	1.5
⅔ cup Harvest Burger for Recipes * protein crumbles (Green Giant)	1.0
2 links Breakfast Links (Morningstar Farms)	3.6
1 patty Breakfast Patties (Morningstar Farms)	1.5
2 strips Breakfast Strips (Morningstar Farms)	0.1
1 patty BurgerBeaters (Morningstar Farms)*	2.4

(continued)

Table 8-1 *(continued)*

Food	*Vitamin B12 Content (micrograms)*
1 patty Chik Patties (Morningstar Farms)	0.9
1 patty Grillers (Morningstar Farms)	6.7
Milk Substitutes	
2 tablespoons Better Than Milk? dairy-free tofu beverage mix*	0.6
8 ounces potato milk (Vegelicious)*	3.0
8 ounces soy beverage (Edensoy Extra)	3.0
Nutritional Yeast	
1 tablespoon T-6635+ Vegetarian Support Formula nutritional yeast flakes (Red Star)*	2.0
Eggs	
1 large whole egg	0.5
1 large egg white	0.1
Dairy Products	
1 ounce part-skim mozzarella cheese	0.2
½ cup ice cream	0.3
8 ounces skim milk	1.0
8 ounces plain, nonfat yogurt	1.5
* Vegan choices	

Making Sure You're Getting It

Our need for vitamin B12 is truly miniscule, but the tiny bit that we might have gotten in years past via contamination of our food or water isn't available to most of us now. If you eat animal products regularly, you've got a source of vitamin B12. If you don't, then you need to find an alternate source. That means that vegans, or people who eat a near-vegan diet, need to pay attention to getting a reliable source of vitamin B12 in their diets.

What about the fact that your body recycles vitamin B12, that it takes years to develop a deficiency, that lack of vitamin B12 in the diet is not a likely reason for people to be deficient, and so on? All of that is true. It's also true that, despite the theoretical risk, few cases of vitamin B12 deficiency in vegans have been reported. There may be several reasons for that, including the fact that folic acid can mask the anemia caused by vitamin B12 deficiency. Folic acid is found in plant foods, especially green, leafy vegetables. Vegetarians, especially vegans, tend to get a lot of folic acid in their diets, so it's possible that a vitamin B12 deficiency could go undetected.

This is part of the vitamin B12 controversy. Some scientists think that vitamin B12 deficiency is rare in vegans, and others think that it's there but is being disguised or underreported.

Take the conservative approach on this one. It's easy to find reliable sources of vitamin B12, such as fortified soymilk and rice milk, fortified breakfast cereals, or even a vitamin tablet. Include them in your diet regularly, just to be on the safe side. It's really very little trouble.

If you've been eating a vegan or near-vegan diet for at least three years and have not been supplementing your diet with a source of vitamin B12, consider seeing a health care provider for a blood test to measure your stores of the vitamin. It may be worthwhile, if only to ease your mind if you have concerns, and it doesn't cost much to do. One of the first symptoms of deficiency is tingling or numbness in your hands, fingers, or toes, although these symptoms can also be caused by conditions other than vitamin B12 deficiency, too.

Distinguishing between different vitamin B12s

Now on to the finer points about vitamin B12 sources. There is vitamin B12, and there's vitamin B12! Or you could say, vitamin B12 by any other name may not be the kind of vitamin B12 that you need.

There are many forms of vitamin B12. The form that you need is called *cyanocobalamin*. This is the form of vitamin B12 that the human body is able to utilize. Other forms of vitamin B12 are known as *analogs*. The analogs are inactive in the human body.

Why would I burden you with this information? There is often confusion over which foods are reliable sources of vitamin B12 for vegans. In the past, sea vegetables, tempeh, miso, and nutritional yeast were touted as being good sources of vitamin B12. When those foods were tested for vitamin B12 content for purposes of labeling the food packages, the labs used a microbial assay that measured for all forms of vitamin B12, rather than specifically for cyanocobalamin. So, people bought those foods, thinking that they were getting the amount of vitamin B12 that the label listed, when, in fact, much of what was listed may have been analogs.

Now, scientists say that up to 94 percent of the vitamin B12 in these foods is actually in analog form, rather than cyanocobalamin. There is some fear that analogs might compete for absorption with cyanocobalamin and promote a vitamin B12 deficiency. Of course, there are other people who think that idea is phooey.

However, the current consensus among nutritionists is that it's better to be safe than sorry. For that reason, vegans are advised to get a *reliable* source of vitamin B12 in their diets. The most reliable sources of vitamin B12 for vegans are vitamin B12 supplements and fortified foods. Vegans should strive to include one or the other in their diets daily.

When you read food packages, be sure to look for the word *cyanocobalamin* to be sure that the food you are eating contains the right form of vitamin B12. You shouldn't have any trouble finding products that have been fortified with cyanocobalamin. Many of these food products, such as breakfast cereals and meat substitutes, are mainstream brands that you can find in any supermarket. Make it a habit to check the food labels regularly, though, because food manufacturers have been known to change the formulation of products from time to time. Other fortified products that are easy to find are soymilk and other milk substitutes. If you can't find them in your neighborhood supermarket, you'll find lots of choices at a natural foods store.

Another product that many vegans enjoy using is nutritional yeast. It has a savory flavor similar to that of Parmesan cheese, and many people use it the same way. You can sprinkle it over salads, baked potatoes, pasta, casseroles, cooked vegetables, and popcorn.

Recognizing good vitamin B12 on food labels

When you read food labels for information about vitamin B12, don't let the labeling format confuse you. The U.S. RDA for vitamin B12 is 2 micrograms per day for adults. That figure has a safety margin worked in and is an amount that covers the needs of most people. But food labels now list nutrients in products as a percentage of the *Daily Value (DV)*. The DV is a goal based on a reference diet of 2,000 calories per day. Your own needs may be more or less,

depending on your individual calorie needs. The DV used for vitamin B12 is 6 micrograms per day, which is three times the RDA. So, if a food label says that one serving of the item provides 50 percent of the DV for vitamin B12, then it provides 3 micrograms of vitamin B12. Aim for the RDA for vitamin B12 (2 micrograms), and you should be fine, but realize that the numbers listed on food labels are a percentage of a higher number (6 micrograms).

If you are using nutritional yeast as a source of vitamin B12, be sure to buy the right kind. The regular yeast used for baking that you commonly find in the supermarket is not what you want. Many brands of nutritional yeast found in natural foods stores contain vitamin B12 analog. You don't want those either. Look for Red Star T-6635+ at your natural foods store. If the store doesn't have it, ask the manager to order some for you. You can also order it by mail through The Mail Order Catalog, P.O. Box 180, Summertown, TN, 38483; phone 800-695-2241, fax 615-964-3518.

Don't be fooled into thinking that many foods that have commonly been considered rich in vitamin B12 actually *are* reliable sources of good vitamin B12. Mostly they contain analogs of vitamin B12, rather than the cyanocobalamin needed by humans. Take a look at some likely imposters:

- Tempeh
- Miso (a fermented soy product used as a soup base or condiment)
- Tamari (a fermented soy sauce product)
- Nutritional yeast
- Sea vegetables such as kombu, kelp, nori, spirulina, and other forms of algae
- Bean sprouts

Considering vitamin supplements

Using a vitamin B12 supplement is a foolproof way to go. You can use a supplement instead of or in addition to eating fortified foods.

Buy the lowest dose of vitamin B12 supplement that you can find. You only need 2 micrograms per day, but you'll probably find that most of the supplements supply much more. Your body adapts its level of absorption according to its needs and the amount in your diet. If you flood yourself with vitamin B12, your body is going to absorb only what it needs and you'll waste the rest. So, there's no point in taking megadoses of the vitamin. If you take a 50-microgram supplement of vitamin B12, your body will probably only absorb about 2 micrograms of it.

Vegans and near-vegans are the only vegetarians who really have to worry about the vitamin B12 content of their diets.

Chapter 9

Other Vitamins and Minerals

• •

In This Chapter

▶ Measuring your needs for vitamin B2, vitamin D, and zinc

▶ Finding these nutrients in vegetarian foods

▶ Considering vitamin supplements

• •

*T*here are a ton of vitamins and minerals out there that work to make a healthy body. Vitamin B2 (also known as riboflavin), vitamin D, and zinc merit discussion because, like the other nutrients covered in this book, they are generally thought of in association with animal products. Dairy products are rich sources of riboflavin and vitamin D, and zinc is found in meat, eggs, liver, and dairy products. And because these three are most commonly associated with animal products, you might worry that they are difficult for vegetarians to get enough of. But don't worry; just read on. Later in this chapter, I also address the question of supplements and whether or not they are necessary.

Vitamin B2 Revisited

Another name for vitamin B2 is *riboflavin*. Riboflavin has multiple functions in the body, primarily related to its role in enabling enzymes to trigger various chemical reactions that take place in your body.

Your requirements for riboflavin are related to your energy intake, so the recommended intakes vary according to your calorie needs. In other words, a person who consumes 3,000 calories a day needs more riboflavin than a person who consumes only 2,000 calories per day.

Riboflavin is present in small amounts in many foods, and many of the foods that are the most concentrated in riboflavin come from animals. Among the richest sources are milk, cheddar cheese, and cottage cheese. Other animal sources include organ meats, other meats, and eggs.

So, vegetarians who eat dairy products and seaweed have options, but what about those poor vegans? Isn't it a challenge for vegans to get enough riboflavin? Not necessarily. Sea vegetables, such as some forms of seaweed, are even more concentrated in riboflavin than are animal products, although most Americans haven't yet developed a taste for them. Green leafy vegetables, enriched breads and cereals, legumes, and several other plant foods also contain some riboflavin.

Some scientists think that the current recommendations for riboflavin intake may not be accurate. In fact, it may be true that vegans, and anyone else who avoids dairy products, may have an easier time meeting their riboflavin needs than was once thought.

However, until there is scientific consensus on the issue, it makes sense for vegetarians to strive to meet the present U.S. Recommended Dietary Allowance (RDA). The recommended riboflavin intake for men is 1.7 milligrams per day and 1.3 milligrams per day for women.

You don't have to eat mountains of mustard greens to get enough riboflavin. Riboflavin is truly spread widely throughout the plant world, and there are many choices. As always, one of the chief strategies for ensuring that your diet is adequate is to limit the junk foods and to pack your meals with as many nutrient-dense foods as you can. Table 9-1 offers some ideas of how you can get the riboflavin you need from vegetarian foods.

Taking a cue from China

The New York Times once called the China Project the "Grand Prix of Epidemiology." The China Project is a huge population study taking place throughout The People's Republic of China and, presently, Taiwan, as well. It's a collaborative effort between Cornell University, Oxford University, and the Chinese government, and its purpose is to study the relationships between peoples' diets and disease rates.

The China Project began in 1983, and in the early years of the study, the Chinese people still largely ate a diet that could be described as "nearly vegan," though the diet has become more Westernized since then. With rare exceptions, dairy products were not a part of the diet. Despite riboflavin intakes well below the RDA, no cases of riboflavinosis, or riboflavin deficiency, were seen.

Dr. T. Colin Campbell of Cornell University, the principal American investigator in this study, and his associates have speculated that human riboflavin needs are actually much lower than those specified by the current RDA. Other studies have also shown that intakes of riboflavin below the RDA do not result in symptoms of riboflavin deficiency.

Table 9-1	Riboflavin Contents of Vegetarian Foods
Food	*Riboflavin Content (milligrams)*
Dairy Products and Eggs	
1 ounce cheddar cheese	0.11
½ cup cottage cheese	0.18
8 ounces skim milk	0.34
8 ounces nonfat yogurt (plain)	0.57
1 large egg	0.25
Fruits	
1 avocado	0.37
1 medium banana	0.12
1 cup raspberries	0.11
1 cup strawberries	0.10
Vegetables	
1 cup cooked bok choy	0.11
1 cup cooked broccoli	0.18
1 cup cooked collard greens	0.20
1 cup cooked kale	0.09
1 cup raw kelp	1.60
1 cup cooked mustard greens	0.09
1 cup cooked peas	0.12
1 cup cooked turnip greens	0.10
Breads and Cereals	
¾ cup bran flakes	0.44
1 cup cooked oatmeal	0.05
1 cup cooked millet	0.14
1 large pocket whole wheat pita bread	0.05
1 cup shredded wheat	0.08
¼ cup wheat germ	0.23
1 slice whole wheat bread	0.06

(continued)

Table 9-1 (continued)

Food	Riboflavin Content (milligrams)
Legumes and Animal Product Replacements	
1 cup cooked garbanzo beans	0.10
1 cup cooked kidney beans	0.10
1 cup cooked lentils	0.15
1 cup cooked navy beans	0.11
1 cup cooked pinto beans	0.16
1 cup cooked soybeans	0.49
8 ounces soymilk (plain)	0.17
1 cup tempeh	0.18
4 ounces firm tofu	0.13
Nuts and Seeds	
1 ounce almonds	0.17
2 tablespoons peanut butter	0.03
2 tablespoons sesame tahini	0.14
Other	
1 tablespoon nutritional yeast flakes (Red Star T-6635+, Vegetarian Support Formula)	2.40

Many nutritionists have concerns that when recommendations for nutrients such as those for riboflavin are set too high, people might be encouraged to consume more animal products in order to meet them. As a result, these people may put themselves at risk for the diseases and conditions that result from high intakes of animal protein — and its accompanying saturated fat and cholesterol — and low intakes of dietary fiber.

Viva Vitamin D!

Vitamin D's primary role is to regulate calcium for proper bone mineralization. In children, too little vitamin D results in bones that are weak and bowed from too little calcium — a disease known as rickets.

The best source of vitamin D is regular exposure to sunlight. We humans are designed to manufacture our own vitamin D when our skin is exposed to sunlight, and theoretically, we don't have to get any from foods. Vitamin D is actually a hormone that regulates the body's calcium balance. Along with calcium, it plays an important role in bone health. (See Chapter 6 for more on calcium.)

It takes about 20 to 30 minutes of summer sun on the hands and face two or three times per week for people with light skin to make enough vitamin D to carry them through the winter. The length of exposure that you need depends in part on how much pigment your skin contains. People with darker skin need more sun exposure, and people with light skin need less. During the summer months, we store enough of what we make to carry us through the winter months when we are exposed to less sunlight.

To get the vitamin D you need from the sun, you need to get exposure to sun without sunscreen. But remember that too much sunlight exposure can cause skin cancer. The best approach to getting enough vitamin D may be to allow yourself limited exposure to sunlight. In other words, go outdoors for brief periods of time without sunscreen, and then wear sunscreen the remainder of the time.

Most of us don't have to worry about getting enough vitamin D, but under certain circumstances, anyone — vegetarian or nonvegetarian — can be at risk of not having enough. In the U.S., though, nonvegetarians and vegetarians who use dairy products have some security measures built into their food supply to help protect them. Vegans — and anyone who doesn't use dairy products — should evaluate their own situations to determine whether or not they need supplemental vitamin D. If in doubt, consult a registered dietitian or your health care professional for an individual assessment.

People at greatest risk of vitamin D deficiency live in large, smog-filled northern cities. Other people at risk include people who have very dark skin (especially those living at northern latitudes), people who are housebound and rarely see the light of day, and people who don't have regular exposure to sunlight because they cover their entire bodies with clothing or sunscreen every time they go outdoors. As we age, our ability to produce vitamin D also diminishes, so older people may also be at greater risk of deficiency.

A few hundred years ago, *rickets* and *osteomalacia* were prevalent in cities throughout the world where people received inadequate exposure to sunlight. The cities were located at latitudes high enough to have short summers and long, gray winters, and the increasing urbanization of the cities created smoggy conditions that further blocked out the sunlight. Peoples' bodies didn't produce enough vitamin D as a result. They ended up with diseases of the bones because without adequate vitamin D, the bones could not utilize calcium properly. In London, for instance, rickets plagued children whose bones were still developing, and osteomalacia, a disease in which the bones soften, was prevalent in adults.

Food sources of vitamin D

Few foods are naturally good sources of vitamin D. And those that are aren't eaten by many vegetarians. Eggs are a source, and so is liver, but liver isn't recommended for anybody due to its high cholesterol content and because an animal's liver is a primary depository for environmental contaminants.

For vegans and vegetarians, there are several sources of vitamin D in addition to sunshine. Some milk substitutes are fortified with vitamin D, as are some brands of margarine and breakfast cereals. Table 9-2 offers some examples.

Table 9-2	Food Sources of Vitamin D
Food	*Vitamin D Content (micrograms)*
Vegetarian Sources	
1 large egg	0.68
1 teaspoon margarine	0.50
8 ounces skim milk	2.50
Vegan Sources	
⅔ cup bran flakes	1.23
1 cup corn flakes	1.23
¼ cup Grape Nuts cereal	1.23
8 ounces potato milk	1.0
½ cup Raisin Bran cereal	1.23
8 ounces rice milk (Rice Dream)	2.5
8 ounces soymilk (Edensoy Extra)	1.0
8 ounces soymilk (Westsoy Plus)	2.5

Foods can be fortified with different forms of vitamin D, including vitamin D2 or vitamin D3. Vitamin D2, called ergocalciferol, is made by irradiating provitamin D (from plants or yeast) with ultraviolet light. Vitamin D3, called cholecalciferol, is made from fish liver oils or lanolin, which is sheep wool fat. Vegans do not use products that have been fortified with vitamin D3 because it is derived from an animal source. Usually the food label will state the form of vitamin D used. If it does not, you may have to check with the manufacturer to determine the source.

When vitamin D is added to milk

Vitamin D is added to fluid milk, but the amount present has been determined to be unreliable. Some samples of milk have contained very little vitamin D, and other samples have contained many times the amount permitted by the government. The problem has to do with difficulties the milk industry has in dispersing the vitamin D evenly throughout large vats or tanks of milk.

In the United States, milk and other dairy products have been fortified with vitamin D for many years as a public health measure to protect people who may have inadequate sunlight exposure. If you drink milk, in effect you get a vitamin D supplement.

Vitamin D supplements

Vitamin D supplements are an option, but anyone taking a daily supplement should be sure not to exceed the RDA. Read labels to be sure that you are not taking too much, or consult a registered dietitian.

Pretty in Zinc

Your body needs zinc for proper growth and development. Zinc plays a role in various chemical reactions that take place in your body, as well as in the manufacturing of new proteins and blood, and it helps to protect your body's immune system.

Because there is some disagreement among scientists as to the appropriate recommended levels of zinc intake, it can be difficult to know how much zinc you need. At the present time, the RDA for zinc is 12 milligrams per day for women and 15 milligrams for men.

Both vegetarians and nonvegetarians have trouble meeting the RDA for zinc. Some scientists think that it's because the RDA has been set too high. Recommendations in other parts of the world are substantially lower than in the United States, primarily due to differences of opinion about how well zinc is absorbed. Like some other nutrients, zinc too is found in relatively high concentrations in animal products, and setting recommendations for intake at levels that are high encourages people to continue eating animal products.

As with many other nutrients, the human body is able to adapt to varying levels of zinc content in the diet. If there's a lot of zinc present, your body absorbs less. If there's a shortage of zinc, your body becomes more efficient at absorbing what is present. This may in part account for the fact that vegetarians tend to have satisfactory zinc status. There may be other reasons, as well.

Zinc absorption

As in the case of dietary iron, there are several factors that either inhibit or enhance the absorption of zinc.

Inhibitors

On the side of inhibiting absorption is phytic acid or phytate. The phytates in whole grains and several other plant products can bind with zinc and prevent the body from absorbing it. Whole wheat breads and cereals, legumes, and nuts all contain phytates. Wheat bran is rich in phytates, which is one reason that bran fiber supplements are generally not a good idea. Excessive amounts of phytates in the diet can upset your zinc balance. So, if you eat a lot of grains, you may not be getting enough zinc.

When calcium is available in meals at the same time as phytates, a complex is formed with calcium, phytates, and zinc, decreasing the availability of zinc to the body. Lacto ovo vegetarians may have high calcium intakes from dairy products, and their zinc status may suffer as a result. Vegans have a more favorable ratio of zinc to calcium because they don't use dairy products.

If you take a calcium supplement, take it between meals or before bedtime so that the calcium doesn't interfere with zinc absorption from your meals.

Enhancers

Various cooking and food preparation methods may increase the availability of zinc. For example, sprouting seeds, cooking or serving foods in combination with acidic ingredients such as tomato sauce or lemon juice, and soaking and cooking legumes, may all be ways of making zinc more available to the body. Vegetarians have an edge when it comes to zinc due to their moderate protein intakes. In contrast, the high protein intakes of meat-eaters cause a substantial increase in their zinc requirements.

Food sources of zinc

Vegetarians should be aware of the need for zinc and strive to frequently eat foods that are rich in zinc. Table 9-3 shows some good food sources of zinc.

Table 9-3	Food Sources of Zinc
Food	*Zinc Content (milligrams)*
Dairy Products	
1 ounce cheddar cheese	0.88
8 ounces skim milk	0.95
8 ounces nonfat yogurt (plain)	2.2
Breads and Cereals	
¾ cup bran flakes	3.75
1 cup cooked oatmeal	1.15
1 cup shredded wheat	0.99
1 tablespoon wheat germ	1.18
1 slice whole wheat bread	0.54
Legumes and Animal Product Replacements	
1 cup cooked garbanzo beans	2.50
1 cup cooked kidney beans	1.89
1 cup cooked lentils	2.52
1 cup cooked millet	1.58
1 cup cooked navy beans	1.93
1 cup cooked pinto beans	1.85
1 cup cooked soybeans	1.98
8 ounces soymilk (plain)	0.56
1 cup tempeh	3.00
4 ounces firm tofu	1.23
Nuts and Seeds	
1 ounce almonds	0.69
2 tablespoons peanut butter	0.93
1 tablespoon sesame tahini	0.07
1 tablespoon nutritional yeast flakes (Red Star T-6635+)	1.00

(continued)

Table 9-3 (continued)

Food	Zinc Content (milligrams)
Vegetables	
1 cup cooked bok choy	0.29
1 cup cooked collard greens	0.80
1 cup cooked kale	1.17
½ cup cooked kelp	0.48
1 cup cooked mustard greens	0.15
1 cup cooked peas	1.90
1 medium baked potato	0.45
1 cup cooked spinach	1.34
1 medium sweet potato	0.41
1 medium raw tomato	0.11

I may sound like a broken record, but I can't emphasize enough the importance of limiting sweets and greasy, junky foods — "empty calorie foods" — that displace nutrient-dense foods that are good sources of zinc, iron, calcium, and other important nutrients and phytochemicals. For more on phytochemicals, see Chapter 2.

Considering a Vitamin Supplement

With the exception of vitamin B12 for vegans, vegetarians can generally get the nutrition they need from foods and don't need supplements unless they have reason to believe that their intake is not sufficient. In the case of vitamin D or calcium, for instance, vegetarians who are in doubt should consult a registered dietitian who is knowledgeable about vegetarian diets for an assessment of their need for supplements.

Recently, the National Academy of Sciences has recommended for the first time that certain population groups take supplements, whether they are vegetarian or not. Specifically, the academy recommends that vegetarian and nonvegetarian adults alike over the age of 50 take a vitamin B12 supplement to ensure that they are getting enough. The academy also recommends that women who are in their childbearing years take a folic acid supplement because it may be difficult for many to reach the recommended level of intake of 400 micrograms per day. Vegetarians do, however, have folic acid intakes that are much higher than those of nonvegetarians.

Vitamin D is a fat-soluble vitamin and we store what we make or consume. Too much can be toxic, so this is definitely a case of "more is not better." The RDA is 5 micrograms or 200 International Units for adults. Be sure not to exceed this level if you are taking supplements. Better yet, consult a registered dietitian or your health care provider if you are unsure whether you need a supplement.

As for supplements of other nutrients, the experts are split on the issues of which ones, how much, and for whom. There are valid differences of opinion because the science is so new and still evolving. If you happen to be a member of the Coke-and-french fries crowd, some nutrition scientists would recommend that you take a multiple vitamin and mineral supplement, just to be on the safe side. On the other hand, others would make a case for redoubling your efforts to clean up your diet and get what you need from whole foods rather than supplements. Admittedly, whole foods contain phytochemicals and other substances not contained in a tablet. So, in order to get all the nutrients your body requires, you mustn't rely solely on vitamin supplements. You've got to eat good, wholesome foods.

If you don't have access to your own registered dietitian, you might be interested in visiting the Web site of Dr. Andrew Weil, author of *Spontaneous Healing* and *8 Weeks to Optimum Health,* at `www.drweil.com`, for an assessment of your supplement needs. His approach is sensible, and at this site you can answer a questionnaire and receive a list of recommendations tailored to your lifestyle and risk factors.

Many nutrition scientists feel that, in addition to vitamin B12 and folic acid for women in their childbearing years, a good case can be made for all people to take supplements of antioxidant nutrients — vitamins A, C, and E; selenium; and mixed carotenes (as opposed to beta carotene alone). That goes for vegetarians and nonvegetarians alike, even though vegetarians tend to have more antioxidants in their diets than nonvegetarians. Because we are exposed to more environmental contaminants than ever before, especially in urban areas, it's possible that our need for antioxidants is greater than could be met through a healthful diet alone. The additional antioxidants are ammunition against the production of harmful free radicals.

Remember, the science of nutrition is in its infancy. A group of British scientists recently published a report saying that a supplement of 500 milligrams of vitamin C — much less than the amount taken by many people — could damage people's genes by promoting the release of free radicals. The scientists found that, while vitamin C is typically described as an antioxidant, it can also have oxidative properties and can convert iron to a form that can damage the heart and other organs. The vitamin C that is present in foods acts as an antioxidant and is health supporting, but the form found in supplements acts as an oxidant and has a damaging effect.

So, the science is changing rapidly, and peoples' individual needs also vary. Your best bet is to check with a registered dietitian or your health care provider for more guidance on whether to use supplements.

Part III
Surviving Among the Carnivores

The 5th Wave   By Rich Tennant

"Relax – another helping of vermicelli, and I'll be done with your precious shredder."

In this part . . .

You've got the nuts and bolts behind you — the various approaches to vegetarianism, some sound reasons to adopt a vegetarian lifestyle, and the nutritional basics of a vegetarian diet. Now it's time for action.

The next few chapters will get you poised to start living the vegetarian way with good-sense advice and strategies for making the transition. You'll learn what you need to know to set up your vegetarian kitchen and for keeping the peace at your nonvegetarian family table, as well as numerous practical tips to smooth the way to a vegetarian lifestyle.

Chapter 10

All Revved Up and Ready to Go

The transition to a more vegetarian diet starts in the kitchen, and this chapter will help set you up. The first step involves making your kitchen as user-friendly as possible. Organization and cleanliness will make your kitchen a much more pleasant and efficient place to spend time. Next, stocking your kitchen with the basics will help ensure that you'll always have the supplies on hand to whip up any number of quick and easy vegetarian meals. I've even included your shopping lists.

Setting Up a Vegetarian Kitchen

You need a clean, well-organized, well-stocked kitchen, even if you don't have a lot of time to cook. When your kitchen is in shape, you'll eat better and you'll feel better, too, because having things in order will give you peace of mind. You might even be more motivated to prepare meals.

Starting out

For some people, the kitchen is the best room in the house. If you're one of these people, you've probably got one of every kind of kitchen gadget there is, and things are in order or you know where to find them. You probably enjoy cooking when you have the time.

For other people, the kitchen is strictly a matter of function — it's where they store food and dishes, but they spend as little time in there as possible. Fixing meals is a necessity of life but not a hobby.

No matter what your attitude about kitchens and cooking meals, there are some things that you can do to make the space more pleasurable and user friendly.

Cleaning up

Some individuals and companies adopt a segment of the highway and vow to keep it clean and neat. Why not start in your own home and adopt your kitchen?

The first thing I recommend doing is getting rid of anything that you don't use, including appliances, party favors and napkins and any other paper goods that have been collecting dust for a year or two, and any items that don't belong in the kitchen but may have made their way into your cupboards and drawers. Throw these things away, add them to your garage sale pile, or donate them to charity. This will help you free up space in your closets and cupboards so that the things you do use are accessible.

Empty your cabinets and drawers a few at a time and wash them out with soap and hot water. Wash your large appliances and microwave oven inside and out. Throw away any foods that have been sitting around unused in your freezer and any foods that are spoiling or otherwise won't ever be eaten in your refrigerator. Check your cupboards, too, and pitch anything that is taking up space and that you know you won't ever use.

Resist the temptation to line your kitchen cupboard shelves with contact paper or shelf paper. Contact paper begins to curl at the edges with time, and crumbs can collect on the sticky edges. Crumbs can also work their way under shelf liners, making them an attractive hiding place for bugs. Instead, wash your cupboard shelves from time to time with soap and water. Paint them with a couple coats of semigloss paint if you prefer a more finished surface.

Getting organized

Over time, you've probably begun shelving items out of place and piling baking sheets, cake pans, and pots and pans on top of each other in unwieldy piles in your kitchen cabinets. Take them out, reorganize them, and store them in such a way that they are easy to see and reach. If you find that you don't have enough room to store items conveniently, consider creative ways of making more space.

For example, you might buy an overhead rack for pots and pans that can hang from the kitchen ceiling or wall. That would free up some cabinet space. If there's room in your kitchen, you could add a baker's rack or a movable island on wheels with extra drawers and shelves for storage. You'll be much happier using your kitchen if all your appliances, dishes, pots and pans, and utensils are easy to access.

Label jars and canisters of baking supplies. Keep spices in a cool, dry place, away from the heat of the stove. Unless you use huge quantities, buy oils and spices in small containers so that you can replace them often and know that they're fresh.

Consider dating groceries, especially canned and packaged goods, when you bring them into the house after shopping. Mark packages with the date they were purchased, using a grease pencil or permanent marker (stick-on labels can fall off of cold or frozen packages). This will help you rotate your stock and use older foods first, helping to ensure that nothing stays in your cupboard or refrigerator too long and that what you have on hand is fresh.

Streamlining your equipment

It's a good idea to equip your kitchen with the utensils and appliances you need to work efficiently, but try not to get bogged down with too many gadgets that you don't use. Nobody likes a countertop that's so jammed with small appliances that there's no counter space to work on. For example, I gave away my electric can opener when I realized that I preferred to use an old-fashioned crank can opener and was able to get one more appliance off my kitchen countertop. The little handheld opener that I use is stored in a drawer.

Not everyone likes to own a large countertop mixer. Some people prefer a handheld mixer. Some people wouldn't use a mixer at all and only need a whisk. Think about your lifestyle and equipment needs, and pare down wherever possible so that you don't waste money and cupboard and counter space.

Here's some kitchen equipment you might want to consider keeping:

- ✔ Spatulas, wooden spoons, and whisks
- ✔ Measuring cups (dry and liquid) and spoons
- ✔ Mixing bowls in various sizes
- ✔ A good set of kitchen knives, including a paring knife, serrated knife, chef's knife for chopping vegetables, and bread knife
- ✔ Countertop or handheld mixer
- ✔ Slow cooker (such as a Crock-Pot)
- ✔ Pressure cooker
- ✔ Heavy-duty blender/juicer
- ✔ Baking pans and sheets
- ✔ Food processor
- ✔ Pots and pans in assorted sizes, some with nonstick surfaces

Stocking up on staples

It's important to keep foods in a variety of forms on hand. There's no question that fresh is best, but it's not always the most convenient option. So, plan to keep a range of fresh, frozen, canned, and packaged foods in your kitchen. The lists that follow will give you an idea of the types of foods you'll want to have on hand. The grocery lists later in this chapter and the descriptions of food choices in Chapter 14 will give you even more detail about the types of staples you'll want to have at home.

Breads, cereals, and other grain products

Grain products are versatile. They can be an accompaniment to a meal, such as a slice of bread or a couscous salad, or they can form the backbone of an entree, such as rice pilaf, a casserole made with buckwheat and vegetables, or a plate of spaghetti.

When you make a pot of rice (or any of a number of grains), make more than you need at one meal. You can store the leftovers in an airtight container in the refrigerator for up to two weeks. Leftover rice can be reheated and served with steamed vegetables, bean burritos, or tacos; topped with vegetarian chili; added to a filling for cabbage rolls; or used to make rice pudding.

When you stock your kitchen, consider buying these types of grain products:

- ✔ Whole-grain mixes such as pancake mixes, pilafs, and baking mixes
- ✔ Bulk grains such as rice, rye, oats, buckwheat, barley, amaranth, quinoa, kamut, teff, spelt, and millet
- ✔ Whole-grain breakfast cereals, hot or cold
- ✔ Pasta in a variety of shapes and flavors
- ✔ Rice in several varieties, such as brown, white, jasmine, arborio, and basmati
- ✔ Breads, rolls, bagels, English muffins, and flour tortillas
- ✔ Frozen waffles and low-fat muffins

Legumes: Beans, peas, and lentils

You can buy legumes dry in bags or in bulk, or you can buy them canned. If you buy them canned, be sure to rinse them in a colander with water to remove most of the added salt.

Remembering less common grains

Amaranth is an ancient grain that was a staple food of the Aztecs of Central America. The seeds can be cooked and used in the same ways as rice or they can be cooked as a hot cereal. You can also bake with amaranth flour. *Quinoa* (pronounced "keen-wah") is a high-protein grain that was used by the Incas in Peru. It, too, can be cooked and used like rice or other cooked grains in casseroles, salads, and side dishes. *Spelt* and *kamut* (pronounced "kah-moot'") are types of wheat that have been popular in Europe for generations. *Teff* is one of the oldest cultivated grains. It is used in Ethiopia today to make the spongy, round, flat Ethiopian bread known as *injera*.

Beans, peas, and lentils are highly nutritious and extremely versatile. You can combine several types of beans (such as garbanzos, pintos, red kidney beans, and white kidney beans) to make many-bean chili. You can mash them for dips, soups, and spreads. You can combine them with rice, pasta, or other grains to make a variety of interesting vegetarian entrees. Be sure to stock up on the following:

- ✔ Many types of beans: black, pinto, kidney, navy, black-eyed peas, garbanzo, cannelloni (white kidney beans), and others
- ✔ Lentils and split peas
- ✔ Dry, canned, and even frozen beans and peas

Small pressure cookers are now available that are safe and easy to use. You can use them to cook dried beans in a fraction of the time that soaking and boiling takes. Although canned beans are fine to use — especially when you rinse off the salt — many people prefer the flavor of beans made "from scratch" and find a pressure cooker a convenient way to cut prep time down substantially.

Fruits and vegetables

The very best fruits and vegetables are those that are locally grown, in season, and fresh. Most of them are packed with vitamins, minerals, and phytochemicals. (See more on phytochemicals in Chapter 2.) Frozen foods run a close second in terms of nutrition, and they're a perfectly acceptable alternative to fresh.

However, there are times when canned fruits and vegetables are more convenient or less expensive than fresh or frozen. Because heat destroys some vitamins, and time on the shelf can allow some nutrients to leach out into the water used in packing, canned fruits and vegetables tend to be less nutritious than fresh or frozen. However, that doesn't mean that they're worthless! On the contrary, canned fruits and vegetables can make a sizable nutritional contribution, so there's no need to avoid them.

When you use canned vegetables, you'll save some of the vitamins and minerals that might have leached out if you can use the packing liquid in the dish you are making. For example, if you are making soup or a sautéed vegetable medley to serve over some kind of grain or pasta, dump the entire contents of the can into the pot. There may be some salt in the packing liquid, but you can leave out any additional salt that is called for in the recipe.

Meat substitutes

Meat substitutes are made from plant ingredients and are low in saturated fat and cholesterol. So, with meat substitute products, you get the convenience and flavor of the "real thing," without the unwanted nutritional baggage. While I usually cringe at the thought of such "substitute" products as sugar substitutes, whipped topping, cream, and butter substitutes, meat substitutes really are wholesome and far better for you than their meat counterparts (see Chapter 16 for more on substitutions). For now, you may wish to try:

- ✔ Veggie burger patties
- ✔ Veggie hotdogs, cold cuts, bacon, and breakfast patties and links
- ✔ Tofu and tempeh
- ✔ Textured vegetable protein (TVP)

Dairy products and dairy substitutes

If you do include dairy products such as cheese, milk, and ice cream in your diet, buy the nonfat varieties. Even the so-called low-fat items are too high in fat. The problem with dairy fat is that two-thirds of it is saturated, so the fat in dairy products is a real artery-clogger.

You'll find some dairy product substitutes in the supermarket, and you'll find even more in a natural foods store. Experiment with some of these:

- ✔ Soy, rice, potato, and oat milks and blends packaged in aseptic (shelf-stable) packages
- ✔ Soy cheeses
- ✔ Soy yogurt with active cultures
- ✔ Soy and rice frozen desserts

Dairy substitute products, such as those I've noted above, tend to be more wholesome and nutritious than many that are found in regular supermarkets. Here I am thinking of such substitute products as nondairy creamers that are filled with artificial flavors and colors, nondairy whipped toppings that are nothing but fluffy filler, and so-called cholesterol-lowering butter substitutes that taste like spreadable plastic. I avoid these like the plague.

Buying convenient vegetarian specialty products

When you're setting up a vegetarian kitchen and are in the mood to try some new products, several are especially helpful. These products have nutritional advantages and/or are especially convenient. You can find some of them in your neighborhood supermarket, and you can find all of them in a natural foods store.

Not all of these may appeal to you, and that's fine. None of them are strictly necessary, but many of the products described here make following a vegetarian or vegan diet much simpler.

- **Soymilk.** Soymilk is a good choice for anyone who is lactose intolerant or just prefers to avoid dairy products. It comes in different flavors, including plain, which has a slight "beanie" aftertaste. It's usually packaged in shelf-stable aseptic boxes that need to be refrigerated after opening. Buy fortified soymilk, because it contains added vitamin B12, calcium, and vitamins A and D. You can use soymilk cup for cup in recipes that call for milk, you can pour it on breakfast cereal, and you can enjoy it when you have a hankering for milk and cookies.

- **Powdered vegetarian egg replacer.** Powdered vegetarian egg replacer is an egg substitute that is made from a mixture of vegetable starches. You just mix a teaspoon and a half of the powder with two tablespoons of water to replace one egg in virtually any recipe. It keeps on a shelf in your cupboard almost indefinitely and is always on hand when you need it. There's no salmonella risk, and it's free of saturated fat and cholesterol.

- **Vegetarian burger patties and hotdogs.** Some vegetarian burger patties are made from soy, and some are grain or vegetable based. There's a wide variety, and they all taste different, so you'll need to experiment to find your favorites. Some are meant to look and taste like meat, and others don't look or taste anything like meat. Vegetarian hotdogs are typically made of soy, and they taste and look like the real thing. They even wiggle appropriately when you take them out of a pan of water with a fork.

  That's one of the advantages of these products: Kids can take them on picnics and to cookouts and not feel too "different" for being vegetarians. You can cook these foods on a grill and serve them the same way their meat counterparts are served. Of course, the nutritional advantage of these foods is that they're low in saturated fat, they're cholesterol free, and many even contain a good dose of dietary fiber. They're quick, convenient, and good tasting, and they work well as transition foods for people making the switch to a vegetarian diet. They can also be the solution to a "What should we make for dinner tonight?" crisis.

- **Whole grain breakfast cereals.** Hot or cold cereals are simply a good way to start the day. They're nutritious and satisfying. Plus, they make a perfectly good supper food from time to time. Once again, if you get stuck on what to fix for dinner, you could do far worse than eating a bowl of cereal. If you're getting a little weary of the choices at your supermarket, check out a natural foods store. You'll be surprised at the variety, and I guarantee you'll hit on some new favorites.

✔ **Tofu.** *Tofu* is soybean curd. It's made much the same way that cheese is made, by using a coagulant to curdle soymilk, separating the solids from the liquid, and pressing the solids into a block. Tofu packaged in aseptic containers is actually coagulated inside the package itself. Tofu is available in different degrees of firmness, depending on how much water has been pressed out.

Different styles of tofu can be used in different recipes. For instance, soft tofu works well for making dips and sauces because it's easy to blend. Firm tofu works well in baked goods and as an egg replacer in many recipes. (See Chapter 16 for more on replacing eggs in recipes.) Extra firm tofu is the style of choice for making stir-fries because the cubes can hold up when they're jostled around in the pan. Unlike cheese, tofu is never coagulated with rennet, an enzyme taken from the stomach linings of baby animals. It's always safe for consumption by vegetarians and vegans alike.

✔ **Tempeh.** *Tempeh* is a traditional Indonesian food that is made from whole soybeans and is sometimes mixed with a grain such as rice. It's fermented and pressed into a flat, rectangular block. You could call it a cultured bean cake. In stores, it's usually sold refrigerated or frozen, vacuum-packed in plastic. You can use tempeh in many of the same ways that meat can be used — in sloppy joe filling, in barbecue, in mock chicken salad, and in a variety of other dishes.

Tofu and tempeh are nutritious and versatile. They're high in protein, low in saturated fat, cholesterol free, and full of beneficial phytochemicals. (For more on phytochemicals, see Chapter 2.) There are many soy cookbooks on the market now. See Appendix A for a selected list of good ones.

✔ **Organic canned beans.** In natural foods stores, you can find organic canned beans, which, in addition to being convenient, have the benefit of being grown without the use of synthetic pesticides and herbicides.

✔ **Dried bean flakes.** You can find dried bean flakes in box mixes and in cardboard milk carton-like containers. The flakes can be made from black beans or pinto beans, and they're especially handy for making burrito and taco fillings as well as bean dip. Just add boiling water to the flakes, and in a few minutes you have a smooth bean purée.

✔ **Whole-grain mixes.** You can find the biggest variety of whole-grain mixes in natural foods stores. They're generally good products because they are free of hydrogenated fats, unnecessary additives, and refined flours, and they are often made with organically grown grains. You can find mixes for a wide range of baked products such as gingerbread, cakes, brownies, cookies, quick breads, pancakes, and waffles.

What does "organic" mean?

The term *organic,* as it refers to foods, is being hotly debated due to proposed government guidelines that will regulate the definition and use of the term on food packages. Up until now, the natural foods industry has used voluntary standards, and state rules for certifying foods as organic have varied. Generally, the term *organic* means that the food has been grown without the use of synthetic fertilizers and pesticides, using farming methods that are ecologically sound. To be certified as *organic,* foods must also be grown in soil that has been free of prohibited substances for at least three years.

✔ **Instant soups.** Many soups are sold in single-serving cardboard cups: You add boiling water, stir, and enjoy. They're good to keep on hand for a quick snack, to pack in a bag lunch, and to take on a road trip (stop at a filling station/market for some hot water). The lentil soup variety makes a good, quick gravy. Just add hot water, stir, and let the soup rest for a few moments until it thickens. Then pour it over a baked potato, mashed potatoes, or toast. Compare labels and buy the varieties with the least amount of sodium.

✔ **Organic canned tomatoes.** Like the organic canned beans, organic canned tomatoes have many practical applications and have the added benefit of being made with organically grown produce. This is especially nice in the case of tomatoes, on which mainstream growers tend to use a relatively large amount of pesticides. You can use organic canned tomatoes to make pasta sauces, to make a variety of toppings for cooked grains, and to use in a wide range of other recipes for soups, stews, casseroles, and other dishes.

The goods on hydrogenated fats

The process of *hydrogenation* changes the chemical configuration of a vegetable oil in such a way that the oil is hardened. An oil such as corn oil can be *hydrogenated* enough to make it hold the shape of a stick (margarine). *Hydrogenated fats* are often used in commercial baked goods, and they are added to many brands of peanut butter to keep the peanut oil in suspension and prevent it from separating and settling at the top of the jar. Like animal fats, hydrogenated fats stimulate your body to produce more cholesterol and are associated with increased rates of coronary artery disease. In fact, experts now believe that hydrogenated fats are even worse for your health than animal fats.

Shopping for Your Vegetarian Kitchen

"Do I have to shop at a health food store?"

"Is there a reason to buy alfalfa sprouts?"

No. And Yes. This section will help you to go beyond your neighborhood supermarket and explore places that you may never before have set foot in search of good foods. It covers shopping tips and strategies, and some interesting new foods that you can try, and sample shopping lists to guide you and help you to remember what you need.

Getting to know natural foods

There's actually no legal definition for the term *natural foods,* but the term *natural* is generally understood to mean that a food has been minimally processed and is free of artificial flavors, colors, preservatives, and any other additives that do not occur naturally in the food.

Assessing the benefits of natural foods

Natural foods are frequently better choices than their mainstream counterparts, in part because they lack the undesirable ingredients of many commercially processed foods, and in part because they contain more nutritious ingredients.

For instance, natural breakfast cereals, baking mixes, and bread products contain no hydrogenated fats. They are usually made with whole grains, so they contain more dietary fiber, vitamins, and minerals than do products made with refined grains. They're usually minimally sweetened, and when they are sweetened, there's often less sweetener used. Fruit juice is frequently used as a sweetener, rather than refined sugar. Natural foods typically contain less sodium than other foods, and they contain no monosodium glutamate or nitrites. The ingredients used in natural foods products are often organically grown, too. (See the sidebar earlier in this chapter.)

Increasing variety with natural foods

Even within a particular category of food products, there are usually more healthful choices in a natural foods store than in a regular supermarket. For instance, in a regular supermarket you may find one or two types of whole-grain pasta. In a natural foods store, you're likely to find an entire shelf of them.

Natural foods stores carry not only natural-style peanut butter, but almond butter and cashew butter, as well. They carry numerous brands of whole-grain hot cereals and cold cereals, and an entire wall of natural fruit juice blends and alternatives to conventional soft drinks. They carry numerous brands of soymilk, as well as rice milk, oat milk, and potato milk, too.

Conventional supermarkets are beginning to carry more natural foods, and they are even beginning to integrate those products with their regular lines, rather than put natural products in a separate "health food" area. However, conventional supermarkets don't yet come close to carrying either the range of products or the number of products within a particular category that is carried by natural foods stores.

Saving money by comparison shopping

Natural foods stores used to be known as health foods stores. Twenty-five years ago, they were holes-in-the-wall that smelled of incense and vitamins and were frequented by the long hair-and-sandals set. The story is totally different today.

The general public is becoming much more familiar with natural foods stores, and natural foods superstores are springing up everywhere. These are large-scale stores that rival the selection and service of even the largest conventional supermarkets. Because natural foods products are being sold in greater quantities now, prices have come down as well. Large natural foods stores can often offer better prices than the small stores can offer on the same products, but conventional supermarkets may or may not offer more competitive prices. It depends on the size of the supermarket and the volume of the item that the store can sell, among other factors. It pays to compare prices, and you may occasionally be surprised at who has the lowest prices.

Finding natural foods in traditional supermarkets

Maybe you can remember when rice cakes and tofu were only found in health food stores. Now most grocery stores have an entire wall devoted to rice cakes in different sizes and flavors, and even several types of tofu in the produce section. Well, things continue to evolve.

Supermarkets are bringing in more and more natural products. Why? Because they're selling. Retailers are being advised by industry specialists to sell the natural products side by side with their conventional counterparts. Put the Muir Glen organic tomato sauces next to the Del Monte and Contadina. Put the Barbara's natural breakfast cereals next to Kellogg's and Post. And stick the soymilk in the area with the dry and canned milk, rather than relegate it to a "health foods" aisle. Better yet, position the soymilk in the refrigerator case, next to the fresh cows' milk.

If there's a favorite product that you can buy at the natural foods store but that your regular supermarket doesn't carry, mention it to the manager of your store. The store may be willing to stock it at a competitive price.

Exploring different types of stores

You may want to shop at more than one place. Many people find that they purchase certain items at one store and others at another store. For instance, you may shop at a natural foods store to buy such foods as frozen vegetarian entrées, specialty baking mixes, whole-grain pastas and breakfast cereals, and your favorite brand of soymilk by the case. Then you might shop at a conventional store for such items as toilet paper, fresh produce, and toothpaste.

Of course, you can usually buy everything at one store or the other. It all depends on your individual preferences. Some people buy everything at a natural foods store, including nonfood items, because they're usually more environmentally friendly than other stores. One factor that might make a difference in where you shop is your access to large natural foods superstores. You'll find them in larger cities, and prices may be better and the variety greater than in cities that have only small stores.

If you've never before set foot in a natural foods store, now's the time to do it. You may not shop there for all of your groceries and supplies, but you should take a look at the many vegetarian specialty items and other great choices that are available. Things are changing in regular supermarkets, but it will still be years before some products finally make it from the natural foods venue to neighborhood grocery stores. Why wait? In the meantime, there are other possibilities to explore.

Ethnic markets

Ever feel like shaking things up a little? Getting tired of looking at the same old items on the same old grocery store shelves? Stopping at an ethnic market might just give your imagination a jump start.

They're usually off the beaten track, hidden away in a strip mall or in the back room of a restaurant, or on the other side of town. They're typically small, sometimes musty and a little unkempt, with ethnic-style music playing in the background. The sights and smells may be different than those to which you are accustomed. That's all part of the fun of it.

There are different types of ethnic grocery stores — Indian, Asian, Mexican, Middle Eastern, kosher, and many more. Each one carries foods and ingredients that are commonly eaten in those cultures but are frequently difficult to find in mainstream U.S. stores.

In Indian stores, for instance, you'll be amazed to see the many types of lentils that you can buy — red, orange, yellow, brown, and so on. You may find small, skillet-sized pressure cookers used in India to quick-cook dried beans and lentils. You'll find unusual spices and a variety of Indian breads.

In Asian stores, you'll find vegetables such as some Chinese greens that are shipped to the store from overseas but that aren't typically found in U.S. stores. You'll find unusual condiments as well.

In all these stores, you'll see a wide range of traditional foods, many of which are vegetarian or just different and can be incorporated into your vegetarian menus at home. More than anything, a trip to one of these types of stores may inspire you to sample foods of another culture and to expand your own repertoire of choices.

Co-ops

Many communities have neighborhood food cooperatives, or co-ops. A *co-op* is a group that has been organized to purchase foods in volume for distribution to its members, usually at a reduced cost. Costs are reduced because of the power of the group to buy in volume, so larger groups may be able to get better prices than smaller groups. Co-ops frequently emphasize natural foods products, and the arrangement can be especially helpful in small towns and rural areas where people don't have access to large natural foods stores with good variety and competitive prices.

Membership rules vary from one co-op to another. Some co-ops ask their members to contribute a certain number of hours each month to helping unload trucks, bag groceries, and distribute groceries. Others don't require that you work but give an additional discount to those who donate their time.

To find a co-op in your area, call your local vegetarian society or ask around among your friends.

Mail-order stores

Another alternative for people who don't have time to shop or can't find certain food items in their local stores is to shop via mail-order catalog. (See Appendix A for sources.) These catalogs often offer such products as TVP, a product made from soy flour that has been denatured by compressing the soy fibers. It's usually sold in granules that, when rehydrated, resemble ground beef. It can also be sold in chunks that, when rehydrated, have the texture and appearance of chunks of meat. Mail-order catalogs also offer a variety of vegetarian mixes, unusual grains, and other vegetarian specialty products.

Let's go shopping! Sample lists to make it easy

So you're ready to hit the stores. Almost. If you're new to vegetarianism, you might want to take a few minutes to think about what items you'll want to buy. It might be helpful to review the shopping list suggestions I present earlier in this chapter.

You don't really have to make a science out of shopping. Write a list, and head to the store. But not everyone likes to shop from a list. It's not that they aren't organized. It's just that they like less structure. That's fine. I, on the other hand, am guaranteed to forget the one item that I actually made the trip to buy. So I carry a list, even if it contains only two items.

People have different shopping styles, just like they have different personalities. Some people like to plan their week's meals, draw up a corresponding shopping list, and buy only what they need to make the meals they've planned. Other people prefer the casual approach, walk up and down the aisles, and put whatever strikes their fancy into their basket. At home, they decide what they're having for dinner based on what they feel like making and the supplies they have on hand.

When you've made a change in your eating habits and are developing new eating skills, it can actually be advantageous to do some planning ahead of time and shop from a list. Planning ahead will give you more control over your meals. Keep that in mind, but do what works best for you.

The grocery lists that follow are only suggestions of what you might buy to stock your vegetarian kitchen. You can adapt them to suit your individual preferences. If you like them just the way they are, you may want to photocopy them and make enough copies to last a few months. Tape a fresh list to the door of your refrigerator after each shopping trip. Check off items that you need or add any that aren't listed. There are separate lists for items that you buy weekly and items that you buy less often.

The lists show vegan options wherever eggs or dairy products are listed. You might have to look for some of these products at a natural foods store if your local supermarket doesn't carry them. While supermarkets frequently carry soymilk these days, they typically don't stock soy yogurt and soy cheeses, for example.

Shopping by the week

The foods on this list have to be purchased fairly frequently because they are perishable and will only keep in the refrigerator for a week or two before spoiling.

Fresh Fruits (especially locally grown)

- ❏ Apples
- ❏ Apricots
- ❏ Bananas
- ❏ Blueberries
- ❏ Cantaloupe
- ❏ Cranberries
- ❏ Grapefruit
- ❏ Grapes
- ❏ Guavas
- ❏ Honeydew
- ❏ Kiwi
- ❏ Lemons
- ❏ Limes
- ❏ Mangoes
- ❏ Nectarines
- ❏ Oranges
- ❏ Peaches
- ❏ Pears
- ❏ Pineapples
- ❏ Plums
- ❏ Strawberries
- ❏ Watermelon

Prepared Fresh Fruits

- ❑ Fresh juices — orange, grapefruit, apple cider
- ❑ Bottled mango or papaya slices
- ❑ Cut fruits
- ❑ Packaged fruit salad

Fresh Vegetables (especially locally grown)

- ❑ Asparagus
- ❑ Bean sprouts
- ❑ Beets
- ❑ Bell peppers
- ❑ Bok choy
- ❑ Broccoli
- ❑ Brussels sprouts
- ❑ Cabbage
- ❑ Carrots
- ❑ Celery
- ❑ Collard greens
- ❑ Corn
- ❑ Cucumbers
- ❑ Kale
- ❑ Leeks
- ❑ Mustard greens
- ❑ Onions
- ❑ Potatoes

Prepared Fresh Vegetables

- ❑ Fresh juices — carrot, carrot/spinach, beet
- ❑ Packaged cut vegetables and mixed greens
- ❑ Fresh herbs — basil, dill, mint, rosemary, others

Fresh Deli Items

- ❑ Four-bean salad
- ❑ Fresh salad dressings (olive oil or fat free)
- ❑ Fresh marinara (seasoned tomato) sauce
- ❑ Fresh pizza (with veggie toppings; try cheeseless)
- ❑ Fresh salsa
- ❑ Hummus

Dairy/Dairy Replacers

- ❑ Skim milk or soymilk
- ❑ Nonfat yogurt or soy yogurt
- ❑ Nonfat cheese or soy cheese

Eggs (or vegetarian egg replacer)

Tofu (fresh or aseptically packaged)

Breads and Other Grain Products (especially whole grain)

- ❑ Bagels (eggless for vegans and lacto vegetarians)
- ❑ Bread loaves
- ❑ Breadsticks or rolls
- ❑ English muffins
- ❑ Pasta (eggless for vegans and lacto vegetarians)
- ❑ Oatmeal
- ❑ Pita pockets
- ❑ Tortillas (not fried)

Shopping by the month

Some items keep for a long time in a cupboard, refrigerator, or freezer, so you can shop for some items fairly infrequently. You may be able to buy many of these nonperishables in large quantities to save money. The following list suggests items you might want to buy on a monthly basis.

CUPBOARD STAPLES

Canned Goods

- ❑ Applesauce
- ❑ Artichoke hearts
- ❑ Beans — vegetarian baked beans, garbanzo, black, pinto, kidney, navy, split
- ❑ Bean salad
- ❑ Fruits — any fruits, cranberry sauce, fruit cocktail
- ❑ Pasta sauce
- ❑ Peas — green peas, lentils, black-eyed peas
- ❑ Pumpkin and fruit pie fillings
- ❑ Soups — lentil, vegetarian, vegetarian split pea, tomato
- ❑ Tomato sauce and paste
- ❑ Vegetables — green beans, peas, carrots, asparagus, corn, tomatoes
- ❑ Sloppy joe sauce
- ❑ Vegetarian refried beans

Snacks and Treats

- ❑ Rice cakes and popcorn cakes
- ❑ Popcorn (bag kernels or low-fat microwave)
- ❑ Baked potato chips and baked tortilla chips
- ❑ Whole-grain, low-fat toaster pastries or energy bars
- ❑ Low-fat granola bars
- ❑ Bean dip
- ❑ Whole-grain crackers
- ❑ Flat breads (including matzo) and bread sticks
- ❑ Whole-grain cookies
- ❑ Tapioca and flan (made with nonfat milk or soymilk)
- ❑ Fruit toppings — prune, cherry, apricot

Herbs and Spices

- ❑ Basil, bay leaves, cinnamon, cumin, curry powder, dill, vegetable bouillon, garlic, ginger, paprika, pepper, others

Beverages

- ❑ Plain or flavored mineral water
- ❑ Plain or flavored seltzer water
- ❑ Club soda
- ❑ Bottled fruit juice
- ❑ Sparkling cider or grape juice
- ❑ Juices — tomato, beet, or carrot
- ❑ Herbal tea
- ❑ Soymilk (aseptically packaged)

Dry Goods

- ❑ Beans and bean flakes
- ❑ Pasta (eggless for vegans and lacto vegetarians)
- ❑ Cold cereal (whole grain) — raisin bran, shredded wheat, bran flakes, others
- ❑ Hot cereal (whole grain) — oatmeal, whole wheat, mixed grain
- ❑ Whole wheat flour, other flours
- ❑ Whole-grain bread, pancake, and all-purpose mixes
- ❑ Rice — basmati, jasmine, brown, wild, arborio, others
- ❑ Other grains — barley, millet, bulgur wheat, kasha, amaranth, spelt, teff, quinoa, kamut, others
- ❑ Couscous (whole-grain if available)
- ❑ TVP

❑ Vegetarian egg replacer

Soup Mixes or Cups

Vegetable Oil Spray

Tofu (aseptically packaged)

Condiments

❑ Butter-flavored sprinkles (for nonvegans)

❑ Chutney

❑ Fat-free mayonnaise

❑ Fat-free salad dressing

❑ Fruit-only or low-sugar spreads, jams, and jellies

❑ Grape leaves in brine

❑ Hoisin sauce

❑ Honey (for nonvegans)

❑ Horseradish, low-fat marinades, BBQ sauce

❑ Ketchup

❑ Mustard

❑ Pickles and pickle relish

❑ Salsa

❑ Spicy brown bean sauce

❑ Stir-fry sauce

❑ Sun-dried tomatoes

❑ Sweet-and-sour sauce

❑ Syrups and molasses

❑ Vinegar — balsamic, herbed, fruited, malt, rice, other

Dried Fruits

❑ Apples

❑ Apricots

❑ Blueberries

❑ Cherries

❑ Currants

❑ Dates

❑ Figs

❑ Mixed fruits

❑ Prunes

❑ Raisins

FREEZER STAPLES

❑ Veggie burger crumbles

❑ Frozen bagels (eggless for vegans and lacto vegetarians)

❑ Frozen entrées

❑ Frozen fruit juice

❑ Frozen fruit bars

❑ Frozen juice bars

❑ Frozen pasta (egg-less for vegans and lacto vegetarians)

❑ Frozen vegetables

❑ Frozen waffles and pancakes

❑ Italian ices

❑ Meatless bacon

❑ Meatless sausage links and patties

❑ Muffins and dinner rolls

❑ Nonfat frozen yogurt

❑ Nonfat yogurt bars (for nonvegans)

❑ Popsicles

❑ Rice-based ice cream

❑ Sorbet

❑ Tofu ice cream

❑ Vegetarian burger patties

❑ Vegetarian hotdogs

Shopping tips to take or leave

Before you head for the store, I'll leave you with a few more pearls of shopping wisdom:

✔ Rotate the stores where you shop to avoid getting into a rut. Go to your neighborhood supermarket this week, try the one across town next time, and stop at the farmer's market when you can. Hit the natural foods store for hard-to-find items, and occasionally take a trip to an ethnic market for inspiration and the odd spice or vegetable.

✔ If you can tolerate lists, keep a running list of items you need taped to the refrigerator door. When you notice that you're low on something, add it to the list. When you're ready to go shopping, grab the list and go.

✔ If you have a problem with buying too many junk foods, eat before you leave for the store. If you're not hungry, you'll be less likely to buy impulsively.

✔ If you have a problem with buying the same things over and over again and are in a rut, go to the store hungry. You'll see things with a different eye and may break out of your rut and buy some new foods.

✔ There are no hard-and-fast rules. If you don't like tofu or alfalfa sprouts, don't buy them.

Chapter 11

Being Vegetarian in a Nonvegetarian Family

● ●

In This Chapter

▶ Keeping the peace between vegetarians and nonvegetarians

▶ Getting the whole family to like your vegetarian meals

▶ Preparing meals when company comes

● ●

Some food fights are easy to settle. He likes chunky and she likes creamy? Keep two jars of peanut butter in the cupboard. Butter versus margarine, mayo against Miracle Whip. Big deal. If only all differences in food preferences were so easy to handle.

If you're a vegetarian, the chances are good that you're the only vegetarian in your household. Like May – December romances, partnerships between a steak-and-potatoes type and a veggie delight can present extraordinary challenges. If you're going vegetarian alone at home, there are numerous issues that will have to be addressed by you, your partner, and other immediate family members. Some will be unique to your living situation, but some problems are common in many peoples' experience. An awareness of the issues and the manner in which you approach those challenges can have a significant effect on your relationships.

Of course, many people will find that going vegetarian poses no particular problems and that their families, partners, or roommates will fall easily into line with their new lifestyle. However, if your choice is being met with some resistance from family and friends, this chapter is for you.

The realities of relationships

If you get into a relationship with someone who isn't a vegetarian, don't bank on him or her changing. If the person does change, great. If not, be prepared to negotiate your lifestyle together. Being realistic about such matters can potentially avert traumatic realizations and disappointments down the road, when the person you thought would eventually see it your way doesn't. "Used-to-be-vegetarians" are often people who were once talked into it by a partner or friend.

Managing Mealtimes

Should you fix a standard meat-two-vegetables-a-starch-and-a-salad meal, and just dodge the meat and fill up on the rest? Or do you fix a separate vegetarian entrée for yourself?

Some families feel burdened by this problem. Nobody wants to get stuck cooking two meals for the same table. Should the meals be vegetarian, so that everyone can eat them? After all, there are lots of meatless dishes that most nonvegetarians enjoy.

I don't have all the answers here. This is a situation that requires discussion and negotiation among all parties concerned. Unless you face it head on, it will bite you from behind.

Preparing meals at home

Let's say that you're the head cook in your household, and you're a vegetarian. Should you be expected to fix meat for nonvegetarian members of the household? Maybe it's time for a nonvegetarian member of your household to learn how to cook meat. You may need a sous-chef in your home. You can prepare meals together, and you can be in charge of everything but the meat.

On the other hand, you might not want to be subjected to the smell of cooking meat, and you might not want meat to touch your kitchen counter or pots and pans. I don't blame you. But you'll have to hash this one out with your family. It may help to know that you're not alone. There are lots of people like you out there.

If there are meat-eaters in your house, sit down and try to work out some compromises that all of you can live with. For example, you might agree that any meat that is brought into the house will be prepared on waxed paper so that it doesn't touch the countertops, and it will be cooked in a pan dedicated to only meat. Another idea: cook meats outdoors on a grill to keep offending odors and drippings out of the house. Yet another option might be buying only pre-cooked meats such as deli or luncheon meats, so that they can be kept wrapped in the refrigerator and do not need cooking or further preparation in the house.

If you are having difficulty negotiating issues surrounding meals with you significant other or other family members, it might help to talk to other vegetarians who have dealt with the same issues. Consider getting online and joining in on some of the vegetarian chats over the Internet. You can locate vegetarian chat groups through some of the resources listed in Appendix A.

Figuring out what to feed the children

What about the kids? If you are a vegetarian parent partnered with a nonvegetarian, what will you feed your children? This situation really has the potential to raise problems. You will have to negotiate what your kids will eat, where, and when.

Nothing seems to charge peoples' emotions like issues surrounding kids. If you have an opportunity to discuss this one before you have children, you may be able to diminish the problems. (You'll still have to deal with your extended family, but that's another book entirely.)

Vegetarian diets can be healthful for children of all ages and can help establish a pattern of good eating habits that will be carried into adulthood. For more information about vegetarian diets for kids, see Chapters 22 and 23.

Some families make the decision that meals at home will be vegetarian, but away from home, it's every man, woman, and child for themselves. Others serve meat at home and let each individual decide for themselves what they will eat, with no pushing or prodding one way or another.

Getting others to try vegetarian foods

Rarely do arguing and cajoling convince others to adopt your vegetarian eating style. In fact, taking the pushy route usually has the opposite result: People will resent the pressure and push right back the opposite way. Instead, play it cool and let people drool over your vegetarian foods. If they're good, let them have a bite. Eventually, they might come around . . . at least part of the time.

If your child's diet is nonnegotiable for you, and you want it to be vegetarian, then you'll have to work that out with your partner and define the terms. A marriage counselor may be able to help if you find your discussions getting contentious.

Letting different folks have their different strokes

Making separate entrées works best when the vegetarian is also the family chef. It's the most obvious solution to the problem of preparing meals that everyone can eat, but it's also the most work.

The idea is simple — fix a full-fledged, standard meat-containing meal for those who eat meat, and fix a separate, vegetarian entrée for those who don't. The vegetarian can eat the vegetarian entrée as well as the nonmeat components of the rest of the meal.

There's a hidden strategy here for the vegetarians. As any experienced vegetarian knows, the vegetarian option tends to look really tasty. Try setting a vegetarian pizza on the table with other pizzas at a party or any gathering. If you're vegetarian, you'd better grab fast, because all the nonvegetarians are going to want the vegetarian choice. Likewise, put a bowl of pasta topped with marinara sauce on the table side-by-side with pasta and meat sauce. Conduct a bit of research, and see which bowl empties fastest. I'll put my money on the marinara — I've seen it happen too many times.

So, the strategy is that if you set out vegetarian entrees, everyone else is going to want them, too. Eventually, you may be making nothing but vegetarian meals. The other people in your household may not even notice the transition. And all that arguing and teeth gnashing will have been for nothing.

Eating what you can of the family's meal

Another option, of course, is for the vegetarian to simply eat large servings of whatever meatless foods are on the table. Mashed potatoes, steamed broccoli, salad, and a dinner roll make a great meal. There doesn't have to be a hole on your plate where the meat should be. You can cover up that bare spot with extra servings of the foods you like.

This is the same approach that many vegetarians use when they eat out at the homes of friends or others who don't serve vegetarian meals. They eat what they can of the available meatless foods. They don't draw attention to themselves (some vegetarians prefer it that way), and they don't give others the impression that it's hard to be a vegetarian in a nonvegetarian culture by whining about not having an entrée.

This approach is passive and fairly nonconfrontational. Problems are most likely to arise if another family member becomes threatened by the fact that you are behaving outside the norm of the family. For some, it may appear that you are rejecting family values and traditions. You're not, of course. You're just changing them.

Finding the vegetarian least common denominator

Another sensible approach is to consider vegetarian foods to be the least common denominator. In other words, everyone — vegetarians and nonvegetarians alike — can eat vegetarian foods, so when you plan meals, start with vegetarian choices. Choose foods that are vegetarian as prepared but to which a nonvegetarian can add meat if he or she so chooses.

For example, make a stir-fry using assorted vegetables, and serve it on steamed rice. A nonvegetarian can cook chicken, shrimp, pork, or beef separately and add it to his own dish. Rather than actually making two different entrées, you're modifying an entrée for a meat-eater. That should be considerably easier than fixing two distinct dishes.

All the following foods are vegetarian, and meat-eaters can add small bits of meat if they so desire:

- Bean burritos, nachos, or tacos
- Italian stuffed shells, manicotti, cannelloni, or spaghetti with marinara sauce
- Vegetable jambalaya
- Mixed green salad (large dinner style)
- Pasta primavera
- Pesto pasta
- Vegetable lasagna with marinara sauce
- Vegetable soup or stew
- Vegetarian chili
- Vegetarian pizza
- Vegetable stir-fry

The role of food in family traditions

Food plays an important role in family traditions around the world. When you make a switch to a vegetarian eating style, you'll find new traditions to replace the old. For instance, instead of a Thanksgiving turkey, your family may serve a stuffed squash, a vegetable-walnut loaf, or a "tofu turkey." Whatever foods you substitute for meat will become the new favorites. Over time, they'll be just as much a source of enjoyment and tradition as the old foods.

Helping Your Family Enjoy Vegetarian Meals

It might help you find solutions to problems if you have some ideas about how other people have solved similar problems. When it comes to handling family meals, there are several options that might work for you as they've worked for others. Because every family is different, though, you might have to adapt these ideas to fit your own circumstances. At the least, they may spur you to think of a workable solution.

You can take some simple steps to make the other members of your household more receptive to vegetarian meals. First, remember that you're asking them to trade in some of their favorite foods. What would it take for you to give up something that you liked, or at least were familiar and comfortable with?

You'd probably want a substitute that tastes as good as or better than the food you gave up. You wouldn't want to be inconvenienced. You wouldn't want the change to leave you feeling less than satisfied with your meals.

Keep that in mind when you ask for your family's support. Make their favorite vegetarian foods often.

Offering vegetarian choices everyone likes

If your family is congenial enough, you may be able to get away with making all vegetarian meals, provided that the group likes the choices. Whether you go vegetarian all the time or part of the time, it's a good idea to go out of your way to make foods that everyone likes. Figure 11-1 shows some favorites.

Figure 11-1:
Vegetarian
foods for
nonvege-
tarians.

So, begin by making a list of all of the family members' favorite foods that just happen to be vegetarian. For instance, your list might include

- Macaroni and cheese
- Grilled-cheese sandwiches
- Bean soup
- Minestrone soup
- Stuffed baked potatoes with grated cheese and chopped broccoli
- Most of the foods listed in the "Finding the vegetarian least common denominator" section earlier in this chapter

To that list, you can add some transition foods — foods that look and taste like familiar meat-based foods — that appeal to most people. These transition foods taste good and can be used in the same ways as their meat counterparts. They serve as crutches or training wheels until people become more comfortable planning meals without meat. Transition foods help meat-eaters cross over to a vegetarian diet. Some examples of common transition foods include

- Vegetarian burger patties and hotdogs
- Vegetarian cold cuts for sandwiches
- Vegetarian bacon and sausage links and patties
- Frozen, crumbled textured vegetable protein (for recipes that call for ground beef)

Finally, experiment with ethnic foods and other new vegetarian recipes. Let family members have input into planning, and incorporate their preferences into the menu. Before long, you'll have a list of family favorites a mile long.

Getting everyone involved

Get the family or your partner involved in meal planning to the extent that they want to be. People who are involved in any aspect of meal planning are more likely to be interested in eating the food. Here are some ways in which everyone in the family can participate:

- Grow some of your own vegetables and herbs.
- Ask for input about daily meal ideas and preferences.
- Shop together.
- Prepare meals together.
- Plan menus together for special occasions and when guests visit.

Setting an example

Don't push. It's that simple. When you preach and push people to do something that they aren't ready to do, you'll probably get the opposite of the result that you want.

Instead, teach by your own example. If your family or partner isn't ready to make a switch to a vegetarian diet, then quietly go about it yourself. Your actions will speak volumes, and the chances are good that, given time, the others will notice, get interested, and make some dietary changes of their own.

Here's a real-life example: My mother has been a vegetarian since I was a child. I remember the day that she went vegetarian.

I grew up in a typical, traditional, Midwestern meat-and-potatoes household. One day, my mother called the family to the table for dinner. We were all seated except my mother. She came to the table, but before sitting down, she briefly announced to us that from that day forward she would be a vegetarian. She didn't say another word about it. No explanation except "this is what I've decided is right for me." She sat down, and we ate our dinner.

My mother didn't discuss her vegetarianism with anyone. With the exception of her family and close friends, most people didn't even realize that she didn't eat meat. At family meals, she continued to prepare meat for my father and my siblings, and then she would make a cheese omelet or toasted cheese sandwich for herself (a Wisconsonite stuck in the cheese-and-eggs-rut) and eat the salad and vegetables along with it.

Time went by. Then, one by one, my sisters and brother and I went vegetarian ourselves. Nobody offered more of an explanation than to say to our mother, "You don't have to fix meat for me anymore." Eventually, the only person my mother was fixing meat for was my father. Many years later, meat also faded out of his diet as well. Decades later, we're all still vegetarians.

There's no reasonable alternative if you want others to change. Ultimately, we all have to concern ourselves with our own food choices and let others choose for themselves, too.

Putting your best food forward

When someone says that all they care about is how the food tastes, don't believe them. Appearances count. Food that is presented attractively *looks* like it tastes better. It sets the expectation that "this food is going to be good."

Set an attractive table. Use a tablecloth or placemats. Place a vase with a sprig of foliage or flowers from the yard on the table. Arrange foods in serving bowls or on plates with a little flair. It doesn't take much to toss a snip of parsley on top or to add a slice of fruit as a garnish on the side.

Let's say that you've made French toast using soymilk and bananas instead of eggs and milk. You'd like your family to love this new breakfast concept. Instead of bringing the French toast to the table in a big stack on a utilitarian plate, slice each piece diagonally, fan the pieces out across a platter, and sprinkle them lightly with confectioner's sugar. Serve warm maple syrup in a small pitcher.

Putting on a happy face

Attitude really is everything. If you present new foods with an upbeat, positive attitude, they're much more likely to be accepted. Show that you're interested in what others think of the food and that you'd like them to like it. Tell them about the dish you've made. Is it a staple in India? Can you eat it with your fingers?

Don't try to fake it, though, unless you're a professional actor. Overzealousness is usually not appreciated, either. Just be yourself, and others will be more likely to share your enthusiasm.

Planning Meals for Invited Guests

In addition to working out a plan for family meals that promotes harmony among all members, you may also have to discuss how you'll handle such regular events as guests coming to stay at your house and friends dropping in and remaining for dinner.

For some people, these situations are nothing to get too excited over. It's business as usual. Whichever way the family has worked things out, it stays that way while the visitors are present. After all, "When in Rome . . ." right?

But it's not that easy for other people. This kind of situation can cause friction, particularly when the lifestyle of the vegetarian in the household is still seen as an intrusion or unwelcome deviation from the norm. Having outsiders come in can cause built-up tensions to flare.

The meat-eater's point of view may be that if eating meat is the norm of the guests, the preferences of the majority should rule. Even attention drawn to the "vegetarian thing" may be unwelcome. In some homes, the nonvegetarian may feel uncomfortable with discussions about vegetarianism in the presence of guests. It's bad enough in the privacy of the home, but exposing such "eccentricities" to people outside the family can be embarrassing for people who think there's something "too different" about it.

In some circles, vegetarianism may be no big deal. In fact, some of your guests may well be vegetarians. Many people are comfortable having some vegetarian dishes and some meat dishes available, with everyone free to choose what they please. But if you are living with someone who doesn't support your choice of diet, it's a good idea to get the issue on the table and resolved before your guests arrive. You may decide to eat out, or you may opt to bring take-out food home. However you solve the dilemma, the important thing is to anticipate the problem and try to find a solution ahead of time. Then enjoy the visit.

Chapter 12

Being Vegetarian in a Nonvegetarian World

You may be a card-carrying vegetarian, but the manner in which you present your lifestyle to the world will make the difference between you being pegged a proselytizer or a model citizen. Hint: People really dislike self-righteous evangelists. You'll find it much easier to get along in the nonvegetarian world if people don't cringe when they see you coming.

There's a greater potential for you to "do good" and make a positive difference in the world if you present yourself in a way that leaves other people open to you and your lifestyle rather than in a way that makes them feel shut out, inferior, and defensive. Your vegetarian lifestyle choice will affect other people, whether they know it or not. It's probably going to make them stop and think about their own choices. This is your golden opportunity to teach others about the advantages of vegetarianism by being a role model.

Honing Your Diplomatic Skills

You may be quite content to live your vegetarian lifestyle without explaining your choice to anyone or attempting to convert them. If so, then you are probably the type who won't rub other people the wrong way. You're an undercover vegetarian rather than a walking-and-talking advocate. That's fine. Even in your relative silence, you're making a statement.

Activism done right

Some people feel that the in-your-face approach has a place. Opinions are neither right nor wrong, of course. The bra burners of the 1960s drew attention to women's rights issues with their very visible demonstrations of activism, and other women advocated for change in subtler ways. Likewise, a peace activist may wage a hunger strike to draw attention to the cause, while others promote peace behind the scenes. Ultimately, it's up to you if — and how — you advocate for vegetarianism. Attacking others, however, is a negative approach that is likely to alienate others and make them less receptive to your message.

On the other hand, if you frequently find yourself engaged in debates or earnest discussions with other people about the merits of a vegetarian diet — whether you initiate the conversations or not — then it's a good idea to give some thought to your approach in handling these interactions.

Whether you just want people to leave you alone and let you live the life you choose or whether you hope to inspire others to consider adopting a vegetarian lifestyle, diplomacy is key. You're going to need to develop skills in dealing with social situations in which your vegetarian lifestyle converges with the nonvegetarian world. Those skills will come with time and experience. In the meantime, the material presented here provides some reality-based suggestions for you to consider in deciding what your own style will be in dealing with others.

Delivering your message the way you mean it

Maybe you've seen the fashion "do's" and "don'ts" features in women's magazines — photos of people who have their looks perfectly and tastefully coordinated versus the ones with visible panty lines, long skirts with short coats, and other fashion gaffes. Your physical appearance can give people the impression that you have it all together or that you're a frazzled wreck.

Similarly, the manner in which you conduct yourself in the presence of others affects the way you are perceived. If you are belligerent, bossy, or brash, you come off as being uncouth. Even if your point of view is valid, others are likely to discount your message at best, or be totally repulsed and reject it outright at worst.

Bumper stickers, buttons, and shirts with vegetarian slogans express your politics loudly and clearly. One makes a statement. Two emphasize the point. But when your car and body are blanketed with these items, you are shouting. Some people may perceive you to be hysterical, depending upon the degree of coverage of your car and clothing. Consider that there may be a point of diminishing returns in terms of the extent to which people will listen to you when you express your views this way.

Responding to questions about your vegetarianism

"Why did you become a vegetarian?"

Most vegetarians have heard that question at least 25 times.

"If you don't eat meat, how to you get enough protein?"

They've heard that one just as many times.

"What do you eat for dinner?"

"Don't you just want a good steak once in a while?"

"If you're a vegetarian, why do you wear leather shoes?"

When someone inquires about your vegetarianism, the best response is a simple, straightforward answer. You don't have to expound on the basics. Just the facts will do. This is generally also not the time for the hard sell, nor is it the time to push someone else's buttons by criticizing their lifestyle.

You'll need to use your own judgment, but most of the time when people ask questions such as these, they're just exploring. They may not know much about vegetarianism, but you've piqued their interest. They may also be testing to determine what you're all about. Answer their questions concisely, but leave 'em wanting more. They'll ask when they want to know — and they may start asking you how they can become vegetarians themselves.

Becoming an Effective Vegetarian Model

The world would be a better place if more people were vegetarians. Those of us who have already made the switch know how nice it can be to live a vegetarian lifestyle. A vegetarian lifestyle is good for you, good for the animals, and good for our environment and planet.

As much as possible, try to be positive in the way you interact with others where food is concerned. Your attitude will affect how people feel about you, and people will associate that feeling with how they feel about the concept of vegetarianism.

The truth is, it's not particularly difficult to be a vegetarian, and there are many benefits. Why not advertise that fact? Some vegetarians present themselves in a way that makes it appear to be difficult and problematic to live a vegetarian lifestyle. Instead, aim for showing people how easy and pleasurable a vegetarian lifestyle can be. Take the positive tack if you'd like other people to give vegetarianism serious consideration.

Filling your plate to show vegetarian variety

Show people that eating a vegetarian diet doesn't mean that you have to go hungry when you eat meals away from home. Fill up your plate with food. Let people see how colorful and appealing a meal without meat can be. Don't leave a hole on your plate or allow it to look empty, as if you're deprived.

Demonstrating flexibility in difficult situations

All vegetarians get stuck at a truck stop or a KFC once in a while, where there's virtually nothing on the menu that they'd eat. Those are the times when you kick into survival mode and take a can of juice or a soft drink and a bag of chips and just hang on until the next opportunity to eat some real food.

Most of the time, though, vegetarians have plenty of food choices, or they can make do with what there is. Whether you're a guest at someone's home, eating out on business, traveling, or out with friends, try to be flexible when it comes to your meals. By being flexible, you show others that you can be a vegetarian in a nonvegetarian society without your lifestyle creating too much conflict. It's a positive message, though it's very easy to project just the opposite message.

Flexibility is especially important for vegans. Vegans do find it more difficult than other types of vegetarians to eat away from home, especially when they're in the company of nonvegetarians or nonvegans and don't have total control over where a group goes to eat.

I was once with a group of people, including two vegans, at a conference in Kansas City. When it came time to find a place to have dinner the first night, we literally roamed the streets for over an hour, wearily walking into one restaurant after another, reading the menus, finding few vegan options, and walking out again. Eventually, after everyone was frustrated and overly hungry, we settled on a Chinese restaurant and ate there every night there-after for the rest of that week. The impression I was left with was that it was no fun at all to be a vegan, and that it was tiresome and difficult to find something to eat away from home.

In a mixed group of vegetarians and nonvegetarians, or vegans and nonveg-ans, it's a good idea to anticipate the limitations and try to preempt them. Steer your party to a restaurant at which you'll be most likely to have choices right from the start. If you can't do that, then do your best to make do wher-ever you land.

Some vegetarians eat a vegan diet at home but occasionally make exceptions and eat foods containing dairy and/or eggs when they're away and have lim-ited choices. The reason? They'd prefer not to isolate themselves socially from nonvegans to the extent that they might have to if they were to adhere strictly to a vegan lifestyle. They feel that by being "90 percent of the way there" they are achieving most of the benefits of a vegan lifestyle without sending others a negative message. In setting an example for others, it may be more important to inspire lots of people to drastically reduce their intake of animal products than it is to inspire one or two to go vegan.

Reconciling Your Approach and Withholding Judgment

Just as your decision to live a vegetarian lifestyle is a personal one, the manner in which you interact with other people is also your call. You can be tolerant or intolerant, kind and compassionate or confrontational.

Your approach may be different than another's. A concession on the part of one near-vegan to eat a food containing dairy or egg when away from home may be completely unacceptable to another vegan, just as someone's deci-sion to eat a piece of turkey at Thanksgiving might be an abhorrent choice to other vegetarians.

In understanding others' choices, it can help to remember how complicated and deeply personal the subject of vegetarianism can be for everyone. Reconcile your approach as you see fit. Then work at projecting a positive image. Show others that you are confident, content, and at ease with your lifestyle.

Chapter 13

Practical Tips to Help You Along

At this point, you may be distracted by such errant thoughts as, "I need a degree in nutrition to get this right," or "I wonder if I'll be vegetarian enough." Your mind may be leaping ahead to such concerns as, "Is my aberrant lifestyle going to ruin my chances of making partner in the firm?" This chapter will help you put some of these issues into perspective.

Taking Charge of Your Nutrition

In the opening of his book, *Baby and Child Care,* Dr. Benjamin Spock wrote these famous words: "Trust yourself. You know more than you think you do." Likewise, while you may not have studied the Krebs cycle or be able to calculate your caloric needs, if you're reading this book, you probably have enough gumption to get your diet mostly right.

The science of nutrition is complicated, but being well nourished is a fairly simple matter. While it may sound strange coming from a nutritionist, there really is no need to become overly anxious about nutrition on a vegetarian diet. Remember that the primary reasons that people get up in arms over vegetarian diets is that they are uninformed and unfamiliar with the many vegetarian societies outside U.S. culture.

Vegetarian diets are not lacking in necessary nutrients. Rather, many people don't eat well, whether they're vegetarian or not. Poor nutrition is a function of lifestyle in general. The greatest threats? Time (the lack of it!) and junk foods.

Finding time to do it right

A friend once said that "time is the only truly nonrenewable resource." He was so right. How you spend your time is just as important as — or maybe even more important than — how you spend your money.

Because time is such a valuable commodity these days, we prioritize how we spend it. After all, there are only so many hours in a day. With all of the obligations that most of us juggle each day — working, being with family members, keeping in shape, mowing the lawn, doing the grocery shopping — it's no wonder peeling potatoes and assembling a casserole have been relegated to the back of the line. Many of us just don't take the time to fix meals from scratch anymore. If it can't be on the table in ten minutes or less, we don't eat it.

While it's true that it may cost more if someone else peels your carrots and washes your lettuce for you, prewashed and precut fresh fruits and vegetables can be worth the extra cost if it increases the amount of them that you eat and the frequency with which you eat them.

When you depend on others — food companies, fast food joints, and the restaurant down the street — to make your meals for you, you lose a great deal of control over what goes into those meals, including how much salt and sugar they contain and what kind of and how much fat is used. You're also more likely to choose impulsively, and choices made when you are overly hungry or stressed are less likely to be healthful.

The challenge, then, is finding ways to prepare good-tasting, health-supporting meals in a minimum of time at home. (See Chapter 15 for some tips and ideas on quick and easy meal preparation.) Some people think that vegetarian meals take longer to prepare than nonvegetarian meals because they contain vegetables that have to be peeled and chopped. Actually, any healthful diet contains plenty of fresh fruits and vegetables that may need some degree of preparation. One way to cut down on the time it takes to prepare a meal is to do some prep ahead of time.

For instance, when you bring groceries home, take 10 or 15 minutes right away to wash, peel, and chop such items as carrots, broccoli and cauliflower florets, onions, and green peppers. Store them in airtight containers in the refrigerator. Later, when you're ready to make a stir-fry, salad, or vegetable lasagna, they'll be ready to use. Prep work is the last thing most people feel like doing when they're hungry and want to fix dinner in a hurry, without much fuss.

Focusing on the foods you need — rejecting the junk

Junk foods are a threat because they're quick, they're convenient, we've acquired a taste for them, and they're everywhere you look. They're empty-calorie foods, and they displace more nutrient-dense foods from your diet.

Whether you're a vegetarian or not, the junk is there to tempt you. It's true that Coke and french fries are vegetarian, but the food of champions they are not. Not for someone who makes a steady diet of them, anyway.

Vegetarians are a more health-conscious bunch than nonvegetarians, generally speaking. But not all vegetarians are immune to the call of junk. The usual suspects? Chips, cookies, cakes, processed snack foods, candy, soft drinks, and that sort of thing.

Vegetarians who shop at natural foods stores do somewhat better than the average folks because many of the treats made by natural products companies contain less salt, sugar, and hydrogenated fat and more whole grains and fiber than other snacks. But even natural foods companies have some products in their line-ups that qualify as nutritional losers.

Sometimes it's hard to be objective about our own diets. Do the best you can to judge the extent to which junk foods displace nutrient-dense foods from your diet. If you have any doubts about the accuracy of your self-assessment, keep a food diary for a week or two. It won't show the whole picture of your diet, but it'll provide a pretty good snapshot of your eating habits.

To assess your own "junk food quotient," keep a food diary for a week or two. Review the results. For most people, one treat a day is a reasonable limit. A couple of cookies, a small dish of sherbet or nonfat frozen yogurt, a large handful of chips, or an ounce or two of chocolate shouldn't wreak too much havoc with your diet. Much more than that, though, and you may start suffering some nutritional casualties.

Avoiding Hidden Animal Products

There are many hidden animal products in foods. Many are present in very small amounts. Some, such as casein and whey — both derived from dairy products — are acceptable for vegetarians to eat but are not acceptable to vegans. Others, such as rennet (which comes from the stomach lining of calves and other baby animals), is unacceptable to all vegetarians. Table 13-1 provides a list of many of these hidden animal ingredients.

Some ingredients can originate from an animal or a plant source, but you can't determine which by reading labels. In those cases, you'll need to contact the manufacturer to inquire. You can also refer to materials made available by some vegetarian organizations. (See Appendix A for resources.)

Table 13-1	Hidden Animal Ingredients	
Ingredient	*What It Is*	*Where You Find It*
Albumin	The protein component of egg whites	As a thickener or texture additive in processed foods
Anchovies	Small, silver-colored fish	Worcestershire sauce, Caesar salad dressing, pizza topping, Greek salads
Animal shortening	Butter, suet, lard	Packaged cookies and crackers, refried beans, flour tortillas, ready-made piecrusts
Carmine (carmine cochineal or carminic acid)	Red coloring made from a ground-up insect	Bottled juices, colored pasta, some candies, frozen pops, "natural" cosmetics
Casein (caseinate)	A milk protein	An additive in dairy products such as cheese, cream cheese, cottage cheese, and sour cream. Also added to some soy cheeses, so read the label.
Gelatin	Protein from bones, cartilage, tendons, and skin of animals	Marshmallows, yogurt, frosted cereals, gelatin-containing desserts
Glucose (dextrose)	Animal tissues and fluids (Some glucose can come from fruits.)	Baked goods, soft drinks, candies, frosting
Glycerides (mono-, di-, and triglycerides)	Glycerol from animal fats or plants	Processed foods, cosmetics, perfumes, lotions, inks, glues, automobile antifreeze
Isinglass	Gelatin from the air bladder of sturgeon and other freshwater fish	As a clarifying agent in alcoholic beverages, some jellied desserts

Ingredient	What It Is	Where You Find It
Lactic acid	An acid formed by bacteria acting on the milk sugar lactose	Cheese, yogurt, pickles, olives, sauerkraut, candy, frozen desserts, chewing gum, fruit preserves, dyes, textile printing
Lactose (saccharum lactin, D-lactose)	Milk sugar	As a culture medium for souring milk and in processed foods such as baby formulas, sweets, medicinal diuretics and laxatives
Lactylic stearate	Salt of stearic acid (see stearic acid)	As a conditioner in bread dough
Lanolin	Waxy fat from sheep's wool	Chewing gum, ointments, cosmetics, waterproof coatings
Lard	Fat from the abdomens of pigs	Baked goods, refried beans
Lecithin	Phospholipids from animal tissues, plants, and egg yolks	Breakfast cereal, candy, chocolate, baked goods, margarine, vegetable oil sprays, cosmetics, ink
Lutein	Deep yellow coloring from marigolds or egg yolks	Commercial food coloring
Natural flavorings, unspecified	Could be from meat or other animal products	Processed and packaged foods
Oleic acid (oleinic acid)	Animal tallow (see tallow)	Synthetic butter, cheese, vegetable fats and oils; spice flavoring for baked goods, candy, ice cream, beverages, condiments, soaps, cosmetics
Pepsin	Enzyme from pigs' stomachs	With rennet to make cheese
Propolis	Resinous cement collected by bees	Food supplements, "natural" toothpaste
Stearic acid (octadecanoic acid)	Tallow, other animal fats and oils	Vanilla flavoring, chewing gum, baked goods, beverages, candy, soaps, ointments, candles, cosmetics, suppositories, pill coatings

(continued)

Table 13-1 *(continued)*

Ingredient	What It Is	Where You Find It
Suet	Hard white fat around kidneys and loins of animals	Margarine, mincemeat, pastries, bird feed, tallow
Tallow	Solid fat of sheep and cattle separated from the membranous tissues	Waxed paper, margarine, soap, crayons, candles, rubber, cosmetics
Vitamin A (A1, retinol)	Vitamin obtained from vegetables, egg yolks, or fish liver oil	Vitamin supplements, fortification of foods, "natural" cosmetics
Vitamin B12	Vitamin produced by microorganisms and found in all animal products; synthetic form (cyanocobalamin or cobalamin on labels) is vegan	Supplements, fortified foods
Vitamin D (D1, D2, D3)	D1 is produced by humans upon exposure to sunlight; D2 (ergocalciferol) is made from plants or yeast; D3 (cholecalciferol) comes from fish liver oils or lanolin	Supplements, fortified foods
Whey	Watery liquid that separates from the solids in cheese-making	Crackers, breads, cakes, processed foods

What you probably didn't know about sugar

White table sugar can be made from sugar beets or sugar cane. About half of the sugar produced in the U.S. is made from sugar cane. Cane sugar is whitened by passing it through activated charcoal, which can be of animal, plant, or mineral origin. About half of the U.S. refineries use charcoal made from animal bones. Because you usually can't determine the type of sugar used in a product (it's just listed on the label as "sugar"), many vegans just avoid any product made with white table sugar (regular vegetarians usually don't boycott table sugar). Brown sugar, confectioner's sugar, and commercial granulated sugar may all be made from cane sugar. Many vegans prefer to use rice syrup, maple syrup, date sugar, or turbinado (raw) sugar when they want a sweetener. Some also use powdered sweeteners made from brown rice, unbleached granulated sugar cane, or fruit juice derivatives, which can be found in natural foods stores.

Doing Your Own Thing

In life, when you play the comparison game, you usually lose. That's because there's almost always someone wealthier, better looking, smarter, and more accomplished than you. If you're vegetarian, there is usually someone who is more "vegetarian" than you, too.

Avoiding comparisons

Some of you know what I mean. Among some vegetarians, there seems to be a hierarchy of vegetarianism. The lacto ovo vegetarians are very pedestrian. They're beginners. They haven't quite "evolved" to the more ethically pure vegan ideal. They consume animal products — dairy and eggs — that subsidize the meat industry or otherwise exploit animals. They haven't yet shed the leather shoes and the wool coats, either.

The lacto ovo veggetarians think the fish-eaters haven't gone far enough, and the vegans think the lacto ovo vegetarians are falling short. Not everyone is judgmental, but many are. In addition to being involved with their own diets, they're also policing everyone else's plates.

My advice is to listen, read, and absorb all the information you care to about vegetarian lifestyles. Then decide what's right for you and do it. Do your best to ignore negative messages from those who feel the need to preach. They, too, have needs to satisfy, but you don't have to be a part of it. The choice of a vegetarian diet — and which kind of vegetarian diet — is highly personal. It's nobody's business but your own.

When people adopt a vegetarian diet, the diet tends to evolve over time as they acquire new skills in meal planning and handling other situations relating to food. Don't let others cajole you into moving at a pace that doesn't feel comfortable for you, and don't let them make you feel bad about whatever level of animal products you include in your diet at any given time. Everyone does the best they can, and we all have different reasons and capacities for making lifestyle changes.

Embracing your choice

When you adopt a vegetarian lifestyle, you may have a sense of being isolated at times. That's especially true when you're surrounded by family members and friends and the differences in your eating styles stand out. It's likely that you'll be the only vegetarian in your household. If feeling different is uncomfortable at first, keep the points that follow in mind:

- ✔ **You're one in a hundred.** More or less. Remember that only about 1 percent of the population is vegetarian. Lots of people call themselves vegetarians, but only a select few actually follow a true vegetarian lifestyle consistently. If you feel a little different, that's because you are.

- ✔ **You alone decide what you put into your body.** You may be different from 99 percent of the population, but you should feel confident in your decision to follow a vegetarian lifestyle. It's healthier and it's better for the environment than a nonvegetarian lifestyle, and it's a nonviolent choice. A vegetarian diet is the thinking man and woman's diet. People that opt for a vegetarian lifestyle tend to be more sensitive and socially responsible than others. They're deeper thinkers. Let's face it, we're brighter! (Of course, meat-eaters reading this don't have to buy into my judgmental statement.)

- ✔ **You owe no one an explanation.** You have every right to do your own thing. Stand tall and take comfort in knowing that you're on the cutting edge of the nutritional curve.

- ✔ **Vegetarian diets are outside our culture.** It bears repeating. Vegetarian diets are not a tradition in our culture. No wonder you feel a little strange. You'd fit right in if you lived in India or any other culture in which vegetarianism has been a tradition for thousands of years.

Keeping It All in Perspective

How far you go in eliminating animal products from your lifestyle is up to you. Like your diet, your use of other animal products, such as wool, leather, and silk, may evolve over time as you figure out which alternatives will work for you. Remember that there are various levels of vegetarianism. You choose what's right for you.

Distinguishing between vegetarian and vegan

While some types of vegetarians eat and use certain animal products — such as milk, eggs, butter, wool, and leather — vegans avoid eating or using any and all animal products — as much as is humanly possible, that is.

Vegetarian

A true vegetarian never eats meat, fish, or poultry, including foods made with by-products of these animal products. The operative word here is "eat," because some vegetarians do use some products that contain meat by-products. For example, some vegetarians use soap made with tallow or shampoo that contains animal proteins.

But a vegetarian doesn't eat these products. A vegetarian doesn't eat soup made with beef stock or rice flavored with chicken broth. A vegetarian also doesn't eat marshmallows or jellybeans made with gelatin.

Technically, a vegetarian wouldn't eat piecrust or refried beans made with lard, or cheese made with animal rennet. It can be hard to avoid these ingredients, though, because it's not always possible to know if a food contains them. That's especially true if you are eating in a restaurant or in any situation in which you don't have a food label to read. In those cases, most vegetarians do their best to ascertain whether the food contains an objectionable ingredient. You can ask the wait staff in a restaurant, for instance, whether the beans contain lard, and you can ask the server in a cafeteria line if the piecrust contains lard.

Vegetarians do not eat animal products that cannot be obtained without the death of an animal. For example, a vegetarian would not eat a chicken leg or drink beef broth. But a vegetarian would drink milk or eat an egg because the use of these foods does not require the animal to die. Most vegetarians do, however, use animal by-products such as leather and silk, even if it means an animal had to die. Vegans, on the other hand, use no animal products whatsoever, regardless of how those foods or products were obtained.

Vegan

So, whereas a vegetarian would eat a pancake that contains eggs and milk or would use margarine that contains casein (a milk protein and thus an animal product), a vegan would not. A vegan would avoid a piecrust containing skim milk solids, pasta made with eggs, and sherbet that contains egg whites. A vegan would avoid clothing and fashion accessories made with fur, leather, wool, and silk.

Vegetarian organizations can refer you to catalogs and stores that carry a wide range of vegan belts, shoes, purses, wallets, and other clothing items.

Some belts, shoes, and purses are now being made of such high-quality synthetic materials that it's difficult to detect that they aren't made with leather. Other vegan clothing options are always in style, such as straw or raffia purses, nylon wallets and purses, and canvas shoes.

Some vegetarians hold the vegan lifestyle to be the ultimate goal. It's the pinnacle of ethical righteousness. The less dependent you are on foods of animal origin and animal by-products, the less you will contribute to the support of industries that exploit and harm animals and the environment. Sooner or later, many vegetarians face a decision about how far they want to take their vegetarianism and whether to shoot for being a vegan.

What's lurking in your lotion?

For anyone who's never given it much thought, it can come as a surprise that so many personal care products, such as lotions, soaps, cosmetics, hair care products — you name it — are made with animal product ingredients. Again, you can check with some of the vegetarian and animal rights organizations listed in Part VII for a complete listing of items made with animal ingredients.

Like the decision to go vegetarian in the first place, the decision to go vegan is highly personal. Given that basic vegetarianism is outside U.S. culture, veganism is even further outside the norms. Most vegetarians would acknowledge that it's far more challenging to aspire to a vegan lifestyle than it is to go for a vegetarian lifestyle.

That's because of the extent to which animal by-products permeate consumer goods. You can begin to understand this when you review the list of hidden animal ingredients in Table 13-1. From photographic film to medicines to personal care products, animal by-products show up everywhere. In many cases, the ingredients are unfamiliar to most people and are listed on labels by their chemical-sounding names, so it's tough to recognize them as having originated from an animal.

It's nearly impossible to be consistently vegan in U.S. culture. Most, if not all, vegans do eat or use animal products at some time or even regularly, even if they aren't doing it knowingly. It's just that it's too difficult to function in this society without taking some chances that an item contains an animal product.

For example, most vegans eat out at restaurants at least occasionally. At some point, they may have to take the chance that the bread they are eating contains skim milk solids or another animal product or derivative. There may be honey in the breakfast cereal or an undetectable dash of Parmesan cheese on the croutons or in the salad dressing. They may go to a salon for a haircut and find that the hairdresser uses a shampoo or conditioner that contains animal proteins, or they may wash their hands at a friend's house or in a public restroom and use soap that contains tallow.

It would be very difficult to avoid all animal products in every situation and still participate as a member of U.S. society. Most vegans simply do the best they can and do not knowingly use animal products. They strive for the vegan ideal and may come close, but they don't necessarily achieve it.

Choosing your course

Whether or not you go vegan depends on several factors, including your ability to make the extra effort required to sidestep animal products as well as to handle the additional social and practical complications. On top of that, people have valid differences of opinion about the effectiveness of adopting a vegan lifestyle.

For example, some people feel that a vegan lifestyle is the most ethical choice because it minimizes or nearly eliminates dependence on animal products and therefore minimizes the exploitation and suffering of animals. They feel compromise is a cop-out, and they simply can't live with themselves unless they always do the best they can to be vegan.

Another point of view is that when people try to follow a vegan lifestyle and are rigid about it and won't ever compromise, outsiders see the lifestyle as overly oppressive or restrictive and are turned off by vegetarianism altogether. Some people feel that it sends the wrong message to others, and that a less restrictive stand might increase the likelihood that others will see vegetarianism as a viable option for themselves.

Many people take a middle-of-the-road point of view and generally strive to minimize their use of animal products while sometimes giving in. By being "90 percent vegan," they feel that they contribute most of the benefits without crossing the line and sending a negative message to others.

Ultimately, you should do what feels right for you. Hopefully, understanding the difficulty of the decision and the many factors that people have to weigh will help you understand and tolerate other peoples' decisions about the choice of vegan or vegetarian and will help them to tolerate yours.

What's a vegan Nazi?

A common term used in vegetarian circles is *vegan Nazi*, as in, "The vegan Nazis won't permit any animal products to be served at the conference site." That unfortunate term is used to refer to vegans who are intolerant of anyone who isn't striving to be a vegan.

Part IV
Meals Made Easy

The 5th Wave   By Rich Tennant

"Do I like arugula? I love arugula!! Some of the best beaches in the world are there."

In this part . . .

Yory don't have to be a good cook to eat well. You
don't even have to enjoy preparing meals to eat
healthfully.

The chapters that follow show you how easy it can be to
plan tasty, nutritious, and satisfying vegetarian meals with
a minimum of fuss. They present menu suggestions based
on the vegetarian food guide pyramid, easy tricks for modifying your favorite recipes, and tips on entertaining —
the vegetarian way.

Chapter 14

The Vegetarian Routine

*Y*ou shouldn't need a degree in nutrition to be able to plan your own nutritious vegetarian meals. You also shouldn't have to wield a calculator to balance your intake of essential nutrients.

Sure, eating well takes some degree of care and awareness of the principles of good nutrition. While you're in the learning stages, it's important to remind yourself to make healthy vegetarian food choices. This chapter presents a simple daily vegetarian food guide to help you plan meals and to remind you of the types of foods you should be including in your diet regularly. The guide also appears on the reference card in the front of this book. Tear it out and tape it to your refrigerator door if you'd like a visual cue to keep you on track.

A Guide to Daily Vegetarian Food Needs

You can use the vegetarian food guide pyramid shown in Figure 14-1 to help you plan meals. It will help you keep the following points in mind:

✔ In addition to a good diet, a health-supporting lifestyle also includes regular physical activity, plenty of fluids, and plenty of fresh air and sunshine (with precautions taken to prevent excessive exposure to the sun).

✔ The foundation of a healthful diet is whole grains, legumes, fruits, vegetables, and nuts and seeds.

✔ Sweets, dairy products, eggs, and vegetable oils are not necessary for anyone and should be limited because excessive consumption of these foods is associated with health problems or displaces more important foods from your diet.

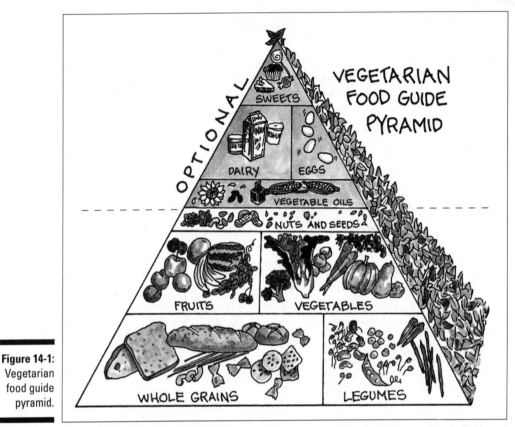

Figure 14-1:
Vegetarian
food guide
pyramid.

Used with permission of Loma Linda University Department of Nutrition and the Third International Congress on Vegetarian Nutrition, 1997.

Measuring and Counting Servings

The number of servings you need from each of the food groups represented in Figure 14-1 varies depending on many factors, including your age, how physically active you are, what type of vegetarian diet you follow, and your size. A good way to approach meal planning is just to look at the types of foods shown below the dotted line in the food guide and to try to eat a mixture of these foods. Eat enough of them to meet your calorie needs. It's really that simple.

If your calorie needs are high, eat a greater number of servings of any of the foods in the guide but especially those below the dotted line. If your calorie needs are low or you are trying to lose weight, eat less but not less than the minimum number of servings shown. If you are limiting your food intake, it's particularly important to include plenty of the foods below the dotted line. Remember that these foods are the most nutrient-rich and are the foundations of a healthful diet.

If you are trying to lose weight, you'll need to cut your calorie intake. You need a deficit of about 3,500 calories a week to lose a pound per week. At the same time as you are cutting calorie intake, you should be increasing your level of physical activity — the number of calories you burn. In fact, the more physically active you can be, the better. If you can burn more calories through exercise, you won't have to cut your food intake as much. That's ideal, because if your calorie intake level is too low, it can be tough to get all of the nutrients you need. You want to lose weight, but you don't want to become malnourished while you're at it.

Table 14-1 shows the number of servings you should aim for from each of the food groups in the pyramid. Recommendations for vegans and lacto vegetarians or lacto ovo vegetarians are shown separately, and the table also gives a suggested number of servings based on whether you want to include more liberal amounts of fat in your diet (for people with high calorie needs) or prefer a low-fat approach.

Table 14-1	Measuring and Counting Servings	
Food Group	*Servings*	*Serving Size*
Whole grains	5 – 12	1 slice bread 1 ounce breakfast cereal (¾ – 1 cup) ½ cup cooked grains, cereal, or pasta
Legumes	1 – 3	½ cup cooked dry beans, lentils, or peas ½ cup tofu, soy product, or textured soy protein 1 cup soy beverage (soymilk)
Vegetables	6 – 9	½ cup cooked vegetables 1 cup raw vegetable or salad ¾ cup vegetable juice
Fruits	3 – 4	1 medium apple, banana, or orange ½ cup chopped, cooked, or canned fruit ¾ cup all-fruit juice ¼ avocado 10 olives
Nuts and seeds	1 – 2	1 ounce (¼ cup) almonds, walnuts, or seeds 2 tablespoons nut butter such as peanut butter
Vegetable oils	4 – 7	1 teaspoon vegetable oil
Dairy	0 – 2	1 cup milk or yogurt (low-fat or nonfat) 1½ ounces low-fat cheese ½ cup ricotta cheese (part skim)
Eggs	0 – 1	Limit yolks to three per week
Sweets	0 – 1	1 teaspoon sugar, jam, jelly, honey, or syrup

Used with permission of Loma Linda University Department of Nutrition and the Third International Congress on Vegetarian Nutrition, 1997.

The foundation of your diet should be whole grains, legumes, fruits, vegetables, seeds and nuts. If your calorie needs are high, eat more servings from the various food groups, especially those below the dotted line on the food guide pyramid. If your calorie needs are low or you are trying to lose weight, eat less food but not less than the minimum number of servings recommended in Table 14-1.

Making Healthy Food Choices

It's not hard to maintain a healthy body on a vegetarian diet. The key is making sure you eat a variety of nutrient-rich foods. This section suggests some ways to help you make the best choices within all the various food groups. Table 14-2 offers some hints to get you going.

Table 14-2	Choosing Foods
Food Group	**Foods to Choose**
Whole grains	Whole wheat or whole-grain products Cereals: wheat, rice, corn, oats, millet Grain products: bread, pasta, tortillas
Legumes	Beans: pinto, navy, limas, soy, garbanzo Peas: split peas, lentils, black-eyed Soy: tofu, soy beverages, textured vegetable protein
Nuts and seeds	Butters and spreads Raw or dry roasted peanuts, almonds, sesame seeds
Vegetables	Includes all vegetables — leafy green and starchy
Fruit	Includes all fruit, but emphasize whole fruit over juice
Vegetable oils	Emphasize those high in monounsaturates such as olive, sesame, and canola Limit tropical oils (coconut, palm kernel, palm oil), and avoid hydrogenated fats
Dairy	Emphasize nonfat or low-fat products If dairy is not included, women, adolescents, children and the elderly need to ensure adequate sources of calcium and vitamin D
Eggs	Limit eggs or use egg whites only
Sweets	Eat in moderation

Used with permission of Loma Linda University Department of Nutrition and the Third International Congress on Vegetarian Nutrition, 1997.

Selecting breads, cereals, pasta, and other grain products

Whole grains occupy the largest section on the food pyramid, so be sure you include plenty of these in your diet. When you choose grain products, keep some general rules in mind:

- ✔ Choose whole grains as often as possible. Whole-grain products contain more dietary fiber and usually contain more vitamins, minerals, and phytochemicals than refined products.

- ✔ It's okay to occasionally eat refined grain products, such as Italian bread, most bagels, and French bread. When you do, try to buy products that are enriched (though most bakery products are not).

- ✔ Eat a variety of different types of grains, including oatmeal, wheat, rye, barley, millet, quinoa, rice, and amaranth.

"Diet" breads are often advertised as having only 40 calories per slice and target people who are watching their weight, playing on the myth that breads are fattening. Ordinary whole-grain breads are not particularly high in calories and are a nutritious part of your diet. You'd be better off cutting down on fat to save calories or exercising a little longer, rather than cutting back on your consumption of bread. The only reason to eat "diet" breads or thinly sliced breads is if you happen to like them better than the regular kind.

Here are some tips for using grains creatively:

- ✔ Many grains can be eaten hot or cold. For instance, rice is good hot with steamed vegetables or vegetarian chili, or it can be eaten cold in rice pudding or vegetarian-style sushi.

- ✔ Mixtures of different grains can be delicious (for example, seven-grain hot cereal, multigrain breads and rolls).

- ✔ Cooked grains keep well in the refrigerator. When you cook grains such as rice, buckwheat, and barley, make more than you need. Store the remainder in the refrigerator and reheat the leftovers to eat with other foods such as cooked beans, vegetable gratins, bean burritos, and bean tacos.

- ✔ Some grains take a long time to cook on the stovetop. To save time, you can often bring a pot of water to boiling, add the uncooked grain, turn off the heat, and take the pot off the stove. Let the grain soak for an hour or two until the water has been absorbed.

Choosing vegetables

When choosing vegetables, keep the following points in mind:

- ✔ Whether they're fresh, frozen, or canned, you can't go wrong with vegetables. They're all nutritious.

- ✔ Some vegetables are nutritional superstars. Shown in Figure 14-2, these include deep yellow, orange, red and green vegetables. These vegetables are especially rich sources of vitamins A and C, iron, and calcium. Examples include sweet potatoes, red and green bell peppers, broccoli, kale, tomatoes, and carrots. Eat them often, and eat lots of them.

- ✔ Cruciferous vegetables are also particularly good choices because they are rich in phytochemicals that may protect your health. Examples include some of the dark green vegetables such as broccoli and kale, as well as bok choy, kohlrabi, turnips, and cauliflower.

- ✔ If you cook vegetables, expose them to heat for as short a time as possible to help preserve their nutrient content. Steam them whenever possible, rather than boiling them in water. This keeps the nutrients in the foods instead of letting them leach out into the water.

- ✔ If you have trouble getting enough calories on a vegetarian diet, eat more cooked vegetables and fewer bulky raw vegetables.

- ✔ Eat large servings of vegetables. One-cup servings are a great idea.

- ✔ Buy locally grown vegetables in season when you can. You'll support local farmers, and fresh foods that don't have to be shipped long distances are more nutritious than foods that have to travel across the country to get to your table.

Here are some good ways to work more vegetables into your diet:

- ✔ Buy some prepared vegetables such as stir-fry mixes, peeled baby carrots, and ready-to-eat mixtures of salad greens. You may pay more, but the convenience is worth the price if it helps you to eat more of these foods.

- ✔ Buy an electric steamer and use it to steam potatoes, sweet potatoes, carrots, onions, and any other favorite cooked vegetables. Just wash the vegetables, cut them into chunks, and toss them into the steamer. Set the timer, go back to your work or relaxation, and there's nothing left to do until the vegetables are ready. No watching the stove or fiddling with the microwave oven.

- ✔ Serve fresh vegetables with a variety of dips, such as hummus, low-fat salad dressing, black bean dip, or salsa.

✔ Chop or finely grate vegetables and blend them into marinara sauce for pasta, or toss them with cooked pasta and olive oil to make pasta primavera.

✔ Grate fresh vegetables and use them to fill pita pockets, along with a scoop of tofu salad, hummus, or a sprinkling of grated cheese.

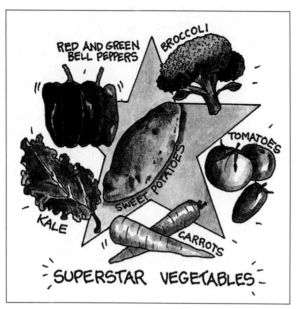

Figure 14-2:
Superstar vegetables packed with nutrients.

RED AND GREEN BELL PEPPERS
BROCCOLI
SWEET POTATOES
TOMATOES
KALE
CARROTS
- SUPERSTAR VEGETABLES -

Picking fruits

When you choose fruits, keep these things in mind:

✔ Buy locally grown fruits in season when you can because they're fresher and more nutritious than foods that are shipped long distances or that may sit for days on a supermarket shelf.

✔ Choose plenty of deep yellow, orange, or red fruits such as papayas, mangoes, apricots, peaches, and oranges. These nutritional superstars are particularly rich in vitamins A and C and other phytochemicals.

✔ Try to eat two pieces of fresh fruit every day.

✔ If you are watching your weight, choose fresh fruits more often than dried fruits or fruit juices, which have considerably more calories for the same volume.

✔ Wash fresh fruits with dish soap and water or use a commercial produce rinse to remove pesticide residues if you are going to eat the peel.

✔ Choose fruit drinks that contain 100 percent fruit juice.

Minimizing your intake of contaminants

Fresh produce contains only a fraction of the amount of pesticides and herbicides that are found in animal products because environmental contaminants accumulate in animal tissues. A vegetarian diet gives added protection against environmental contaminants because dietary fiber from plant matter helps to move contaminants through the body faster than in people with low fiber intakes, so there's less time for contaminants to be in contact with the lining of the intestines. However, you can remove some pesticide residues by washing produce with dish soap and water or using special produce rinses available in stores. You can also buy organically grown produce.

Even though you don't plan to eat the peel, be sure to wash the outsides of melons, grapefruit, and other fresh fruits before slicing them. If you don't, you will likely drag any bacteria or contaminants that may be present on the surface into the interior, edible portion of the fruit. In some cases, these bacteria can cause sickness.

Here are some strategies to work more fruit into your diet:

- ✔ Keep a bowl of fresh fruit on your kitchen table or counter. Keep a variety of fruit on hand.

- ✔ When fresh fruits have been sitting untouched for several days, cut them up and make a fruit salad.

- ✔ Serve sliced fruit with meals. Use slices of apple and pear as garnishes on a plate, add chunks of fruit to salads, and serve fresh or cooked fruits for dessert.

- ✔ Cut up fruit and store it in an airtight container in the refrigerator right at eye level. Somehow, fresh fruit can be more appealing when it's already cut up for you, and you're most likely to eat it if it's the first thing you see when you open the refrigerator to hunt for a snack.

Selecting legumes and meat substitutes

Here are some general rules of thumb for choosing legumes and meat substitutes:

- ✔ You can't go wrong nutritionally with beans, peas, or lentils of any kind.

- ✔ Feel free to use canned beans. To eliminate some of the sodium introduced in the canning process, rinse them with water in a colander before using.

✔ Buy organically grown canned and dry beans when it's feasible, but the regular kind are fine, too.

✔ When you compare meat substitutes such as veggie burgers, hotdogs, and breakfast "meats," choose the ones that are lowest in sodium and fat and the highest in dietary fiber.

Here are some good ways to include more legumes in your diet:

✔ Add a can of any kind of beans to a pot of soup

✔ Serve bean salads with meals. Marinated black beans with corn and diced red peppers make a colorful side dish to serve with sandwiches. Try a four-bean salad made with green beans, wax beans, dark red kidney beans, and garbanzo beans.

✔ Serve bean chili and onions over a vegetarian hotdog on a bun.

✔ Use mashed pinto beans or black beans as the base for a bean dip that can be seasoned with different herbs and spices. Serve bean dips with raw vegetables, tortilla chips, or toasted pita bread wedges brushed with olive oil and minced garlic.

✔ Serve a variety of bean soups often as accompaniments to meals. Good choices are navy bean soup, lentil soup, minestrone soup with white kidney beans, split pea soup with diced carrots, and black bean soup topped with minced onions.

A number of products are made from soybeans, including tofu, tempeh, soy nuts, canned soybeans, soymilk, and textured vegetable protein. All of these are good choices, and when they replace meat and high-fat dairy products in your diet, they can dramatically reduce your intake of saturated fat and cholesterol.

Eating nuts and seeds

Nuts and seeds sometimes get a bad rap because they're high in fat. The truth is, they *are* high in fat, and they're also a concentrated source of calories. So, if you're watching your weight, use them sparingly. A sprinkle here and there is fine. For instance, adding a tablespoon or two of sunflower seeds or pumpkin seeds to a salad adds flavor and crunch. A dash of slivered almonds adds flavor and nutrition to a plate of green beans.

Using seeds or nuts in this way is not a problem. In fact, nutrition scientists now recognize that in addition to being a good source of vitamins, minerals, and protein, nuts and seeds also contain beneficial phytochemicals. Also, the fat contained in nuts and seeds is mostly monounsaturated fat, a form of fat now generally thought to be better for health than either saturated or polyunsaturated fats.

While people who struggle with extra pounds may want to limit nuts and seeds because of their calorie content, people having trouble getting *enough* calories on a bulky vegetarian diet can add seeds and nuts to meals for extra calories. Overall, seeds and nuts are beneficial to your health. So as long as you keep in mind the extra calories they contain, there's no reason not to eat them.

Buy unsalted seeds and nuts when you have a choice, to keep your sodium intake down. It's also better to eat seeds and nuts that are raw or dry roasted than those that are cooked in additional oil.

Considering dairy products and eggs

If you eat dairy products, use only nonfat dairy products such as milk, cheese, yogurt, and frozen desserts. If you are vegan or otherwise don't eat dairy products at all, be sure that you eat plenty of plant sources of calcium and that you get enough vitamin D from sunshine or other sources. (See Chapters 6 and 9 for information on good vegetarian and vegan sources of these nutrients.)

If you eat eggs, limit the yolks. There's no exact science to figuring out how many egg yolks are too many for you, but generally speaking, the fewer the better. If you eat eggs, it's best to use the whites only. Of course, there are many good egg substitutes. See Chapter 16 for more on replacing eggs in recipes.

Working in sweets, treats, and other extras

How can you put your finger on how much dessert or candy or any other treat you can have and still maintain a healthful vegetarian diet? The best way to say it is that you can have treats in moderation. The term *moderation* is widely used to mean "just enough, but not too much." How much is too much? To many people, *moderation* means "less than what the other guy eats." Too often, it means that anything goes. Robert Pritikin, director of the Pritikin Longevity Centers, has said, "In this country [the U.S.], we're dying of moderation."

Coming from the point of extremes (extremely high intakes of fat, cholesterol, sugar, salt, and so on) typical of many people's diets, the term *moderation* can be hard to determine.

When sweets such as honey, jam, jelly, syrup, sugar, and so on are used as condiments — a teaspoon here and there to flavor your foods — they are generally not a concern and can be used on a daily basis. As long as you aren't using half the jar, it's doubtful that you could be eating too much.

On the other hand, when sweets are eaten in the form of desserts and snacks, too much can displace more nutritious foods from your diet. So, in the case of desserts and sweet snacks, one serving a day is a reasonable goal. If you are trying to lose weight, you might want to limit yourself to less — one serving every few days or once a week.

The same goes for junk foods such as chips and candies. Aim for not more than one serving of any of these each day. In other words, one serving of either a sweet dessert or snack or a junk food snack or treat. (Not one serving of each!)

Chapter 15

Eating Well When Time Is Short

- -

In This Chapter

▶ Building your breakfast repertoire

▶ Managing quick and easy meals

▶ Simplifying snacking

▶ Fixing foods ahead of time

- -

*Y*ou don't have to be a professional chef to fix adequate vegetarian meals. You don't even have to impress your friends. All you have to do is satisfy yourself (and your family — maybe).

Are you already a gourmet cook? Yes? Then you probably need no reassurance that you'll be adept at fixing vegetarian masterpieces once you've figured out what you want to make . . . which won't take long because you're already skilled and creative.

On the other hand, you may be one of the rest of us — just regular people who somehow manage to put together reasonably appealing meals most of the time. Sometimes we even do it with a little flair. But most of the time, we're talking whipping meals together in a half hour or less, with the emphasis on less.

If you need a little head start or a leg up in planning meals, this chapter's for you. There's some good-sense advice about ways to simplify meal preparation, and there are plenty of mix and match sample menus to give you some ideas of where to begin. You can use them and modify them until you feel confident enough to begin creating your own. See Appendix A for a list of selected vegetarian cookbooks.

To help you think of things to fix, make a list of your favorite vegetarian foods and post it in the kitchen (behind a cabinet door is a good place). Some may be foods that are favorites even for nonvegetarians, such as macaroni and cheese, grilled cheese sandwiches, vegetarian pizza, and bean burritos. It may help you to have this list to refer to at times when you can't think of something vegetarian to make for lunch or dinner. Vegetarian breakfasts are a little easier to plan than other meals because many traditional breakfast foods are already vegetarian, such as cereal, toast, fruit, yogurt, bagels, and muffins.

Beginning with Breakfasts

Okay, so you may not be a breakfast eater. How about a very early lunch?

Really, breakfast is an excellent way to fire up your gray cells. Boost your blood sugar with a good, high-carbohydrate meal first thing in the morning, and you'll function better for the rest of the day than you would without it. What's more, if you are a breakfast eater, you'll find that there couldn't be an easier vegetarian meal to prepare.

Breakfast basics

When you think about what you want to fix for breakfast, consider the following:

- There's nothing wrong with having leftovers from last night's dinner, cold pizza, cold Chinese takeout, or a bowl of soup for breakfast. Nobody says that breakfast has to be cereal or toast.

- A glass of juice and a bowl of cereal make a substantial breakfast. So do a couple of pieces of toast and a banana. Breakfast doesn't have to be particularly creative, and it doesn't have to be a five-course meal.

- Because a vegetarian breakfast can consist of exactly the same things a nonvegetarian would ordinarily eat for breakfast, it's a good meal to serve when you are entertaining nonvegetarian guests. You could serve freshly squeezed orange juice and French toast with apple compote and warm maple syrup, for example. Everyone would be happy, and your guests probably wouldn't notice they were eating a vegetarian meal.

- You can also modify a traditional breakfast to be vegetarian or vegan. For instance, for a meal consisting of juice, pancakes, and sausage, you could substitute vegetarian sausage for the regular sausage, and the meal would be essentially the same. Instead of a breakfast consisting of scrambled eggs, bacon, toast, juice, and coffee, you could serve scrambled tofu, vegetarian bacon, toast, juice, and coffee.

- If you like cold cereal in the morning, try mixing two or three varieties in the same bowl for a change of pace.

- Just as leftovers from yesterday's dinner can be a fine breakfast, breakfast foods can be a great change of pace for lunch or supper or a late-night snack. So, don't feel guilty if you like a bowl of cereal for dinner now and then, or even once a week. It's okay.

A week of breakfasts

The sample menus that follow represent a range of ideas for healthful vegetarian breakfasts. They've all been planned without animal products so that they're appropriate for any type of vegetarian. If you'd prefer to use dairy products or eggs in some cases, just substitute them for the vegan option in the menu. For example, if soymilk is listed, you can substitute skim milk, or if tofu scrambler is listed, feel free to use scrambled eggs. Realize, though, that the nutritional analyses will be different if you make changes.

You may notice that I've specified fortified orange juice and soymilk wherever those foods are listed. That's a nod to the fact that many people — especially vegans — have trouble meeting the recommended intake levels for calcium without including substantial amounts of high-calcium foods, supplements, or fortified foods in their diets. If you use dairy products regularly, you may opt not to use fortified juice or soymilk.

Surprise your family and friends with a delicious breakfast juice blend of freshly squeezed orange juice mixed with fresh carrot juice. Experiment to find the ratio of orange to carrot juice that you prefer, but a 50:50 blend is good. You can use orange juice concentrate instead of fresh orange juice if need be, but fresh carrot juice tastes much better in this drink than canned carrot juice. If your supermarket doesn't carry fresh carrot juice (check the deli area), you'll need a high-speed blender or juicer to make your own.

Breakfast one

¾ cup calcium-fortified orange juice

2 slices eggless French toast (made with whole-grain bread, bananas, vanilla, and soymilk)

½ cup sliced apple compote, lightly sweetened with sugar or any other sweetener

4 tablespoons warm maple syrup

Hot beverage

Nutrition: *Calories 724; Total fat 5g; Saturated fat 0.5g; Cholesterol 0 mg; Protein 10g; Dietary fiber 9g; Sodium 509.5mg; Iron 6mg; Calcium 508mg; Zinc 1.5mg; Vitamin B12 0.5µg.*

Breakfast two

½ cup prune juice

1 cup cooked oatmeal with cinnamon, 1 tablespoon brown sugar, and 2 tablespoons raisins

1 cup fortified vanilla soymilk

Hot beverage

Nutrition: Calories 491; Total fat 5.5g; Saturated fat 0.5g; Cholesterol 0 mg; Protein 13g; Dietary fiber 4g; Sodium 103mg; Iron 5mg; Calcium 416mg; Zinc 2mg; Vitamin B12 1μg.

Breakfast three

½ grapefruit

2 slices multigrain toast with 1 teaspoon soy margarine and 1 tablespoon raspberry preserves

¾ cup bran flakes

1 cup calcium-fortified soymilk

Hot beverage

Nutrition: Calories 489; Total fat 9.5g; Saturated fat 1.0g; Cholesterol 0mg; Protein 15g; Dietary fiber 11g; Sodium 671.5mg; Iron 11mg; Calcium 432mg; Zinc 5mg; Vitamin B12 3μg.

Breakfast four

¾ cup calcium-fortified orange juice

¾ cup scrambled tofu

½ cup hash brown potatoes

2 slices whole wheat toast brushed with olive oil

Hot beverage

Nutrition: Calories 588; Total fat 29g; Saturated fat 7g; Cholesterol 0mg; Protein 28g; Dietary fiber 8g; Sodium 343.5mg; Iron 16mg; Calcium 593mg; Zinc 3mg; Vitamin B12 0μg.

Breakfast five

¾ cup grapefruit juice

1 whole bagel with 2 tablespoons soy cream cheese

1 banana

Hot beverage

Nutrition: Calories 443.5; Total fat 12g; Saturated fat 3.0g; Cholesterol 0g; Protein 10g; Dietary fiber 3g; Sodium 284.5mg; Iron 2mg; Calcium 44mg; Zinc 1mg; Vitamin B12 0.1μg.

Breakfast six

¾ cup calcium-fortified orange juice

½ cup mixed fruit compote

1 medium bran muffin

Hot beverage

Nutrition: Calories 289; Total fat 5g; Saturated fat 1g; Cholesterol 0mg; Protein 5g; Dietary fiber 5g; Sodium 177mg; Iron 2mg; Calcium 56mg; Zinc 1mg; Vitamin B12 0.1μg.

Breakfast seven

¾ cup freshly squeezed orange juice

1 cup hot whole-grain cereal with 1 tablespoon chopped dates and 2 tablespoons brown sugar

1 cup calcium-fortified vanilla soymilk

1 slice multigrain toast with 1 teaspoon strawberry jam

Hot beverage

Nutrition: Calories 421; Total fat 5g; Saturated fat 0g; Cholesterol 0mg; Protein 14g; Dietary fiber 4g; Sodium 780mg; Iron 3mg; Calcium 216mg; Zinc 2mg; Vitamin B12 1μg.

Other Meals to Keep You Going

It's always important to eat well — to make conscious choices about the foods you eat. You need to do this to keep your energy level up and to maintain a healthy body. But, even when you're short on time, you don't have to run short on nutrition. This section presents some quick and easy light meals to help you start thinking about what to fix.

A week of light meals

The light meal menus that follow can be used for lunches, snacks, or light suppers.

You may notice that the sodium levels of some of the menus are extremely high due to the fact that canned soups and canned beans are included. In a few cases, sodium levels are 1,000 milligrams to 1,500 milligrams per meal. This is a dramatic example of how much sodium prepared convenience foods can add to your diet.

You can cut the sodium content of these meals in half or more by

✔ Making your own soups, using minimal or no added salt.

✔ Buying reduced-sodium soups. Many natural foods brands are much lower in sodium than conventional store brands.

✔ Rinsing canned beans before using them.

Light meal one

6 baby carrots with salsa

1 hummus sandwich (2 slices cracked-wheat bread with ¼ cup hummus, sliced tomato, and alfalfa sprouts)

¾ cup vinaigrette coleslaw

Water with lemon

Nutrition: *Calories 431.5; Total fat 15g; Saturated fat 2g; Cholesterol 0mg; Protein 14g; Dietary fiber 9g; Sodium 1,044mg; Iron 4.5mg; Calcium 139mg; Zinc 1mg; Vitamin B12 0μg.*

Light meal two

1 bean burrito (1 8-10 inch flour tortilla, ½ cup refried beans, chopped tomatoes, lettuce, onions, ¼ cup rice, and 2 tablespoons salsa)

Several orange slices

Herbal iced tea

Nutrition: *Calories 371; Total fat 4g; Saturated fat 1g; Cholesterol 0mg; Protein 14g; Dietary fiber 4g; Sodium 651mg; Iron 4mg; Calcium 174mg; Zinc 2mg; Vitamin B12 0μg.*

Light meal three

1 cup black bean soup topped with minced onions

1 mixed-greens salad with tomato slices and 2 tablespoons spicy vinaigrette dressing

1 sourdough roll with 1 tablespoon balsamic vinegar and 2 teaspoons olive oil

Water with lemon

Nutrition: Calories 394; Total fat 18g; Saturated fat 3g; Cholesterol 0mg; Protein 12g; Dietary fiber 4g; Sodium 1,522mg; Iron 4g; Calcium 84mg; Zinc 2mg; Vitamin B12 0μg.

Light meal four

1 vegetarian burger on a kaiser roll with lettuce and tomato

½ cup sweet corn and red bean salad

½ cup home fries

Herbal tea

Nutrition: Calories 465 ; Total fat 12g; Saturated fat 4g; Cholesterol 0mg; Protein 23g; Dietary fiber 10g; Iron 5mg; Calcium 138mg; Zinc 2mg; Vitamin B12 0μg.

Light meal five

1 cup split-pea soup with minced carrot

1 sandwich of 1 teaspoon pesto and tomato on 2 slices whole wheat toast

¾ cup fresh fruit salad

Water with lime

Nutrition: Calories 433; Total fat 9g; Saturated fat 2g; Cholesterol 0mg; Protein 16g; Dietary fiber 7g; Sodium 1,329mg; Iron 5mg; Calcium 81mg; Zinc 3mg; Vitamin B12 0μg.

Light meal six

½ cup grapefruit sections

1 sandwich of ½ cup tofu salad on 2 slices marble rye bread

½ cup three-bean salad

Herbal iced tea

Nutrition: Calories 260; Total fat 7g; Saturated fat 1g; Cholesterol 0mg; Protein 9g; Dietary fiber 5g; Sodium 529mg; Iron 2mg; Calcium; 108mg; Zinc 1mg; Vitamin B12 0μg.

Light meal seven

1 cup vegetarian chili

1 medium corn muffin

1 apple

Hot beverage

Nutrition: *Calories 496; Total fat 6g; Saturated fat 1g; Cholesterol 0mg; Protein 21g; Dietary fiber 19g; Sodium 1,051mg; Iron 7mg; Calcium 150mg; Zinc 2mg; Vitamin B12 0μg.*

A week of main meals

These menus are suggestions for dinner or a heavier midday meal. You can reduce the sodium content of these main meals by following the instructions given in the section "A week of light meals" earlier in this chapter.

Main meal one

1 tempeh sloppy joe (½ cup filling) on a whole grain bun

2 ears corn on the cob

¾ cup cooked kale with minced garlic and sesame seeds

Fresh pear, sliced

Water with lemon

Nutrition: *Calories 650; Total fat 13g; Saturated fat 2g; Cholesterol 0mg; Protein 29g; Dietary fiber 21g; Sodium 680mg; Iron 14mg; Calcium 306mg; Zinc 5mg; Vitamin B12 0μg.*

Main meal two

1 large salad of mixed baby greens with chopped walnuts and 3 tablespoons raspberry vinaigrette dressing

6 ounces vegetable lasagna

1 multigrain roll

1 cup mixed berries

Water with lime

Nutrition: *Calories 479; Total fat 14g; Saturated fat 1g; Cholesterol 0mg; Protein 30g; Dietary fiber 6g; Sodium 1,292mg; Iron 3mg; Calcium 85mg; Zinc 1mg; Vitamin B12 0μg.*

Main meal three

¾ cup sweet-and-sour cabbage

1 cup stir-fried vegetables and tofu over 1 cup steamed white rice

½ cup sautéed Chinese greens

Several orange slices

Hot beverage

Nutrition: Calories 440; Total fat 6g; Saturated fat 1g; Cholesterol 0mg; Protein 12g; Dietary fiber 11g; Sodium 121mg; Iron 5mg; Calcium; 311mg; Zinc 1mg; Vitamin B12 0μg.

Main meal four

½ cup hummus with 6 pita wedges and raw vegetable sticks

2 stuffed cabbage rolls made with garbanzo beans, steamed rice, raisins, lemon juice and seasoning

¾ cup cooked mixed vegetables

2-inch piece of baklava (made with honey alternative if vegan)

Hot beverage

Nutrition: Calories 695; Total fat 20g; Saturated fat 1g; Cholesterol 0mg; Protein 32g; Dietary fiber 8g; Sodium 1,135mg; Iron 6mg; Calcium 175mg; Zinc 2mg; Vitamin B12 0μg.

Main meal five

1 mixed-greens salad with strawberry halves and 2 tablespoons poppy seed dressing

2 bean tacos

¾ cup seasoned rice (or alternative cooked grain for a change of pace)

¾ cup steamed broccoli

½ cup vanilla pudding

Hot beverage

Nutrition: Calories 602; Total fat 10g; Saturated fat 1g; Cholesterol 0mg; Protein 24.5g; Dietary fiber 11g; Sodium 994mg; Iron 8mg; Calcium 471mg; Zinc 4mg; Vitamin B12 0μg.

Main meal six

1 cup minestrone soup

2 cups fettuccine tossed with 1 cup steamed mixed vegetables, garlic, and 1 teaspoon olive oil

½ cup sautéed spinach

2-inch piece Italian bread

1 large wedge cantaloupe

Water with lemon

Nutrition: *Calories 429; Total fat 8g; Saturated fat 1g; Cholesterol 0mg; Protein 17g; Dietary fiber 10g; Sodium 1,436mg; Iron 6mg; Calcium 255mg; Zinc 2mg; Vitamin B12 0μg.*

Main meal seven

1 black bean burger on a multigrain bun with red onion

¾ cup steamed, fresh green beans with 1 tablespoon slivered almonds

¾ cup roasted red potatoes with olive oil, minced garlic, and parsley

½ cup peach crisp

Hot beverage

Nutrition: *Calories 557; Total fat 9g; Saturated fat 1g; Cholesterol 0mg; Protein 25g; Dietary fiber 11 g; Sodium 465mg; Iron 5mg; Calcium 169mg; Zinc 2mg; Vitamin B12 0μg*

Satisfying Your Snack Attack

A snack may have to be nonperishable and portable enough to pack in a briefcase, purse, gym bag, or backpack. On the other hand, it may be left-overs from dinner earlier in the day, or a glass of soymilk and a couple of cookies grabbed in the middle of the night during a wee-hours fit of the munchies.

A midmorning or midafternoon snack can be a good strategy for many people. A snack can help stave off a headache, especially if it's been more than three hours since you last ate a meal and if another meal is still a few hours away. A snack can also help boost your energy level when there's going to be a long stretch of time between meals. A snack can even help prevent you from overeating. For example, a light snack just before leaving work or school in the late afternoon can take just enough of the edge off your hunger that you don't eat everything in sight when you arrive home.

So, your choice of a snack may vary depending upon circumstance. You've got lots of options, though. Here are a few ideas to get you started:

- Soymilk and fruit smoothie
- Cookies and soymilk
- Graham crackers and milk
- Bowl of cereal and milk
- Half a sandwich
- Soy yogurt
- Bran muffin
- Low-fat popcorn
- Bagel with jelly
- Soup cup with whole-grain crackers
- Bowl of three-bean salad
- English muffin or toast with jam
- Baby carrots with hummus or salsa
- Baked tortilla chips with black bean dip
- Fresh fruit
- Frozen banana
- Frozen fruit bar
- Bean burrito
- Bean taco
- Bowl of fruit salad
- Bowl of rice pudding
- Freshly picked strawberries topped with nonfat or rice- or soy-based vanilla ice cream
- Oatmeal cookies
- Fig Newtons

See how many more you can add to the list yourself. The snacks listed here range from about 100 to 300 calories each.

Planning Ahead to Stay on Track

Planning ahead can help you gain control over meals. That's especially important when you're working on changing your eating behavior. If you're new to a vegetarian diet, meal planning may be easier for a while if you think about the meals a day in advance. That way, you'll help to avoid a last-minute crunch when you're tired and hungry and can't think of anything to fix. You might even have time to prepare part of the meal the night before — a salad or a sandwich filling, for instance.

One effective way of planning ahead is to prepare a few foods that can be stored in the refrigerator for several days or in the freezer for even longer and are available to take out and use whenever you need them.

Set aside a couple hours one day a week to fix a few meal items for the coming weeks. Because some of those foods can be frozen, over time you'll build up a good supply of ready-made foods to have on hand for times when you're too tired or too busy to cook a complete meal.

Filling the fridge

Lots of foods can be fixed ahead of time and kept in the refrigerator until you need them. Some will only keep for a few days, such as fresh fruit and vegetable salads. Others, such as some dips and grain-based salads, may last a little longer — several days to a week. Still, having a salad or a sandwich filling or two on hand can be a tremendous help when it comes time to put dinner on the table. Who wants to wash and peel vegetables and toss a salad when they get home from work? Sometimes it's all you can do to fix a quick pasta dish or sauté some vegetables for a stir-fry.

Here's a list of a few salads that will keep two or three days in the refrigerator:

- Cucumber and tomato salad (best if eaten within two days)
- Three-bean salad
- Greek salad (best if eaten within two days)
- Mixed fresh fruit salad (add bananas just before serving)
- Mixed berry salad
- Melon salad
- Winter salad with apples, pears, raisins, chopped figs, and cinnamon
- Green bean and boiled potato salad
- Coleslaw

These dips and salads will keep for several days to a week in the refrigerator:

- ✔ Tabouli salad
- ✔ Wheat berry with cranberries salad
- ✔ Hummus
- ✔ Rice pilaf
- ✔ Marinated vegetable salad made with broccoli, cauliflower, mushrooms, and carrots
- ✔ Broccoli salad made with broccoli, sweet onions, dried cherries, sunflower seeds, and soy mayonnaise
- ✔ Black bean dip or spread
- ✔ Pinto bean spread (refried beans)
- ✔ Potato salad

Stocking the freezer

It's nice to have a few things in the freezer — casseroles, soups, main dishes, breads, and muffins — that you can take out as needed. Of course because they're frozen, they'll keep for several weeks, until you use them.

You can freeze bread products, such as pancakes, waffles, cookies, and muffins. Store them in small batches or single servings so that you can take out only what you need for a few days at a time. If you freeze pancakes, put a layer of waxed paper between each so that they don't stick together and are easier to separate.

Other foods that freeze well include:

- ✔ Vegetarian chili
- ✔ Soups
- ✔ Lasagna
- ✔ Grain and vegetable casseroles
- ✔ Stuffed shells or manicotti
- ✔ Grapes and bananas (Peel bananas first. These make great frozen snacks or you can use the frozen bananas for smoothies.)
- ✔ Fresh berries and melon balls
- ✔ Spinach pie
- ✔ Tofu quiche
- ✔ Fruit crisps and pies

Chapter 16

Reinventing Your Favorite Recipes

· ·

In This Chapter

▶ Substituting for eggs in baked goods, casseroles, and more

▶ Replacing milk, cheese, butter, sour cream, and yogurt in recipes

▶ Trying meat alternatives in your favorite nonvegetarian recipes

▶ Discovering vegetarian sources of gelatin

· ·

*W*hen I think about vegetarian substitutions for animal products in recipes, I immediately think of Gilligan, the Skipper, palm trees, deserted islands, and big coconut cream and banana cream pies.

You may not want to admit it publicly, but surely you remember the TV show *Gilligan's Island*? As a kid, I was intrigued by those pies and wondered how the castaways managed to make them without eggs, butter, and milk. Okay, they had coconut milk. No eggs or butter, though. And those pies looked so good.

You may not have known that you don't need eggs, milk, or butter to make your favorite desserts — because standard cookbooks don't give you any other choices. Think about it. Your old *Betty Crocker* and *Joy of Cooking* call for animal products in nearly every recipe they contain for baked goods and desserts. Cookies, cakes, pies, quick breads — they all call for eggs, milk, and butter. What holds a meatloaf together? Eggs, of course. How do you make French toast? With eggs and milk, naturally.

It's our tradition. In our culture, animal products play a major role in nearly every meal we eat. They are incorporated into nearly every recipe. Even the standards by which many foods are judged are dependent upon animal product ingredients for the qualities that have come to be considered desirable.

For example, a piecrust or biscuit is supposed to be flaky and tender. How does it achieve that texture? By the use of lard (or more recently, hydrogenated shortening). If you were to use vegetable oil instead, the crust or biscuit would not be as flaky. Similarly, if you used soymilk and mashed bananas in place of milk and eggs to make French toast, you'd get delicious French toast, but it wouldn't be quite the same as the French toast to which you may be accustomed. The color and flavor would be a little different.

So, when you make substitutions for animal ingredients in recipes, the characteristics of the finished product may be different from those made with animal products.

If you want to substitute nonanimal ingredients in your favorite traditional recipes, you will probably be on your own in figuring out how much of each ingredient to use. Unless you're using a vegan or vegetarian cookbook in which the recipes have already been tested, you'll have to fiddle around with regular recipes yourself until you hit on the ingredients that work best and the proper amounts.

This chapter shows you how to make many of your favorite foods without using any animal products whatsoever. Of course, if you're a vegetarian who eats dairy products and eggs, you won't care to work those ingredients out of your recipes. However, if you're a vegan or you just want to lower your intake of saturated fat and cholesterol, you may find the information here useful.

In many cases, you can use any of several different foods as a substitute for an animal product in a recipe. You'll need to experiment to find the one that gives you the best result. The information in this chapter will help guide you in working the animal products out of nonvegetarian or nonvegan recipes and give you a sense of where to start. Figure 16-1 shows some common substitutions.

 When you modify a recipe, use a pencil to make notes on the original recipe of what substitutions you made and how much of each ingredient you used. When the product is finished, jot down suggestions for improvements or any minor adjustments that you'd like to make next time. Whenever you make an adjustment, erase and update your notes on the recipe.

Getting Rid of Eggs

How many times have you wanted to bake a batch of cookies, only to find that you're missing a vital ingredient, such as eggs?

Bet you didn't know that those eggs weren't so vital. If you had known that you could substitute any number of other foods for the eggs in your recipes, you wouldn't have had to waste a minute running to the store.

Eggs perform a number of different functions in recipes, including binding other ingredients together, leavening, affecting texture, and affecting color (such as in a sponge cake or French toast). So your choice of a substitute will depend upon how well it can perform the function needed. In some cases, the effect of the egg in the recipe is so slight that you can leave the egg out altogether, not replace it with anything else, and not even notice that it's missing.

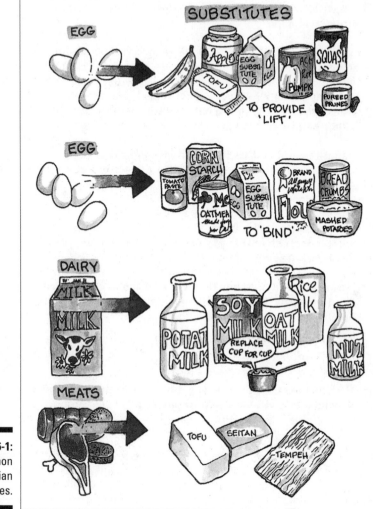

Figure 16-1:
Common
vegetarian
substitutes.

In this section, we'll look at some of the foods that can be used to replace eggs in recipes.

Baking without eggs

In baked goods, eggs are usually used for *leavening*, or lightness, and to act as a binder. In some recipes, eggs are beaten or whipped, incorporating air into the product and decreasing the product's density. The type of baked good determines whether you can leave out the egg entirely, or whether you need to replace it with another ingredient to perform the function of the egg in the original recipe.

For example, in baked goods that are relatively flat and don't need a lot of leavening, such as cookies and pancakes, you can oftentimes get away with leaving out the egg and not replacing it. That's particularly true when the original recipe calls for only one or two eggs. In recipes that call for more eggs, the eggs probably play a much greater role in leavening or binding, and you'll find that the recipe fails if you don't replace them.

If you omit the eggs in a recipe and don't replace them, you might want to add a tablespoon or two of additional liquid — soymilk, fruit juice, water, and so on — for each egg omitted, just to help the product retain its original moisture content.

In baked goods that are light and have a fluffy texture, you'll want to replace eggs with an ingredient that provides some lift. Try any of the following to replace one whole egg in a recipe:

- ½ **ripe mashed banana:** This works well in recipes in which you wouldn't mind a banana flavor, including muffins, cookies, pancakes, and quick breads.

- ¼ **cup any kind of tofu, blended with the liquid ingredients in the recipe:** If you use light tofu, you'll reduce the fat and calories in the finished product.

- 1½ **teaspoon commercial vegetarian egg replacer, such as EnerG Egg Replacer, mixed with 2 tablespoons water:** This product is a combination of vegetable starches and works wonderfully in virtually any recipe that calls for eggs. Natural foods stores usually sell this by the 1 pound box.

- ¼ **cup applesauce, canned pumpkin or squash, or pureed prunes:** These fruit or vegetable purees may add a hint of flavor to foods. If you want a lighter product, also add an extra ½ teaspoon of baking powder to the recipe because using fruit purees to replace eggs can make the finished product somewhat denser than the original recipe.

- 1 **heaping tablespoon soy flour or bean flour mixed with 1 tablespoon water:** This thickens and adds lift.

- 2 **tablespoons cornstarch beaten with 2 tablespoons water:** This also thickens and adds some lift.

- 1 **tablespoon finely ground flax seeds whipped with ¼ cup water:** This also thickens and adds some lift.

Holding food together without using eggs

In foods such as vegetable and grain casseroles, lentil loaves, vegetarian burger patties, and other foods in which the ingredients need to stick together, you need an ingredient that acts as a binder. Eggs traditionally serve that function in nonvegetarian foods such as meatballs, meatloaf, hamburgers, and many casseroles, but there are plenty of alternatives if you want to omit the eggs.

To replace eggs that act as binders in recipes, keep in mind the following:

- ✔ Begin with 2 or 3 tablespoons of replacer for each egg you're replacing, and adjust the amount as needed.

- ✔ When working with dry ingredients such as arrowroot or cornstarch, some recipes may work best if you mix the dry ingredient with water, vegetable broth, or another liquid (about 1½ teaspoons of dry ingredient to 2 tablespoons of water).

- ✔ Moist foods such as casseroles or some vegetarian loaves may not require any additional moisture when you're removing or replacing eggs.

Try any of the following to replace one whole egg in a recipe where egg is used to bind food:

- ✔ ¼ cup any kind of tofu, blended with 1 tablespoon flour
- ✔ Tomato paste
- ✔ Arrowroot starch
- ✔ Potato starch
- ✔ Cornstarch
- ✔ EnerG Egg Replacer
- ✔ Whole wheat, unbleached, oat, or bean flour
- ✔ Finely crushed breadcrumbs, cracker meal, or matzo meal
- ✔ Quick-cooking rolled oats or cooked oatmeal
- ✔ Mashed potatoes, mashed sweet potatoes, or instant potato flakes

With these substitutions, you'll probably find that you have to experiment a bit to determine just the right amount of an ingredient to serve the purpose in a specific recipe. A good starting point with most recipes is 2 or 3 tablespoons of any of the ingredients listed, or a combination of them, to replace one whole egg. If the original recipe calls for 2 eggs, start with 4 to 6 tablespoons of egg substitute.

Some of the ingredients listed may affect the flavor of the finished product, too, so you should consider that when you decide which ingredients to use to replace the eggs in your recipe. For instance, if you add sweet potato to a burger patty, you may be able to taste it in the finished product, whereas if you mix some into a casserole, its flavor may be more disguised by the other ingredients. On the other hand, the extra flavor that some of these ingredients add may be a nice change of pace.

Imitating egg with tofu

Tofu can stand in for eggs in all sorts of recipes. Usually it's invisible as an ingredient, but sometimes it appears simply as an egg imposter. Here are some examples:

✔ You can use chopped firm or extra firm tofu in place of egg whites in recipes for egg salad sandwich filling. Just make your favorite egg salad recipe, but use chopped tofu instead of hard-boiled eggs. You can even use soy mayonnaise instead of regular mayonnaise for a vegan version.

✔ Add chopped firm tofu to mixed-greens salads or spinach salad in place of chopped hard-boiled eggs. You can also add chopped or minced tofu to bowls of Chinese hot and sour soup.

✔ Make scrambled tofu instead of scrambled eggs. Natural foods stores stock "tofu scrambler" spice packets, and you may also see them in the produce section of your regular supermarket, next to the tofu. Vegetarian cookbooks also give recipes for making scrambled tofu. The recipes usually include turmeric to give the tofu a yellow color similar to that of scrambled eggs.

✔ Use scrambled tofu to fill pita pockets or as a sandwich filling on hoagie rolls.

Dumping Dairy Products

It's not nearly as tricky to replace dairy products in recipes as it is to replace eggs. The dairy products that you're most likely to find in recipes are milk, yogurt, sour cream, butter, and cheese. There are good nondairy alternatives that can easily be substituted for all of these.

Move over, milk!

Cows' milk can be replaced in recipes with soymilk, rice milk, potato milk, nut milk, or oat milk. Just substitute any of these milk alternatives cup-for-cup for cow's milk. While oat milk has a neutral flavor without sweetness, some nut milks, such as almond, are too sweet for savory dishes. Use them in desserts and smoothies.

Soymilk is made by grinding soybeans that have been soaked and cooked. The soymilk is pressed out of the beans. A similar process is used to make other kinds of milk substitutes.

Soymilk is generally more nutritious than any of the other milk alternatives, such as rice milk and almond milk. Fortified soymilk has extra calcium and vitamins A, D, and B12, too. If you use substantial amounts of a milk alternative, fortified soymilk is usually the best choice in terms of nutrition.

Plain and vanilla flavors are the most versatile varieties of soy milk because the mild flavors blend in with just about any recipe. I use vanilla-flavored soymilk exclusively, and it's worked well in any recipe I've ever made. You can try plain soymilk in savory recipes such as some main dish sauces and soups. Use vanilla soymilk in sweeter dishes, such as puddings and custards, on cereal, in baking, and for smoothies. Carob soymilk is also delicious in some smoothies and puddings.

Soymilk, rice milk, almond milk, oat milk, and blends of soy and rice milk can all be found in shelf-stable, aseptic boxes in natural foods stores, and many brands are now carried at regular supermarkets, too. Potato milk is sold in natural foods stores in powdered form. Some soymilk is still sold in powdered form, too. You may find the liquid soymilk to be more palatable and much more convenient, though.

You can save money at many supermarkets and natural foods stores if you buy soymilk (or other milk alternatives) by the case. Because the aseptic packages can keep for several months or more in your cupboard, you may find it convenient to buy one or two cases at a time. There are usually 12 boxes to a case, and many stores will give you 10 percent off each case.

Simply soymilk

If you try soymilk for the first time and don't care for it, give it a second chance and try another brand. Soymilk varies in flavor considerably from one brand to the next. You may have to taste three or four before you find your favorite. Most of the soymilk sold in the United States and Canada is made from whole soybeans, so it has a bit of a beany aftertaste, which some people find pleasant but others don't like. If you object to the mild bean flavor, you may prefer a flavored soymilk to plain. Soymilk grows on you. If you use it for a while, you'll probably grow to love it.

Sayonara, sour cream and yogurt!

If you prefer not to use dairy yogurt, you'll find soy-based plain and flavored yogurts at any natural foods store. They're delicious. Natural foods stores also sell soy-based sour cream. Nutritionally, the biggest advantage to both of these products is that they contain no cholesterol and far less saturated fat than their dairy counterparts. Some soy yogurts also contain active cultures, just like many dairy yogurts.

You can use soy yogurt and sour cream in most of the same ways that you would use the dairy versions, including baking, making sauces and dips, and eating as is. Because these substitutes sometimes separate when they're heated on the stove, they may or may not work in certain sauce recipes. Most of the time, however, you'll find you have no problems substituting them for dairy yogurt and sour cream.

You can make your own version of nondairy buttermilk by adding 2 teaspoons of lemon juice or vinegar to one cup of soymilk or any other milk substitute.

Cheesy options

Full-fat dairy cheeses are loaded with saturated fat and cholesterol, but many people find that the nonfat varieties are short on flavor (they taste like plastic) and don't melt well. You can avoid dairy cheeses altogether by trying some of the good nondairy alternatives on the market.

Cheese alternatives are usually sold in natural foods stores — only a few regular supermarkets carry them at this time — and are usually soy or nut based. They come in a variety of flavors and types, such as mozzarella style and jack or cheddar style. Parmesan-style cheese and cream cheese are also widely available in natural foods stores. Most taste reasonably good, and they are free of cholesterol and much lower in saturated fat than their dairy counterparts.

Nondairy cheese alternatives don't all melt as well as regular, full-fat dairy cheeses, but they generally melt better than nonfat dairy cheeses. That's due, in part, to the fact that they tend to be high in fat, albeit vegetable fat. The sodium content of cheese alternatives varies. Some are higher, some are lower, and some are about the same as their dairy counterparts. Remember to read the labels to ensure that you're getting what you want.

You can make your own nondairy substitute for ricotta cheese or cottage cheese. Mash a block of tofu with a fork and mix in a few teaspoons of lemon juice. You can use this "tofu cheese" to replace ricotta cheese or cottage cheese in lasagna, stuffed shells, manicotti, Danish pastries, cheese blintzes, and many other recipes. Nutritional yeast works well as a substitute for

Parmesan cheese on casseroles, salads, baked potatoes, popcorn, and pasta. It has a savory, cheesy flavor. You'll find it in natural foods stores.

Experiment with cheese replacers to find the brands you like the best and the varieties that work best in your recipes. Most cheese substitutes do well as an ingredient in a mixed dish, such as a casserole, in which the cheese doesn't have to stand alone but is mixed throughout the dish. Cheese substitutes, including nonfat dairy cheeses, melt better this way, too.

If you are a lacto or lacto ovo vegetarian and you do eat dairy-based cheese, remember that full-fat and even low-fat cheeses can add a substantial amount of saturated fat and cholesterol to your diet. You might want to consider using some soy- or nut-based cheeses in place of some of the dairy cheese that you eat.

Better butter choices

Soy margarine is available at natural foods stores. It's free of casein and other dairy byproducts that other brands of margarine usually contain. So, vegans can use soy margarine.

In terms of your health, though, it's even better if you switch to olive oil for as many uses as possible. For instance, instead of spreading margarine on your bread and vegetables, it would be healthier to brush your foods with a little olive oil (use a pastry brush).

That's because the vegetable oils used to make all forms of margarine, including soy margarine, have been chemically altered, resulting in a form of fat that scientists call *trans fatty acids.* These vegetable fats have had their chemical compositions changed through a method of processing that hardens the vegetable oil into a form that can hold the shape of a stick. If you consume trans fatty acids, you'll increase your risk for coronary artery disease even more than you do when you use butter.

If health is your only consideration in choosing a fat, olive oil is by far the best form of fat to use, followed by other vegetable oils. Butter is better than margarine, even though it is high in saturated fat. If you choose to use margarine, choose the brand that is lowest in saturated fat. Check the food label, and choose a brand that contains not more than 1 gram of saturated fat per serving.

Use about ⅞ of a cup of vegetable oil to replace 1 cup of butter in recipes. This substitution may not work as well in recipes for baked goods as it does in other recipes, so you may need to experiment to find the amount that works best.

Messing Around with Meat Substitutes

Some vegetarian dishes are originals — they've been meatless from the start, and they don't cry out for a meat-like ingredient. Some good examples are falafel (a Middle Eastern food made with deep-fried chick pea balls, often served in pita pockets), muttar paneer (an Indian dish), lentil or black bean soup, spinach pie, ratatouille (a spicy vegetable dish), pasta primavera, and many, many more.

Other dishes were made with a meat-like ingredient in mind. Without meat — or a suitable substitute — they're lacking something. Examples include chili, burgers (a burger without the burger is just a bun), sloppy joes, and recipes that call for chunks of meat, such as stews and stir-fries.

Some meat products are stand-alone traditions — hotdogs, hamburgers, sausage, cold cuts, and bacon, for instance. Believe it or not, there are some very good imposters to replace even these. Whatever the recipe, you've got lots of choices when it comes to replacing the meat.

Trying tofu and tempeh

People often talk about tofu and tempeh (pronounced "TEM-pay") as if they're bookends and go together like a matching pair. The fact is, they look and taste very different, and their functions in recipes vary, too.

Tofu

Tofu is a smooth, creamy food, and it has very little flavor or odor. It picks up the flavor of whatever it's cooked with. It blends well, so it can be used to replace dairy products in sauces, dips, puddings, fillings, and a host of other recipes. Bean curd is another name for tofu, so at Chinese restaurants, when the menu lists bean curd dishes, it means that these dishes are made with tofu.

 Cream soups can be made without milk or cream. Just puree some cooked potato with vegetable broth and mix it into the soup. You can use pureed soft tofu the same way. Blend the soft tofu with a little vegetable broth, and then mix it into the soup. Works wonderfully.

When tofu is used as a meat substitute, it's usually cut up into cubes and stir-fried (extra firm tofu works best for this), or it's marinated and cooked in slabs or chunks. If it's frozen first, and then thawed, tofu develops a chewy texture that resembles that of meat.

Tempeh

Tempeh is more limited than tofu in its usefulness because it's made with whole soybeans and can't be blended the way that tofu can be to make foods that have a smooth or creamy texture. But it can be crumbled, and many people use crumbled tempeh to make such foods as tempeh sloppy joes, tempeh mock chicken salad, and tempeh chili.

Tempeh can also be used in ways that meats are more traditionally used. For instance, strips or blocks of tempeh can be grilled, barbecued, baked, and broiled. Chunks of tempeh can be used with vegetable pieces for shish kebobs. Chunks of tempeh can also be used to make stews, casseroles, and other combination dishes.

Sampling seitan

Seitan (pronounced "SAY-tan") is a chewy food made from wheat *gluten*, or wheat protein. You can buy mixes for seitan at natural foods stores, but most people find it far more convenient to buy it ready-made. It's usually found in the refrigerated sections of natural foods stores.

One of the best ways to sample seitan is at a Chinese or Thai restaurant, where you can try it prepared in different ways. It can take different forms, but it's often served in chunks or strips in a stir-fry. Seitan dishes are absolutely scrumptious. Many people (me included) get totally hooked on the stuff. But you may have to go to a restaurant in a big city to find it. Because seitan is relatively unfamiliar to most Westerners, you aren't likely to find it in small-town or even medium-sized-city restaurants. You'll usually see it in big-city Asian restaurants where the menu is fairly extensive.

Tucking in some textured vegetable protein

Textured vegetable protein (TVP) can replace the ground meat in taco and burrito fillings, sloppy joe filling, and spaghetti sauce. If you toss a handful into a pot of chili, people won't likely be able to tell the difference between the TVP and ground meat. You can buy it frozen in bags at supermarkets or dried in small bits or chunks in boxes, bags, or in bulk at natural foods stores.

TVP is much more widely used in Great Britain and Western Europe than it is in the United States and Canada, and it's been sold overseas in natural foods stores, especially in bulk, longer than it has in North America. British vegetarian cookbooks, for instance, are more likely to call for TVP in recipes than are American or Canadian cookbooks. That may be changing, now that interest in TVP is growing and manufacturers are "mainstreaming" it in regular supermarkets.

Trying bulgur wheat

Bulgur wheat is rolled, cracked wheat. It has a nutty flavor, and it can be used in some of the same ways that TVP is used. For example, you can toss a handful of bulgur wheat into a pot of chili and get much the same effect as you would if you used TVP. It absorbs the liquid in whatever it's cooked with, and it has the appearance of ground meat and a chewy texture.

Using Vegetarian Forms of Gelatin

Vegetarian sources of gelatin are usually made from sea vegetables and are available in natural foods stores. Agar is one form, and it's made from red algae. Natural foods stores carry plain and fruit-flavored powdered vegetarian gelatin. These products can be used in the same ways that commercial gelatin found in regular supermarkets is used.

If you use vegetarian gelatin in recipes in which regular gelatin is usually liquefied and then added to cold ingredients, you may need to change the process a bit. Vegetarian gelatin may begin to set immediately, so you'll need to add the rest of the recipe's ingredients right away. If a recipe doesn't turn out well using the original preparation method, try blending the vegetarian gelatin into cold liquid first, and then bringing the liquid to a boil.

Chapter 17

Entertaining: Holidays and Special Occasions

*I*f you're a new vegetarian, you may be a little apprehensive the first few times that you have family, friends, or business associates over to your home for holiday meals and other special occasions. That's understandable. You've changed your way of eating, and your old menus may not fit anymore. Now you've got to plan a new menu. You'd like to fix a nice vegetarian meal, but you want to ensure that your guests will like the food as much as you do.

Holidays can be especially tough because so many people associate specific animal foods with various holidays, and those foods are as much a part of the holiday tradition as any other part of the observance. For some people, Thanksgiving just isn't Thanksgiving without the turkey. Easter means ham, and people drink eggnog at Christmastime. Maybe your family has always celebrated anniversaries or birthdays with a steak dinner.

Can Passover be Passover without traditional foods made with eggs? Thanksgiving without the turkey? Easter without the ham? All possible. All you need is a little imagination, a bit of know-how, and a room full of hungry guests. This chapter helps you get started.

Taking a Fresh Look at Your Traditions

If a vegetarian diet is new to you, planning vegetarian meals for special occasions and holidays, or just entertaining guests in your home, will require you to plan with an open mind. You'll need to acquire a new way of thinking about what holiday meals look like and how to set a table without making meat the centerpiece. To do this, a little creativity helps. So do some common-sense strategies.

Translating traditions

We expect turkey on Thanksgiving and ham for Easter dinner because they're traditions. We've simply done it that way for so long that those specific foods have become associated with those specific occasions. The food and the occasion seem to be inextricably linked. But they're not — not necessarily.

You can easily create new traditions, and you can even do it without forgoing all memories of the way it used to be. The first few times that you celebrate the new way, it may seem a little odd to you or to some of your guests. But if you leave other components of the celebration in place, the change won't seem so drastic.

There are times when it may also work well to entertain guests at a restaurant rather than in your home. That's especially true if you think that everyone's food preferences may be difficult to accommodate. At a restaurant, everyone can choose what she likes.

Let's say that in your family, Thanksgiving dinner has always meant turkey with stuffing, mashed potatoes, green beans, candied sweet potatoes, a mixed-greens salad, dinner rolls, fruit salad, and pumpkin pie for dessert. How could you modify that meal to make it vegetarian?

Actually, very easily. The vegetarian version of a Thanksgiving dinner doesn't have to be much different at all. You could replace the turkey with a meatless entrée, and leave everything else the same.

For instance, in place of a turkey, you might serve a large, baked squash stuffed with apple-cinnamon-nut filling or any number of favorite stuffing recipes. Stuffed squash is very much in keeping with the spirit of a late autumn meal, it makes an eye-catching centerpiece, and it tastes good. Here are some other options:

- ✔ Serving a "tofu turkey." Some people use a seasoned tofu mixture to make a loaf in the shape of a turkey. It's baked and may be served with stuffing on the side.

- ✔ Serving a lentil loaf, a cheese-and-nut loaf, or a hearty casserole as the main dish.

- ✔ Serving small, individual stuffed pumpkins as the main course.

- ✔ Serving a different favorite entree, such as vegetable lasagna or spinach pie. Fix something that takes more time to make and that you perhaps don't make every week, so that it seems more special.

Choose any of these options or think of another, but in planning the meal, also include the foods that you've always associated with that occasion that happen to be meatless or that can be modified to make them vegetarian, such as cranberry relish for Thanksgiving, or potato latkes for Hanukkah.

There's no rule that says you must have an entrée at each meal. Another option for adapting holiday meals or meals for entertaining is to simply not have a specific entrée at all. Instead, serve several interesting dishes, such as casseroles or gratins, quiches or savory pies, along with salads, breads, and desserts. The chances are good that no one will miss that piece of meat they're used to. Figure 17-1 shows a festive vegetarian holiday spread.

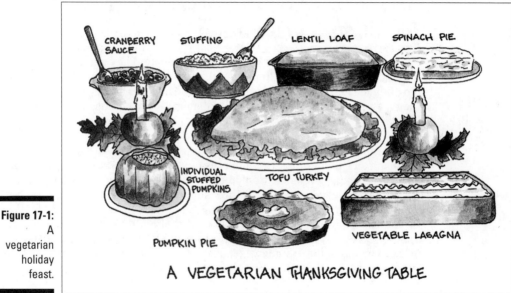

Figure 17-1:
A vegetarian holiday feast.

No matter what the holiday or special occasion, it helps to take the point of view that you are creating new traditions. What's new today with time will become tomorrow's tradition. You'll look forward to the new tradition just as you did the turkey, ham, or any other meat or animal product.

Re-creating traditional recipes

There's no need to scrap all of your favorite holiday foods just because they aren't vegetarian. Many of them can simply be modified. Soy margarine, soymilk or other milk alternatives, and egg replacers can be used to bake holiday cakes and cookies. You can work the meat, dairy products, and eggs out of recipes for side dishes, casseroles, breads, and other foods, too. (See Chapter 16 for more on making recipe substitutions.)

Coleslaw can be made with a vinaigrette dressing instead of mayonnaise, or you can use soy mayonnaise to make both coleslaw and potato salad. Use vegetarian bacon to make German potato salad or to add "bacon" bits to a salad. Use pureed soft tofu to make cream soups. Pumpkin pie filling can also be made using tofu instead of eggs and milk.

Challah (a rich Jewish egg bread) can be made with vegetarian egg replacer instead of real eggs. Even mincemeat pie filling can be made without the meat. You'll find lots of good recipes for all these foods in vegetarian cookbooks. See Appendix A for a list of some especially good ones.

Browsing vegetarian cookbooks for holiday inspiration

Many vegetarian cookbooks have an ethnic theme. They emphasize foods from one or more cultures in which meatless foods are a tradition. For example, they may contain lots of recipes for foods of Middle Eastern origin, or they may emphasize vegetarian pasta dishes. These can be great resources for planning special meals.

On the other hand, if you want vegetarian versions of traditional American recipes, you can find those, too. Scores of vegetarian cookbooks give recipes for hearty soups, chili, macaroni and cheese, potato salad, coleslaw, pumpkin pie — you name it — all made without animal products.

Go to the library and check out cookbooks that interest you. If you find a few that are especially good, go to a bookstore and buy them (you can also shop by catalog and online). Some vegetarian cookbooks even provide menus and suggestions for holiday meals and entertaining.

Taking cues from other vegetarians

It's a good idea to take opportunities to share meals for special occasions and holidays with other vegetarians. It can be helpful to see what others serve. Many local vegetarian societies hold covered dish get-togethers, restaurant gatherings, or catered events for holidays. Oftentimes these events are held a week or two before the actual holiday date because many people have family obligations then.

Many large cities have caterers that specialize in vegetarian cooking. Some restaurants also do catering. Depending upon your budget and time constraints, having a special meal catered can be very convenient. Most caterers will set up the meal at your house using their own equipment, or you can arrange to pick up the food at their place of business and serve it yourself. Some upscale supermarkets also provide this service.

Planning to Make the Most of Special Events

Never underestimate the value of planning when you're entertaining. If you have any anxiety at all about serving a vegetarian meal to your guests, taking some time to plan ahead will boost your confidence and increase the likelihood that your event will be a success.

Choosing a theme

Sit down when you're relaxed and have a few minutes to yourself, and think about what kind of meal you'd like to serve. If it's late summer and corn on the cob, tomatoes, and melons are in season, maybe you'd like to serve a simple, informal summer meal featuring fresh, locally grown produce. If it's wintertime, you might want to fix a hearty grain-and-vegetable casserole and serve it with a green salad and some good bread.

As you try to visualize the meal that you'd like to serve, keep the following in mind:

✔ The types of foods you think your guests would enjoy

✔ The degree of formality you prefer

✔ The setting

While you consider these questions, look for a theme or an overall mood you'd like to create with the meal, and let that serve as your starting point. Once you decide what kind of experience you want to create, you can go on to add appropriate decorations, music, and activities.

Keeping your guests in mind

If your guests are vegetarians themselves, they're probably familiar with many different types of vegetarian dishes and will like whatever you serve. If they're not, you might want to serve "crossover" foods that are enjoyed by vegetarians and nonvegetarians alike. These are foods that don't scream "meatless" to a nonvegetarian.

For a cookout, you could serve

✔ Veggie hotdogs and veggie burgers cooked on a grill

✔ Baked vegetarian beans with veggie franks

- ✔ Potato salad or coleslaw made with soy mayonnaise
- ✔ Corn on the cob
- ✔ Chips and salsa
- ✔ Watermelon
- ✔ Oatmeal cookies
- ✔ Lemonade or herbal iced tea sweetened with fruit juice

For a Super Bowl party, you could serve

- ✔ Vegetarian pizza
- ✔ Cut vegetables and a variety of chips with salsa and/or black bean dip
- ✔ Fruit salad
- ✔ Brownies
- ✔ Beverages

For a more formal meal, you might serve vegetable lasagna, spaghetti, pasta primavera, or stuffed shells or manicotti filled with cheese or a tofu mixture as a main course. You could serve bean chili with cornbread and a salad, or a hearty lentil or bean soup with a salad and a loaf of good bread.

Serve your guests ethnic foods

Many of the vegetarian foods that nonvegetarians like are ethnic. Most people like bean burritos, bean tacos, nachos, Chinese stir-fried vegetable dishes, Italian pasta dishes, and Greek spanikopita (that is, spinach pie). Look through ethnic vegetarian cookbooks for ideas. Planning a meal with an ethnic theme can be fun. If your guests have never tried these foods before, they may enjoy experimenting with something different. When your meal has an ethnic theme, it can also be simple to plan, because side dishes and accompaniments are easy to "match."

For example, you might serve a mixed-greens salad, black bean soup, hard rolls, and vegetable paella for a meal with a Spanish theme. You could serve green papaya salad, a vegetable curry over jasmine rice, and hot jasmine tea for a meal with a Thai theme. Check bookstores, catalogs, and online resources for good ethnic vegetarian cookbooks.

If you're serving a meal with an ethnic theme, consider ordering out for part of the meal. For example, you might order take-out Chinese soup and egg rolls for four, and then fix a vegetable stir-fry to go with it at home. Or you might fix a Middle Eastern meal featuring hummus and pita bread wedges, salad, and spinach pie, but order out for the baklava dessert. Ordering out for part of the meal can cut down substantially on the amount of time and work for you. Plus, some ethnic foods are hard to make at home and never seem as good unless they're made by the experts!

Think about other foods that happen to be vegetarian that your guests would find familiar and satisfying. You'll probably find that it's not hard to fix a vegetarian meal that is made up of foods that most people know and enjoy.

Spreading out the work

Even a fairly simple holiday meal or dinner party can be a time-consuming affair. If you can break down the task into its component parts, you'll see that much of the preparation can be staggered over several days leading up to your event. If you can get much of the work done ahead of time, you will be less stressed the day of your meal and will be in better shape to handle any minor glitches that may crop up.

A few days to a week before your meal, you can

- ✔ Wash and iron tablecloths and napkins

- ✔ Polish silver

- ✔ Set out any decorations that you're going to use

- ✔ Bake and freeze some desserts, such as cookies or cake layers

- ✔ Pick out music

- ✔ Draw up a grocery list and buy any supplies that aren't perishable

A day or so before the meal, you can

- ✔ Pick out and chill wine if it's being served

- ✔ Buy fresh fruits or vegetables and other perishable groceries

- ✔ Prepare any parts of the meal that can keep in the refrigerator for a day, such as marinated salads, salad dressings, and casseroles

- ✔ Buy fresh flowers — or pick them from your garden

On the day of the meal, start early in the day washing, chopping, and trimming vegetables; assembling salads and appetizers; and setting the table. Spread the work out over the course of the day, rather than wait until a few hours before. In the two or three hours before your guests arrive, you'll want to be putting finishing touches on the table, getting some last-minute meal items together, and watching any foods that may be in the oven or on the stove. You'll also want time to shower and change your clothes so that you'll feel refreshed before your guests arrive.

Presenting your vegetarian creation

Some people will tell you that they don't care about how foods look. They only care about how they taste. Don't believe them. Appearances do count.

Foods that are presented with a flair — with an eye to aesthetics, neatly arranged in appealing bowls and platters, with a garnish — look like they're going to taste good. It's important to pay attention to presentation. See Figure 17-2 for an example.

Figure 17-2:
Garnishes
add flair.

If you make your food look good, people will expect it to taste good, too. They'll go into the meal with a positive attitude. That's especially important when people are trying foods with which they may not be familiar. If you're serving a vegetarian meal to friends, it pays to "put your best food forward."

Any of the following embellishments can make your dishes look lovely:

- Garnishes such as slivers or twists of fresh fruits (oranges, lemons, limes, apples, strawberries); edible flowers; sprigs of fresh herbs; black olives; cherry tomato halves; a handful of sweet potato chips; or a pickle wedge

- A paper doily placed on a plate under the dessert

- A charger or liner (a large, often contrasting, plate upon which the smaller dinner plate is placed)

- A sprinkling of grated cheese, chopped parsley, or cilantro, or a dusting of cinnamon, powdered sugar, or cocoa

- Chocolate sauce, raspberry or vanilla sauce, or cheese sauce, drizzled over the food itself or in a zigzag pattern over the plate before the food is arranged on top

Put some thought into the dishes and bowls in which you serve your food, too. Colorful fruit and vegetable salads can be stunning served in a clear glass or crystal bowl. Hearty stews and casseroles look nice served in rustic pottery bowls.

In addition to making your food look good, give some attention to the setting of your meal. Remove distractions. Turn off the television. Put on some pleasant music, but not so loudly that people can't hear themselves talk.

Dim the lights if it's evening, and light some candles. Have some fresh flowers nearby or on the table. Your table should be neat and not too cluttered. Use place mats if you aren't using a tablecloth. An interesting quilt or Oriental rug can make a nice table cover for a change of pace.

Part V
Movin' on Out!

The 5th Wave   By Rich Tennant

@RICHTENNANT

"Gordon's always had trouble controlling his appetite at restaurants. I had to explain to him that you're not supposed to pull your chair up to the salad bar."

In this part . . .

It's one thing to be a vegetarian in your own home, where you can choose the foods you have on hand and what you fix for meals. It's quite another when you're a guest at someone else's home, when you're traveling, or when you're eating out. You lose a measure of control once you leave home, and most of the time you're surrounded by a society for which a vegetarian lifestyle is not the norm.

The chapters that follow provide some insights into being a vegetarian away from home — whether you're visiting relatives or friends, traveling, eating at the office or school cafeteria, or looking for meatless meals at restaurants.

Chapter 18

Vegetarian Etiquette: Minding Your Peas and Quinoa

. . . .

In This Chapter

▶ Being a gracious dinner guest

▶ Arranging for vegetarian foods at weddings, banquets, and other events

▶ Negotiating the dating scene

▶ Managing your vegetarian choices in professional situations

. . . .

*1*t's one thing to maintain a vegetarian lifestyle at home. It's another to do it away from home with style and grace.

Actually, no explanation of your eating preferences should be required, but remember that vegetarian diets are outside U.S. culture. That means that your eating style — particularly if you are vegan — is at odds with the ways of most everyone else you'll meet. True, that's changing. In general, people are becoming increasingly health conscious, and more people are aware of the environmental and ethical advantages of a vegetarian diet. But the vast majority of folks still eat meat, and you're the one who will have to do most of the adapting when you're out with them socially.

This chapter focuses on some common situations for which you'll need to develop skills in relating with nonvegetarians. You'll become more comfortable with these situations as you have more experience with them.

Accepting Dinner Invitations

Being invited to a nonvegetarian's home for dinner is one of the most common and most stressful events that many vegetarians encounter. How you approach the situation depends upon the degree of formality of the occasion and how well you know your host.

Notifying your host ahead of time

You're a vegetarian. Out with it. You need to find the right moment to tell your host that you're a vegetarian, but do say something. If the invitation comes by phone, the best time to say something is at the time that you get the invitation. Something as simple as, "Oh, thanks, I'd love to come. By the way, I'd better tell you that I'm a vegetarian. You don't have to do anything special for me — I'm sure I'll find plenty to eat — but I just didn't want you to go to the trouble of fixing meat or fish for me."

The chances are good that your host will ask if you eat spaghetti or lasagna or some other dish that he is familiar with serving and thinks will suit your preferences. If your host suggests a shrimp stir-fry, you can also nip that one in the bud by letting him know that you don't eat seafood (if you don't). In that case, it would also be a good time to toss out a few more suggestions of foods you do eat, or you could reassure your host that you'll be fine with extra servings of whatever vegetables, rice, potatoes, salad, and other side dishes he plans to serve.

If you get an invitation to dinner by mail, through a spouse or partner, or in some other indirect way, you have two choices.

✔ You can show up for dinner and eat what you can.

✔ You can call your host, thank him for the invitation, and mention that you're a vegetarian.

If you've been invited as the guest of the invitee (your spouse, partner, date, etc.), you might want that person to call the host on your behalf. Examine the situation and do what feels most appropriate and comfortable.

It may feel a bit awkward to initiate a conversation about your vegetarianism. But telling your host that you're a vegetarian up front may be less uncomfortable than showing up for dinner and finding that there's nothing you can eat, or finding that something special has been made for you that you have to decline. In either of these situations, not only do you run the risk of not getting enough to eat, but your host is bound to notice if you are overly selective about what foods you take and may not understand the reason unless you explain that you're a vegetarian.

It may make some people a little nervous when you say that you're a vegetarian. Most people who invite guests to dinner want them to enjoy the food and have a good time, and they may not be very familiar with what a vegetarian will and won't eat. It's important to reassure your host that you'll be fine so that he won't worry too much. On the other hand, most people appreciate knowing ahead of time that you won't be eating the meat or fish. It saves them from preparing something that won't be eaten and is therefore possibly wasted. It also saves everyone the embarrassment of scurrying to find something for you to eat. And it also saves you from being stuck in a situation where the rice is cooked with chicken stock, the salad is sprinkled with bacon, the appetizer is shrimp cocktail, and steak is the main course. It can be a bit conspicuous if all you have on your plate is a dinner roll.

Tell your host that you're a vegetarian.

If you think that you may have trouble finding something you can eat at your host's home, have a snack before you leave home. That way, you won't be starving if you find that there isn't much to eat.

Offering to bring a dish

Another way to handle dinner invitations is to offer to bring a dish that you and everyone else can share. This works best in casual situations when you know your host well or the setting is going to be relatively informal. You might not feel as comfortable suggesting this, for instance, if you are being invited to a formal company function at the home of someone with whom you don't interact regularly. In that case, bringing your own food could look tacky.

Offer, but don't push. If you tell your host that you're a vegetarian and she sounds worried or unsure about how to handle it, you might say something like this:

> "If you'd like, I'd be happy to make my famous vegetable paella and saffron rice for everyone to try. It would go well with many other entrées that you might make for the others, and a salad and bread would go well with it."

If your host bites, great. If she brushes the suggestion aside, just consider your job done and leave it at that. Reassure her that you think that you'll be fine eating the salad and side dishes that don't contain meat or seafood and that you're looking forward to coming.

Someday, it may happen that you've told your host that you're a vegetarian, and he's tried to fix a special vegetarian meal for you, but has "missed." For example, he may have prepared a gelatin mold salad, used eggs in the baked goods, put bacon on the salad, or served the salad with Caesar dressing. What should you do? Be the best actor that you can be and just eat whatever you can of the other parts of the meal. Make your plate look as full as you can so that your host doesn't feel as though you don't have enough to eat. Assure your host that you're fine. You won't starve. Enjoy the company, and then eat when you get home.

Keeping quiet about your vegetarianism

If you decide for whatever reason not to tell your host in advance that you're vegetarian, then downplay the fact during the meal or stay undercover. Pointing out that you can't eat the food will make everyone uncomfortable and may put a damper on the gathering. Your host may feel badly and may even ask why you didn't say something sooner. Eat what you can. If you have to ask about ingredients in the food or you have to say that you can't eat something because it's not vegetarian, be sure to play down any inconvenience, and reassure your host that you'll be just fine with what there is.

If you're a dinner guest at a nonvegetarian's home, it's a major faux pas to carry on about the evils of meat. Even if another guest eggs you on and attempts to engage you in an earnest discussion or debate about the merits of vegetarianism, resist the temptation to participate. To do otherwise is just plain uncouth.

Accepting Invitations to Weddings and Other Special Functions

It's fairly easy to manage invitations to weddings, banquets, and other functions at which there will be lots of people and where the food is served from a buffet line. Even if a sit-down meal is served, a hotel or restaurant usually caters the food. You may find it much easier to speak to hotel or restaurant staff about getting a vegetarian meal than to ask the host directly.

Attending an event at a private home

If the function happens to be held at a private residence, you can follow the advice given earlier in this chapter for dinner invitations. Because the occasion is likely to involve a large number of guests, it's likely that lots of food will be served, and even more likely that your host won't have to do anything special for you. You'll probably find plenty of foods that you can eat.

Meeting your vegetarian needs at hotel and club functions

If the event is planned at a hotel, country club, community center, or restaurant, call ahead and ask to speak with the person in charge of food service. You don't have to say anything to your host. It's perfectly fine to speak to the chef or caterer and request a vegetarian or vegan entrée as a substitute for whatever the other guests will be served. It would be very unusual if there would be an extra charge to the host for an alternate dish, but if you are worried, you can ask to be sure.

Be clear about what you can and can't eat. For example, if you eat no meat, fish, or poultry, be sure to say so. Otherwise, you may end up with fish or chicken because *vegetarian* may only mean "no red meat" to some people. You might ask about how other items will be prepared. For instance, if Caesar salad is being served, see if a salad with a different type of dressing can be set aside for you (and remind the kitchen that you don't eat bacon on your salad).

When talking with a member of the food service staff, be sure to mention whether you eat dairy products or eggs. If you aren't explicit, and you're vegan, you may end up with egg pasta, an omelet or a quiche, grated cheese on your salad, or cheese lasagna.

If you call the restaurant or hotel kitchen to request a vegetarian meal for an event, feel free to suggest a dish that you know you can eat and that the kitchen is likely to be able to make. For example, most kitchens have the ingredients on hand to make pasta primavera or a large baked potato topped with steamed vegetables. They're simple to fix, too. They can also be preferable to that ubiquitous steamed vegetable plate.

When the meal is served and the waiter arrives at your table, quietly mention that you have ordered a vegetarian meal. If the waiter whisks a regular plate of food under your nose before you can say a word, let the food sit there until you can flag the waiter down again to request your meal.

Navigating buffet lines

If the meal is served as a buffet, you may not even need to mention to your host that you're a vegetarian unless you think there's a chance that the menu will be limited. If the meal is served at a restaurant or hotel, it's very likely that the menu will include a wide variety of dishes and plenty of foods that you can eat.

If you are vegan, however, it may still be wise to phone ahead and ask about the menu, just to be certain that there will be some dairy- and egg-free choices for you. You may find that you'll need to ask for some rice, pasta, or vegetables to be set aside for you if everything on the buffet line is going to be doused with butter or cream sauce. The chef might even be able to make a suitable dish for you and serve it to you at your seat.

Mixing Vegetarianism and Dating

If your date is also a vegetarian, you're off to a good start. All you'll have to worry about (food-wise anyway) is whether you're in the mood for Mexican or Thai or Ethiopian food. Even if you're a lacto ovo vegetarian and he's a vegan, at least you're simpatico. You'll work it out.

On the other hand, if your date is not a vegetarian, it's best to broach the subject early on. You don't have to make a big deal out of the fact that you don't eat meat, but it's probably best to mention that fact sooner rather than later, and probably before you get together for a meal. And before your relationship gets really serious, ask yourself the following:

- ✔ Would you expect that person to stop eating meat eventually?
- ✔ What would the ground rules be if you decided to live together or get married?
- ✔ Would you have meat in the house?
- ✔ Would you cook two different meals, or each fend for yourselves?
- ✔ What would you do if you had nonvegetarian guests over for dinner — serve them meat or not?
- ✔ How would you resolve the conflict if you and your partner had different views about what to do?
- ✔ Can you live and let live, or would you need your partner to see things as you do and maintain a vegetarian lifestyle with you?

This last question is especially important if your vegetarianism is rooted in ethical beliefs or attitudes. It's difficult to compromise when your personal philosophy is at issue. You'll have to decide whether there's room in your life for someone who marches to a different drummer than you do. Some vegetarians find it harder to connect with a partner who doesn't share the same sensitivities. If it doesn't matter now, it may later. You don't have to arrive at any hard-and-fast conclusions about these issues today, but if you've never faced them before, it's a good idea to begin thinking about them.

If you do decide to get serious with a nonvegetarian, be sure to think about the following:

- ✔ Will your mixed relationship survive?
- ✔ Could you live with a nonvegetarian? Be married to one?
- ✔ What about children — would you raise them vegetarian or not?

These are weighty questions for many vegetarians. It's a good idea to think about them and begin to formulate some answers, even though your ideas might change after you've met someone and are in a relationship.

Only, but not lonely

Vegetarian singles groups are active in some cities. Check with your local vegetarian society to see if such a group exists in your area. You might also check some of the resources listed in Part VII of this book. These groups plan restaurant outings, outdoor activities, and other events with the needs and interests of singles in mind.

But some vegetarians won't even date a nonvegetarian. (Kiss someone with greasy cheeseburger lips? No way!) Would you? If you restrict yourself to dating only fellow vegetarians, you may find yourself spending many a Saturday night alone in front of the television. After all, vegetarians make up only 1 percent of the population, and only a fraction of that number is in the market for dating.

Managing Your Vegetarianism on the Job

In many professions, your success at the office is partly dependent upon how well you blend into the culture of the organization. If your job involves entertaining clients or meeting with colleagues over lunches and dinners, your eating habits will be on display for all to observe. If you're a vegetarian, the manner in which you conduct yourself can lead others to mark you as either sensible and health conscious or eccentric and difficult to please. Your vegetarianism may be an asset or a liability, depending upon how you play it. So behave!

This may matter more in some work settings than in others. An advertising agency or a marketing department within a company, for instance, is likely to be comfortable with creative people who do things differently and may be better able to tolerate an "eccentricity." It may be more important for you to appear compatible with your peers if you're in a more conservative line of work such as law or banking.

Why should you care about what your coworkers think about your eating habits? You should care because the perception that you are a social standout may negatively affect your chances of getting a promotion or a choice job opportunity. If you play your cards right, however, you can turn the difference in your lifestyle into an asset that will reflect positively on you and enhance the company's impression of you.

To increase your likelihood of success, don't preach about the benefits of being a vegetarian. With your actions, you can communicate an understated message to your coworkers that they'll get loud and clear. Show them that you care about your health and have the self-discipline and determination to persevere with healthy lifestyle habits such as diet and exercise.

Interviewing over lunch or dinner

Job interviews often involve lunching with your prospective employer and colleagues. If that happens, there's no need to hide the fact that you're a vegetarian. At the same time, it's best not to make a big deal of it. Just approach the subject in a confident, matter-of-fact way. Remember the following:

- ✔ **First impressions count.** In job interviews, you want your prospective employer and colleagues to focus on your skills and ideas, rather than on the fact that you don't eat meat. When they reflect back on their meeting with you, you want them to think about how well you'll fit into their environment and about how your unique set of abilities will be an asset to their organization.

- ✔ **Do your best to downplay any inconveniences due to your diet.** When you're on a job interview, it's common for the people interviewing you to choose the restaurant where you'll eat, so you may not have an opportunity to steer them to a restaurant with lots of vegetarian choices. If that happens, size up your menu options as quickly as possible. It's fine to ask the waiter whether the soup is made with chicken stock or a beef base or if the beans contain lard. But if you do, make it as low-key as you can. If the answer is affirmative, have an alternative choice in mind so that you don't hold up the table's order while you struggle to find another choice.

- ✔ **Have an off-menu choice in mind, in case you have trouble finding something on the menu.** In a restaurant that serves pasta, for example, it's usually easy for the kitchen to whip up pasta tossed with olive oil, garlic, and vegetables or served with a marinara sauce. If you find yourself at a steak house, go for a baked potato, salad, and vegetable side dishes. It'll be easy to eat while you're fielding questions.

You may find yourself at a job interview being served a catered luncheon in a conference room. If they serve you a preplated ham sandwich, eat what you can from your plate and leave the rest. No explanation is necessary unless someone asks why you've left the food. In that case, all you have to say is, "I don't eat ham." You might also reassure your host that you'll be fine, that you aren't particularly hungry, or whatever sounds appropriate to you. The key is not to make a big deal out of the fact that they served you meat and you aren't eating it.

Making your vegetarianism a professional asset

The best way to handle your dietary difference is to present yourself with confidence and to present your diet in a matter-of-fact way. Let your cowork-ers view you as being sensible and health conscious, virtues that would reflect upon you positively in most business settings. Even if your coworkers have a vague sense that you may be motivated by ethical or political ideals, remain above it all and keep your views in these regards to yourself. After all, if one of your coworkers has beliefs that don't suit you, you don't want to hear about them every day.

Whatever you do, don't allow yourself to be sucked into silly conversations or debates about the political or ethical issues relating to vegetarianism. Certainly these subjects have merit, but you'll be a loser if you bring them up in a business setting. You may find that some of your officemates won't be able to resist prodding you a bit, especially if they think that they can elicit an emotional reaction out of you or instigate an argument. Don't fall for it. Don't engage them. If you do, you'll be branded a standout, a radical, or worse. You'll be the loser; they won't. All your opinions may be valid, but the work setting is not the best place to air them unless you're prepared to accept the consequences. Unfortunately, it's just a fact of life. You might as well be realistic about it.

Chapter 19

Dining in Restaurants and Other Venues

In the land of 16-ounce steaks, chicken halves, and pint-sized servings of vegetables, it's becoming quite easy to find vegetarian entrées on restaurant menus. It's even becoming somewhat easier to find vegetarian options in the workplace, in schools, and, of course, on college campuses. Natural foods stores with deli or restaurant components are becoming increasingly common in many communities. This is good news for vegetarians because it is making it easier and easier to dine out and still exercise your vegetarian choice.

Still, you'll need to have a few tricks up your sleeve to find a satisfying vegetarian meal away from home. This chapter covers some of the strategies and know-how that seasoned vegetarians rely on when they go out to eat in non-vegetarian territory.

Dining in Vegetarian Eateries of All Sorts

Many natural foods stores have a café tucked away in a corner of the store in which you can get a quick bite to eat. Some carry cold salads and ready-made sandwiches, and others have a more extensive menu including a "soup and salad" bar, hot foods, and baked goods. Natural foods store cafés are popular places for many people to pick up a take-out meal for lunch during the work-week or for dinner on the way home from work.

Vegetarian restaurants, on the other hand, can run the gamut from raw foods or macrobiotic eateries and homey little vegetarian hideaways to large metropolitan restaurants that stay packed during business hours. Many serve foods with an ethnic bent such as Indian or Middle Eastern, and some blend various ethnic cuisines.

Vegetarian restaurants often have an "alternative" feel to them — an earthy atmosphere that is usually quite casual. They tend to serve foods made with natural ingredients. For instance, you're likely to find brown rice served instead of white rice, and whole-grain breads rather than plain dinner rolls. Even desserts such as cookies and piecrusts tend to be made from whole grains. Some menu items may be flagged as vegan. You'll find raw sugar on the table, and the menu will offer natural soft drinks, herbal teas, dishes made with tempeh and tofu, and foods made with minimally processed ingredients. You may find soymilk on the menu, too. All these features — as well as a rustic, homey atmosphere — give many vegetarian restaurants a distinctive personality that sets them apart from other restaurants.

Surviving Nonvegetarian Restaurants and Cafeterias

If you live in a major metropolitan area, you can eat at a vegetarian restaurant every time you go out to eat. If you live anywhere else, you'll need to rely on the meatless options served at regular restaurants, or you can go ethnic. Frequent meals at a cafeteria — school or company — can also prove challenging for vegetarians. This section suggests ways to find the vegetarian foods you need at nonvegetarian places.

Making selections from a meat-centered menu

The good news for vegetarians is that the restaurant industry has gotten the word that a sizable percentage of the population wants meatless foods when they eat out. Not all of these folks are vegetarians per se, but they see vegetarian menu choices as being healthful and tasty.

Even some of the most traditional restaurants have responded by adding at least one or two vegetarian options to their menus. Many have added veggie burgers to their menus because burgers are so familiar and popular. It's also not uncommon to see a vegan option now and then, although it may not be labeled as such. An example is pasta primavera tossed with olive oil and garlic and made with egg-free noodles. For more ideas on how to get a vegetarian meal at a decidedly nonvegetarian restaurant, see the section "Making the Most of Restaurants: Tips and Tricks" later in this chapter.

Exploring ethnic restaurants

Many countries, such as India and China, have vegetarian traditions. Not everyone in these countries is vegetarian, but many are, and everyone — vegetarian or not — is familiar with the concept of vegetarianism and vegetarian foods.

Other countries, such as those of the Mediterranean, the Middle East, and parts of Latin America, have some traditional foods that happen to be vegetarian, despite the fact that the diets in these cultures rely heavily on meats and other animal products. For example, in the Middle East, lamb is eaten in large amounts, and falafel, spanikopita, and hummus are also traditional favorites that happen to be vegetarian.

What you order when you eat at an ethnic restaurant will depend upon what type of vegetarian diet you follow and how that restaurant prepares specific foods. In one Italian restaurant, for example, the eggplant Parmesan sandwich may contain cheese, and in another it may not. If you are vegan, you probably won't eat the spanakopita at a Greek restaurant because it's usually made with cheese. On the other hand, you might be perfectly happy with a Greek salad (minus the feta cheese), some pita bread, and an order of boiled potatoes with Greek seasonings.

Wherever you eat, you'll need to ask the wait staff for specifics about how the food is prepared, especially if you're vegan. One restaurant's baked ziti in marinara sauce may be vegan, while another's may come to the table smothered in melted mozzarella unless you request otherwise. Also, some restaurants prepare marinara sauce using beef broth, so be sure to ask about it. The following are some common vegetarian foods (not all of them vegan) served in a variety of ethnic restaurants:

At Italian restaurants, try

- Fresh vegetable appetizers (sometimes called antipasto) with or without mozzarella cheese
- Mixed-greens salad
- Minestrone soup, lentil soup, or pasta e fagioli (pasta with beans)
- Focaccia
- Italian bread with olive oil or flavored oil for dipping
- Vegetable-topped pizzas (with or without cheese)
- Pasta primavera
- Spaghetti with marinara sauce
- Pasta with olive oil and garlic
- Other pasta dishes tossed with vegetable combinations

- Italian green beans with potatoes
- Cappuccino or espresso
- Italian ices
- Fresh fruit desserts

At Mexican restaurants, try

- Gazpacho
- Bean nachos
- Mixed-greens salad
- Tortilla chips with salsa and guacamole
- Bean soft tacos
- Bean tostadas
- Bean burritos
- Spinach burritos or enchiladas
- Cheese enchiladas
- Bean chalupas (fried tortillas layered with beans, lettuce, tomato, guacamole, and beans)
- Chiles rellenos (cheese-stuffed green pepper, usually batter-dipped and fried, topped with tomato sauce)
- Flan (custard dessert made with milk and eggs)

At Chinese restaurants, try

- Vegetable soup or hot and sour soup
- Vegetarian spring rolls or egg rolls
- Sweet-and-sour cabbage (cold salad)
- Vegetable dumplings (fried or steamed)
- Minced vegetables in lettuce wrap
- Sesame noodles (cold noodle appetizer)
- Sautéed greens
- Steamed rice
- Chinese mixed vegetables
- Broccoli with garlic sauce
- Vegetable lo mein
- Vegetable fried rice

- Szechwan-style green beans or eggplant
- Family-style tofu
- Other tofu and seitan (or gluten) dishes
- Fortune cookies (but note that they usually contain eggs)

At Indian restaurants, try

- Dal (lentil soup)
- Cucumber and yogurt salad
- Chutney
- Steamed rice
- Chapati, pappadam, naan, and roti (Indian breads)
- Samosas and pakoras (vegetable-filled appetizers)
- Muttar paneer (tomato-based dish made with cubes of cheese and peas)
- Vegetable curry
- Palak paneer (spinach-based dish with soy cheese)
- Lentil, chickpea, and vegetable entrées
- Fresh fruit
- Rice pudding

At Ethiopian restaurants, try

- Mixed-greens salad
- Injera (large, round, flat, spongy bread — tear off small pieces with which to pinch bites of food from a communal tray)
- Bean, lentil, and vegetable-based dishes served directly on a sheet of injera on a tray or platter

At Middle Eastern restaurants, try

- Hummus
- Spinach salad
- Dolma (stuffed grape leaves)
- Baba ganoujh (a blended eggplant appetizer)
- Fattouche (minced fresh green salad)
- Tabouli salad (wheat salad)
- Spanikopita (spinach pie)

- ✔ Lentil soup

- ✔ Falafel plate or sandwich (chick pea patties)

- ✔ Vegetarian stuffed cabbage rolls (filled with rice, chick peas, and raisins)

- ✔ Halvah (sesame dessert)

- ✔ Muhallabia (ground rice pudding; contains milk but no egg)

- ✔ Ramadan (cooked, dried fruit with nuts, often served with cream and nutmeg)

- ✔ Middle Eastern lemonade

Lunching at school

Finding satisfactory vegetarian options in elementary, middle, and high school cafeterias can be difficult, though the situation is slowly improving. For now, the reality is that many vegetarian kids have to bring food from home if they want a good meal at school. If your child has to take a bag lunch to school, vary the contents. Figure 19-1 shows some popular school lunch box items. Some good choices include

- ✔ Small, aseptic cartons of fruit juice or vanilla- or carob-flavored soymilk

- ✔ Small boxes of raisins

- ✔ Single-serving containers of pudding or canned fruit

- ✔ Fresh fruit

- ✔ Peanut butter or almond butter sandwiches

- ✔ Hummus in a pita pocket

- ✔ Peeled baby carrots with salsa or hummus for dipping

- ✔ Muffins

- ✔ Whole-grain cookies, bagels, graham crackers, and granola bars (try natural product brands)

If a weekly menu is available, sit down with your child and discuss ahead of time which days she will eat at school and which days she will bring a bag lunch from home. On some days, it may work for an item or two from the school cafeteria to be supplemented with a piece of fruit from home. Also consider meeting with school food service staff to discuss your child's dietary needs and learn about any options that might exist for the school to better meet your child's needs.

Figure 19-1:
Popular
vegetarian
choices for
school
lunch boxes.

If your child is old enough to operate a microwave oven and has access to one at school, soup cups and hot cereal cups are also convenient and come in many varieties. If your child has access to a refrigerator, you can also pack a tofu-salad sandwich, pasta salad, yogurt, and other perishable items. See Chapter 23 for more on feeding vegetarian children and teens.

If your child is college age, you have less to worry about. Most college and university campuses offer vegetarian choices on their menus these days, and many offer them at every meal. Requests for vegetarian foods are common, and colleges and universities do not have to adhere to the kinds of regulations that local public schools have to follow when planning menus. So, vegetarian college students generally have a much easier time finding something to eat at school than their younger counterparts.

Eating in the company cafeteria

Isn't it nice to be an adult? Nobody is standing over you making sure that you take two servings from the meat group anymore. You don't have to take the milk, either. But, dining in the company cafeteria can still be a challenge sometimes.

Company cafeterias vary considerably in what they offer employees. Some employ their own cooks or chefs, who prepare foods on site, and others contract with a food service company to provide the meals. The food can range from burgers and fries to more sophisticated sandwiches and salads. Some companies offer more, some less.

The nice thing is, you probably don't care anymore if someone looks at you cross-eyed because you've brought a bag lunch to work. You can use some of the same strategies in dealing with your meals at work as you do with your kids' meals at school. Here are a few ideas:

✔ If a weekly menu is available, plan ahead of time which days you'll eat the company's food and which days you'll bring your own from home. On some days, you might take an item or two from the company cafeteria and supplement it with a piece of fruit from home.

✔ If you are having difficulties dealing with meals at work, arrange a meeting with the person in charge of food service. See if there is any room for them to provide choices that meet your needs.

You may not be the only one at your work site who would like more meatless choices. Even the nonvegetarians may want meatless options from time to time. See if you can recruit some others to lend support to your request.

Making the Most of Restaurants: Tips and Tricks

There are going to be times when there's virtually nothing on the menu for a vegetarian. Some fast food restaurants and truck stops are good examples — the baked beans contain pork, the biscuits are made with lard, the vegetables are cooked with bacon, and the staff just chuckles and looks incredulous when you ask if there's anything vegetarian on the menu. You're stuck.

In most cases, though, there are plenty of choices. You just have to get creative. With a little practice, the ability to get a vegetarian meal at a nonvegetarian restaurant can be a relatively simple matter.

When a restaurant isn't vegetarian friendly, scan the menu to get an idea of the ingredients they have on hand. In many cases, you can ask for a special order using ingredients used to make other menu items. For example, if the restaurant serves spaghetti with meat sauce, you know they have pasta. The tomato sauce may already be mixed with meat, but they may have vegetables on hand for side dishes. Ask for pasta primavera made with olive oil and garlic and whatever vegetables they can add. If all else fails, you can usually ask for a baked potato and a salad, or a salad and a tomato sandwich on whole wheat toast. Be creative.

Vegetarian choices on the run

Fast food restaurants usually have a limited number of vegetarian options, but some have several. Some choices include pancakes with syrup, muffins, mixed-greens salad, bean burrito (you can order it without the cheese), bean soft taco or regular taco, bean tostada, beans-and-cheese side dish, veggie burger (or ask for the cheeseburger, hold the meat, or a tomato sandwich on a bun), baked potato with toppings from the salad bar, veggie wrap sandwich, or a big salad from the salad bar.

If you find yourself at a restaurant with limited vegetarian options, try some of these tried-and-true ideas for hunger prevention and possibly even a very good meal:

- At finer restaurants, peruse the menu for interesting side dishes that may be served with meat entrees. You may be able to combine some of them into a vegetarian plate that will be the envy of everyone else at your table.

- If the restaurant serves baked potatoes, ask for one as your entrée. You can top it with items from a salad bar if the restaurant has one. Try adding broccoli florets, salsa, black olives, sunflower seeds, or whatever looks good to you.

- Combine several appetizers and/or side dishes to create a vegetarian plate. For example, you might order a mixed-greens salad, a bowl of gazpacho, an order of stuffed mushrooms, and an appetizer portion of grilled spinach quesadilla.

- Take a good look at meat-containing entrees and determine whether they can be prepared as vegetarian dishes instead. For instance, a pasta dish mixed with vegetables and shrimp could easily be made without the shrimp. A club sandwich could be fixed with grilled portabello mushroom, avocado, cheese, or tomato slices instead of the meat. This is most likely to work at restaurants where the food is made to order and not premade.

If you want to find a good meal and avoid disappointments when you go out to eat as a vegetarian, you need to be aware of some of the realities of the restaurant industry. The good-sense suggestions that follow will make it easier for you to get what you need:

- Finer and family-run restaurants are often in a good position to accommodate special requests. They tend to prepare their menu items to order. Family restaurant chains are less likely to be able to help you out because many of their menu items are preprepared. They might not be able, for instance, to cook the rice without chicken stock — it may have been made in a large batch the day before — or to fix the pasta without meat in the sauce.

✔ When you speak with restaurant staff about your order, be clear about what you would like. For instance, instead of just saying, "I'm a vegetarian," explain specifically what you do and do not eat. Let the wait staff know if dairy and eggs are okay, or if you don't want your foods flavored with chicken broth or beef broth.

✔ If you have plans to go to a restaurant that is unfamiliar to you, try to get a copy of the menu ahead of time. If you have a fax machine at home, ask them to fax you a menu. Look it over and call the restaurant to discuss options if needed. You can also ask to speak with the chef and ask for recommendations.

✔ Given enough notice, finer restaurants are usually happy to prepare a special meal for you. Give them a day or two's notice, if possible.

✔ Be reasonable about special requests, especially if you can see that the restaurant is very busy. If it's a Friday or Saturday night and the place is packed, make your requests as simple as possible.

✔ Ask questions about how the food is prepared *before* you order. If you prefer to avoid cream, butter, grated cheese, anchovies, and other animal products, check to be sure that these ingredients aren't added to the food, rather than sending the food back once it comes to the table with the offending ingredient.

✔ Ask your server whether your special request will increase or decrease the cost of the meal.

✔ Be aware of cooking terms that can be clues that a menu item contains an animal product. For example, *au gratin* usually means that the food contains cheese, *scalloped* means that the food contains cream, *sautéed* can mean that the food is cooked with oil or butter, and *creamy* usually means that the item is made with cream or eggs.

Avoiding Hidden Animal Ingredients

Unless you know you're at a restaurant where everything served is vegetarian or vegan, you'll need to be on the lookout for hidden animal ingredients in foods that you order. Some foods are more suspect than others. For instance, the beans in Mexican restaurants are notorious for containing lard. If you think the beans taste a little unusual, you may well be tasting an animal ingredient. Likewise, those flaky biscuits and piecrusts that you've been eating at your favorite diner may be made with lard. Ask your server to check with the cook or read the ingredients label if the food comes from a package or can.

Table 19-1 lists some common foods that may contain animal ingredients. There are many others besides these. Remember to be assertive and ask questions *before* you order so that you're not disappointed when the food comes to the table and you have to send it back.

Table 19-1	Hidden Animal Ingredients in Restaurant Food
Food	*Likely Culprits*
Refried beans	Lard
Flour tortillas	Lard
Biscuits, pie crust	Lard
Bean soup	Bacon
Split pea soup	Ham
Caesar salad	Anchovies in the dressing
Stir-fry	Oyster sauce
Greek salad	Anchovies on top
Steamed rice	Chicken stock
Sautéed vegetables	Chicken stock (fatback or salt pork is often used in the South)
Green beans	Bacon
Cooked greens	Fatback or salt pork in the South
Potato salad	Bacon if German-style potato salad; eggs
Spinach salad	Bacon; eggs
Baked beans	Pork

Also note that most baked goods are made with eggs and/or dairy products, that many vegetables and other menu items may be seasoned with butter, and that cream, cheese, or eggs may be added to creamy-style foods and foods served with a sauce.

Chapter 20

Staying on Course When You Travel

● ●

In This Chapter

▶ Facing special travel-related challenges

▶ Preparing for a car trip

▶ Maintaining your vegetarian diet in the middle of the ocean

▶ Arriving meat-free (and not hungry) when you travel by plane

● ●

*T*raveling puts many people into "survival mode" where meals are concerned. When you travel, you're off your home turf. You've got less control over meals, you may be in unfamiliar surroundings, and you have to contend with the challenges that a change in your normal routine can bring. That can put you at risk of eating poorly, either because you can't find what you need or because you get distracted by foods that you ordinarily wouldn't eat.

Traveling makes you vulnerable to impulsive food choices. You're also susceptible to the "I'm on vacation so I'm entitled to eat whatever I want to" mentality, which can be especially problematic for frequent travelers.

For vegetarians, avoiding meat and possibly other animal products requires a set of skills that can be acquired with time and experience. In this chapter, I'll help you get started by explaining some of the ways you can improve your chances of getting what you need when you're on the road, on the sea, or in the air.

Hitting the Road

If you want something to eat when you're traveling by car, you're usually limited to whatever is near the exit off the highway you're on. Your choices are likely to be a family chain restaurant or a truck stop.

A better choice than relying on roadside restaurants — especially if you travel by car a lot — is to pack a cooler or bag of food to take along with you in the car. Take your own food, and you're likely to

✔ **Save time:** You won't have to stop to eat a meal, unless you want to take the time for a picnic along the way. If you eat in the car while you're en route, you'll only have to stop for stretch breaks, to fill up with gas, and to use the restroom. (If you're the driver, be careful that whatever you are eating doesn't cause enough of a distraction from driving to endanger you or others on the road.)

✔ **Save money:** Food that you take from home is likely to cost less than food that you eat at a restaurant.

✔ **Eat more healthfully:** Let's face it: Planning ahead helps to ensure that you eat well. You'll also be less likely to eat junk out of desperation if you have trouble finding vegetarian options on the road.

The following list gives you some ideas of handy vegetarian foods that you can pack in a cooler or bag to take along with you in the car. You can add to this list yourself by giving some thought to foods that you have in your cupboard and refrigerator that might travel well:

✔ Individual aseptic packages of soymilk (buy carob-flavored for a change of pace)

✔ Small cans or aseptic packages of fruit juice

✔ Bottles of mineral water or flavored seltzer water

✔ Bagels

✔ Peanut butter or almond butter sandwiches on good bread

✔ Fresh fruit

✔ Peeled baby carrots

✔ Instant soup cups that you can mix with hot water from the coffee maker at a gas station/food mart

✔ Instant hot cereal cups that you can mix with hot water from the coffee maker at a gas station/food mart

✔ Snack-sized cans of fruit or applesauce

✔ Homemade, whole-grain quick breads, muffins, and cookies

✔ Graham crackers

✔ Individual boxes of dry breakfast cereal with soymilk or rice milk

✔ Deli salads

✔ Hummus sandwiches

✔ Tofu salad sandwiches

If you like to take trips by bicycle, or if you hike, you'll need to pack foods that are light and portable and don't require refrigeration. Dried fruit and nut mixtures, small containers of soymilk or fruit juice, crackers and peanut butter, and fresh fruit are good choices. You can munch during the day while you're active, and then pile on the calories that you need when you stop for the night and have time to prepare a meal or have dinner at a good restaurant.

Many people fall into the trap of thinking that a bag lunch has to have a "main course," which usually means a sandwich. Not so. Your meal can be much more interesting — and you won't run out of ideas as quickly — if you mix and match odds and ends instead, such as muffins, bagels, fresh fruit, leftovers, instant soup cups, and so on.

Cruisin' Without Losin'

If it's been a while since you've been on a cruise, stand informed: Today's cruise ships are spas on the waters, with a wide selection of all types of food, including healthful options. As such, food is not a problem for most people, unless you buckle under the temptations of five-course meals and rich desserts. After all, even fat-free calories count, and on cruise ships, the kitchen never seems to close.

Any vegetarians on board are usually in luck. It's fairly common now for cruise ships to see vegetarian passengers, and most can accommodate them.

Some cruise lines have separate menus for "health conscious" people, or they flag specific entrées and menu items as being "healthy." In many cases, that means meatless. If meat is included in the dish, it's often something that can be left out of meals that are cooked to order. For example, a pasta dish mixed with vegetables and seafood can easily be made without the seafood.

If you do find that the menu choices on a particular day don't include enough options for you, handle the situation the way you would at a fine restaurant. Explain your needs to your server or the chef and ask for a special order. If possible, let the kitchen know what you want the day before, especially if the ship is going to be serving a large number of people in that sitting (for the captain's dinner, for instance).

If you have concerns about whether a cruise line will able to accommodate your food preferences, have your travel agent request information about meals and get sample menus to examine. You can also call the cruise line's customer services office yourself and ask for more details.

In lieu of or in addition to sit-down meals, cruise ships are known for their elaborate buffets. The sheer volume and variety of foods served makes it easy for most vegetarians to find enough to eat. You'll have to sidestep the gelatin salads, and vegans may have to bypass items made with cream or mayonnaise. But think of it this way: The foods with those ingredients are the ones that give other people traveler's remorse after the vacation when they get on the scale and see the pounds they've gained. You can sit smug and satisfied with your fresh tropical fruit salads, rice and pasta and vegetables, and good breads, and have just as much fun.

Taking Flight

Airlines are cutting back on meal service, especially on shorter flights. So don't be too surprised if the next time you fly, you try to request a vegetarian meal and discover that you won't be served anything more than peanuts and a beverage.

On many short flights, a beverage and a handful of peanuts or pretzels is all that may be served, whereas a few years ago passengers would have been served a snack. Flights on which passengers may once have been served complete meals are now being serviced with a light snack instead. Some airlines give passengers an opportunity to make special requests for their snacks as well as their meals, whereas some only permit special requests for full meals.

Meal service in business class and first class cabins is customarily more complete than in coach class. On flights in which coach class passengers are served a snack, first class passengers are often served a light meal. The airline representative (or travel Web site) will probably inform you of meals scheduled to be served when you reserve your flights, but you can always ask to be sure. You can also put in a standing order for vegetarian meals with your travel agent or corporate travel office if they handle your reservations.

Ordering a vegetarian in-flight meal

It's easy enough to order a vegetarian meal when you fly. Just call the airline's reservation desk or go to its Web site at least 24 hours before your flight to make your request, or make the request at the time that you make your flight reservations. In either case

- ✔ Ask the agent if meals or snacks will be served on any of the flights.

- ✔ Explain that you'd like to request vegetarian meals.

- ✔ Indicate what type of vegetarian meal you'd prefer. Be sure to say something if you prefer no eggs and/or dairy.

On domestic flights, most airlines offer several options for vegetarians. They typically include

- Lacto ovo vegetarian meal
- Vegetarian meal, with no eggs or dairy (some airlines also use the term *vegan*)
- Fruit plate

Fruit plates can be a great idea for any traveler. If you've never ordered one before, consider it the next time you fly. They're light, and it's a good way to get some fresh fruit into your diet when you're traveling and fresh foods are few and far between, causing many people's diets to suffer.

On airlines that fly to Asia, you may be offered "Asian vegetarian" or "Indian vegetarian" meals. Some airlines designate the Indian option as "Hindu." You can specify whether you want the meal to include dairy and eggs. These special meals can be a nice change of pace from the standard airline issue.

On some flights, the crew will have a list of passengers who have ordered special meals, and they may identify you as you are taking your seat, or they may ask you to ring your flight attendant call button just before they begin meal service. On other flights, you'll get served a regular meal unless you speak up and tell the flight attendant that you've ordered a vegetarian meal. If you are seated near the back of the plane, you may want to ring your call button early in the meal service to let the attendants know that you are expecting a vegetarian meal. That's to ensure that they don't give it away before they get to you, which can happen when someone seated in front of you asks for a vegetarian meal despite not having ordered one (and the flight attendant doesn't check the name on the meal), or when the airline hasn't loaded enough of a particular special request onto the aircraft.

Working it out when you don't get what you ordered

As any frequent flyer will tell you, ordering a vegetarian meal doesn't ensure that you'll get it. This isn't always the airline's fault. Sometimes a last-minute change of aircraft can mean that the meals meant for your flight aren't on that plane. If you miss a flight and have to take an alternate flight, you won't get the meal that you special ordered. If you upgrade your ticket to first class just before you board your flight, your vegetarian meal may be back in coach and you may have another (maybe better) menu from which to choose in first class. Your flight attendant can usually retrieve your meal from coach if you still want it.

If you have a particularly long travel day and want to be extra sure that your vegetarian meal has been ordered, you may want to phone the airline a day or two before you leave, just to reconfirm that the request has been noted. This is especially important if you've made a schedule change because the agent may not have carried your meal request over to your new reservations.

If you find yourself stuck with a ham sandwich instead of your vegetarian meal, there are a few things that you can do:

✔ Eat what you can of the meal that you have been served. Picking the meat off a sandwich and eating the rest of it isn't an option for many vegetarians, nor is pushing the sausage away from the stack of pancakes that it's been leaning against. But your only other option may be peanuts and tomato juice, so if you're really hungry, you may at least be able to eat the salad or crackers.

✔ Ask your flight attendant for cookies, crackers, nuts, pretzels, or juice. If your flight attendant knows that you haven't received your special order, he or she should be able to help you out with some extra snacks or beverages.

✔ Pull out the reserves (fresh fruit, a bagel, a sandwich) that you might have taken along in your carry-on bag just in case.

Planning for plane problems

You know what they say about best-laid plans. Missed connections happen, and airlines make mistakes. There's always a good probability that you won't get the special meal you ordered. For that reason, it's a good idea to eat a full meal before you leave home. If you don't have time or if you're going to be traveling all day, pack a few small items in your carry-on bag to hold you if you miss a meal or can't get something that suits your needs.

If you are traveling internationally, you may not be able to take fresh fruits and vegetables back and forth between countries. Instead of packing fresh foods in your carry-on bag, take small containers of aseptically packaged soymilk or fruit juice, packaged crackers, pretzels, nuts, trail mix, or dried fruit.

You may find yourself roaming the airport terminal during a lengthy layover and decide to stop for a meal or a snack. Or you might even have to grab something to go if you're hungry, you're racing to catch a flight, and you know that the flight won't be offering meal service. If so, your food choices will vary considerably, depending upon the size and location of the airport.

At worst, you'll be stuck with vending machines and newsstands selling candy, packaged cookies and crackers, and maybe some nuts. That's the disadvantage of small airports, although the trade-off is an easy time getting to your connecting gate. At larger airports, you may find several full-service restaurants, cafeterias, and food stands with a huge variety of food choices.

Many hotels have bowls of fruit at the checkout desk. Before you leave your hotel, pick up a piece and stow it in your carry-on bag. If you don't find fruit at your hotel, buy a piece or two in the airport terminal at a food stand or cafeteria. It's good to have on hand in case you get hungry while you're traveling, and it's a good source of dietary fiber and other nutrients that tend to be neglected when people travel.

At larger airports with a wide range of places to eat, the restaurants are essentially the same as those outside the airport. Ethnic restaurants (such as Mexican and Chinese) have the most options for vegetarians, and one or two others may serve veggie burgers. In some airports on the west coast, you'll find juice bars, and on the east coast you'll find bagel stands that sell New York – style bagels and bowls of fresh fruit salad, both good choices for anyone. Some airport vegetarian options include

- ✔ **Newsstands:** Packaged cookies, crackers, pretzels, nuts, and trail mix

- ✔ **Food stands:** Frozen yogurt, soft pretzels, nuts, fresh fruit and fruit salad, bagels, fruit juice, bottled water, trail mix, muffins, popcorn, and pizza

- ✔ **Cafeterias:** Mixed-greens salads, bagels, fresh fruit, fruit salad, fruit juice, bottled water, yogurt, frozen yogurt, muffins, pizza, and French fries

- ✔ **Restaurants:** Bean burritos, bean tacos, bean tostadas, mixed-greens salads, vegetable stir-fry, veggie burger, vegetarian pizza, vegetarian-style sandwiches, and many others, depending upon the restaurant

- ✔ **Airline clubs or lounges:** Hot and cold beverages — including coffee, tea, fruit juices, soft drinks, and bottled water — and cookies, crackers, nuts, and bagels

Part VI
Vegetarianism for Special Needs

The 5th Wave   By Rich Tennant

"For the last time— pregnant vegetarians do NOT give birth to Cabbage Patch Dolls."

In this part . . .

You're planning a vegan pregnancy? Congratulations. Or maybe your baby is already here and you're having food fights over peas and carrots. Mom and Dad are eating a low-fat, vegetarian diet and want to know if the whole family can eat that way, including Grandma and Grandpa, who have their own needs because they're getting up there in age.

Maybe you have a vegetarian teenager who would like you to think that she's one of those "air plants" that can basically live on nothing, with an occasional Twizzler and Coke at the movie theater. Or you're an athlete consuming 4,000 calories a day, all of them vegetarian, and you just want to know if you're getting what you need.

The chapters that follow are for all of you who have (or know someone who has) special needs and want to know how to meet them on a vegetarian diet.

Chapter 21

Taking Care of Mommy-to-Be

· ·

In This Chapter

▶ Preparing for your pregnancy

▶ Managing your nutritional needs during pregnancy

▶ Simplifying your food preparations

▶ Taking care of the queasies and the munchies

· ·

*N*ever mind all the free advice from your mother-in-law and the inquiring minds asking if you plan to read to your baby in utero. Tell people that you're pregnant and that you're a vegetarian, and all sorts of alarms go off. Take all the outside assistance that most pregnant women experience and multiply that by 100 if you proclaim to maintain your vegetarian lifestyle for the duration of your pregnancy. The reactions you receive just might be enough to tempt you to make your reservations at the funny farm right now.

You probably know that it's perfectly safe and healthful to eat a vegetarian diet — and even a vegan diet — when you're pregnant. Then why is it that other people get so anxious when a vegetarian becomes pregnant? After all, vegetarians all over the world have been having healthy babies with little fanfare or angst over their diets for centuries.

But that's just the point. Remember that vegetarian diets are still a large part of a lifestyle choice that is not the U.S. cultural norm. Many or most of your family members and friends probably haven't had personal experience with a vegetarian diet, and most have not been raised in a vegetarian tradition. So, they're anxious, and anxieties heighten when there's a baby involved. All the concern over your vegetarian diet when you're pregnant may seem like an irritating intrusion, but try to take comfort in knowing that these people care. The information in this chapter can help you put to rest some of the most common worries.

Planning for a Vegetarian Pregnancy

Not every pregnancy is planned, but if there's a chance that you might get pregnant in, oh, say the next nine months or so, then it's a great time to be proactive and get yourself into great nutritional shape. The longer you have to eat well before you become pregnant, the better for you and your baby.

The prepregnancy advice for vegetarians is pretty much the same as for non-vegetarians:

✔ Consider taking a regular-dose, daily multivitamin and mineral supplement for several months before you get pregnant. In particular, it's important to have adequate folic acid before pregnancy because it may help prevent a neural tube defect in your baby.

✔ Limit sweets and junk foods that displace more nutritious foods from your diet.

✔ If you drink coffee and haven't already quit for your pregnancy, limit it to two cups a day. Avoid alcohol and tobacco.

✔ Get regular physical activity and drink plenty of water.

✔ Vegans need to have a reliable source of vitamin B12 before, during, and after pregnancy.

But, vegetarians often go into pregnancy with an edge because they are more likely than other women to have close-to-ideal body weights and to have been consuming plenty of folic acid – rich foods, which help to prevent neural tube defects such as spina bifida. Paying careful attention to your diet and fitness level can go a long way toward ensuring a healthy pregnancy — and a healthy baby.

Eating smart for a healthy start

The longer you can eat well before you become pregnant, the better off you and your baby will be. People who are well nourished have strong immune systems, and they're less likely to succumb to many common illnesses such as colds and the flu.

By limiting your intake of junk foods and stocking up on plenty of nutritious vegetables, whole grains, and fresh fruits, you can substantially increase your intake of folic acid, a nutrient that is instrumental in preventing neural tube defects, a type of birth defect that involves an incomplete closure of the spinal cord, in babies. What's more, having high folic acid intakes *before* pregnancy increases the chances that your baby will be protected, since the period of risk for neural tube defects occurs in the very earliest stage of pregnancy, before many women even realize that they're pregnant.

Before you become pregnant, it is also important to ensure that your iron stores are high. Many U.S. women go into pregnancy with low iron stores and put themselves at risk for iron deficiency while they're pregnant. Maternal blood volume increases by about 50 percent during pregnancy, and women who go into pregnancy with low iron stores risk becoming anemic.

Starting out physically fit

The beginning of pregnancy is not the time to start a new or vigorous exercise program, but if you establish an exercise routine prior to pregnancy, then it's likely that you can continue that level of activity throughout your pregnancy. (Your health care provider can advise you about specifics of exercise during pregnancy.) Staying physically active will help you maintain muscle tone and strength as well as help to promote normal stools during a time when many women experience problems with constipation and hemorrhoids. Drinking plenty of fluids, especially water, and getting plenty of rest round out a healthful prepregnancy lifestyle.

Vegetarian women are likely to have higher dietary fiber intakes than nonvegetarian women, and having plenty of fiber in the diet, along with fluids, helps to promote normal stools and diminish problems with constipation and hemorrhoids.

If you smoke tobacco or use illicit drugs, or if you are a habitual alcohol user, the time to stop is before you become pregnant because there are substantial advantages for you and your baby to beginning pregnancy in top physical condition.

Eating Well for Two

Okay, the test strip turned blue, and you're on your way to becoming a mommy. The questions are beginning to trickle in:

- Now that you're eating for two, how are you going to get enough protein?
- Are you getting enough calcium, iron, and vitamin B12?

The questions you have now that you're pregnant are probably the same ones that you had when you first went vegetarian. Understanding the ways that pregnancy changes your nutritional needs and how those needs can be met on a vegetarian diet will give you the confidence you need to enjoy your vegetarian pregnancy and minimize worries. Figure 21-1 shows some vegetarian foods that are especially good for you during pregnancy.

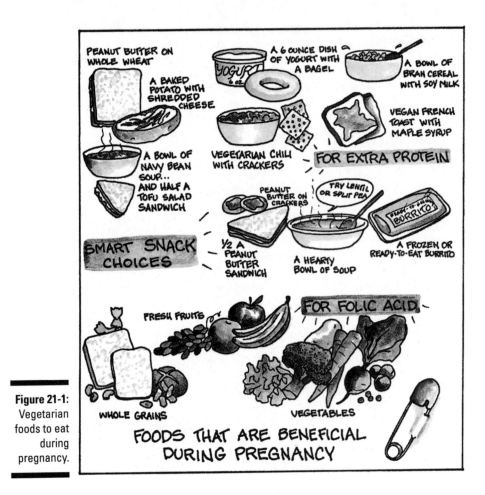

Figure 21-1:
Vegetarian
foods to eat
during
pregnancy.

Gaining the right amount of pregnancy weight

Vegetarians are more likely than nonvegetarians to go into pregnancy at body weights that are close to ideal. Women who go into pregnancy at close to their ideal weight can expect to gain from 25 to 35 pounds. If you are overweight when you begin your pregnancy, you may gain less — between 15 and 25 pounds — and if you are thin when you become pregnant, it's healthy to gain more weight — between 28 and 40 pounds. Weight gain varies with individuals, however, so it's important to get prenatal guidance from a health care provider, whether that's your medical doctor, nurse practitioner, or midwife.

In the first three months of pregnancy, it's commonplace to gain very little weight — a few pounds at most. Weight gain picks up in the second and third trimesters of your pregnancy, and a weight gain of about one pound a week is typical. Once you begin gaining weight after the third month of pregnancy, you'll need about 300 calories per day more than what you needed before you became pregnant. Women who need to gain more weight will need slightly more calories, and women who need to gain less weight will need fewer calories to maintain a healthy pregnancy weight.

Most vegetarian women have weight gains that follow similar patterns to those of nonvegetarian women. However, vegan women are more likely to be slender going into pregnancy. They may be more likely than other women to have low calorie intakes because their diets tend to be bulky. If you are having trouble gaining weight, consult your health care provider for individualized advice. The following tips may also be helpful:

✔ **Eat snacks between meals.** Even something light and easy to fix, like a bowl of cereal with soymilk, half a peanut butter sandwich or peanut butter on crackers, a bowl of hearty soup such as lentil or split pea soup, or a frozen, ready-to-heat bean burrito are a few suggestions.

✔ **Substitute starchy, calorie-dense foods for bulkier, low-calorie foods.** For example, instead of filling up on a lettuce and tomato salad, try a thick soup made with vegetables and barley. Choose starchy vegetables such as potatoes, sweet potatoes, peas, and corn more often than low-calorie choices such as green beans and cucumbers. (Don't give up the folic acid – rich greens, though!)

✔ **Drink extra calories.** When it's calories you need, you may find that shakes and smoothies are an easy way to get them. If you use dairy products, you can make shakes or smoothies using ice milk or frozen yogurt mixed with fresh fruit. Vegans can use tofu, soymilk or other milk substitutes, and nondairy ice cream substitutes.

If you happen to have the opposite problem and are beginning your pregnancy overweight, now is not the time to actively reduce. At most, you'll want to control your weight gain by limiting sweets and fatty or greasy foods that are concentrated in calories and offer little in the way of nutrition in return. Plan to lose weight gradually with diet and exercise after the baby is born.

Banishing nutritional worries

Friends and relatives mean well, but constant badgering about your vegetarian diet can make even the most confident woman worry that her diet and pregnancy don't mix. Not true. Here's some information you can use to reassure others that you're just fine.

Protein

Protein is the first thing people question vegetarians about, and it's the nutrient about which most vegetarians have the least need to be concerned. If you're a pregnant vegetarian or vegan, it still should be the least of your concerns.

The recommended level of protein intake during pregnancy is 60 grams per day for most women. That's about 10 grams more protein than a woman needs when she's not pregnant. Most women, including vegans, are already exceeding that level of protein intake before they become pregnant. They typically get even more during pregnancy because their calorie intakes increase by 300 calories a day, and protein makes up part of those 300 calories. So, you can see that getting enough protein during pregnancy is nothing to worry about.

Each of these food choices adds an extra 10 grams of protein or more to your diet:

- A peanut butter sandwich on whole wheat toast
- A baked potato topped with 1 ounce of shredded cheese (regular or soy)
- A 6-ounce dish of flavored yogurt (regular or soy) with a bagel
- A bowl of vegetarian chili and a couple crackers
- A bowl of bran cereal with soymilk
- Two pieces of vegan French toast with maple syrup
- A bowl of navy bean soup with a half a tofu salad sandwich

Calcium

Counting the milligrams of calcium in your diet wouldn't be much fun, and fortunately it's not necessary. And getting enough is not a problem even if you're vegetarian.

In general, pregnant women need more calcium than women who are not pregnant. Current recommendations call for 1,200 milligrams of calcium per day during pregnancy and while a woman is breast-feeding her baby. Because vegans typically get less calcium than other vegetarians and nonvegetarians, it may be more challenging for them to meet this level of calcium intake.

On the other hand, there is some evidence that the body becomes more efficient at absorbing and retaining calcium during pregnancy, and that may offset lower calcium intakes. Until this can be confirmed, however, vegans and other pregnant women should aim for the 1,200 milligram target. The best way to do this is to try hard to get three or four servings of calcium-rich foods each day. See Chapter 6 for a list of good calcium sources.

If you need help getting enough calcium in your diet when you're pregnant, try these ideas:

- Go for big portion sizes of calcium-rich foods. Instead of a wimpy ½ cup serving of cooked kale, go for it and take a 1 cup helping.
- It may be easier to drink your calcium than to chew it. Have some calcium-fortified orange juice, or make smoothies with calcium-fortified soymilk, fresh or frozen fruit, and tofu that has been processed with calcium.

Vitamin D

Vitamin D goes hand-in-hand with calcium to ensure that your baby's bones and teeth develop normally. If you're pregnant, be sure that your vitamin D intake is adequate. Vegetarian women and nonvegetarian women alike need vitamin D, but it's easy to come by. You can get vitamin D from exposure to sunlight or from fortified foods. Either way, just make sure you get it. For more on vitamin D, see Chapter 9.

Iron

With any luck, you stocked up on iron before you got pregnant, so that you began your pregnancy with adequate iron stores. This is important because going into pregnancy with low iron stores can result in iron deficiency anemia in the later stages of pregnancy.

All pregnant women need additional iron during the second and third trimesters of pregnancy when maternal blood volume skyrockets and iron levels plummet. It's common for health care professionals to advise women to take an iron supplement of 30 milligrams per day during this time.

During pregnancy, it's important to keep the junk foods in your diet to a minimum to ensure that there will be enough room in your diet for the good stuff, including foods that are high in iron. Is there an echo in here?

Vitamin B12

Vegetarian pregnant women don't need any more vitamin B12 than any other pregnant women. However, if you're a vegan woman, you have to make a special effort to get it because vitamin B12 is found in eggs and dairy products. The importance of this cannot be stressed enough. Not only does your baby need vitamin B12 from you while she's developing, she also needs it while breast-feeding. So, vegan women need to have a reliable source of vitamin B12 before, during, and after pregnancy. See Chapter 8 for more on vitamin B12.

Caffeine and pregnancy

Whether you're a vegetarian or not, it's best to limit or eliminate your use of caffeine when you're pregnant. Studies have demonstrated problems in pregnancies resulting from the equivalent of five cups of coffee or more per day. Until otherwise demonstrated to be benign, it's best to err on the side of caution and eliminate caffeine during pregnancy, or limit your use to one or two cups of caffeine-containing beverages per day, including coffee, tea, cola, and other soft drinks that contain caffeine.

Making Mealtimes Easy on Yourself

What most pregnant women need is someone to make their meals for them. Now *that's* meal planning made easy! Okay, so you don't see that happening within the next nine months. Here's what you do: Permit yourself to take some shortcuts for a while. Here are some suggestions:

- ✔ **Use more convenience foods.** Frozen vegetarian entrees and snacks such as burritos and ready-to-heat sandwiches and veggie burger patties can reduce meal prep to minutes.

- ✔ **Order out for meals when you're too tired to cook.** Chinese vegetable stir-fry with steamed rice, a falafel sandwich and a side of tabouli, or a vegetarian pizza may be just what you need.

- ✔ **Open a can or carton.** Eat a can of lentil soup with whole wheat toast, or have a bowl of cereal with soymilk for dinner. Canned beans, canned soups, breakfast cereals, frozen waffles, burritos, and microwave popcorn are all nutritious and quick.

- ✔ **Become a weekend cook.** Make a big batch of vegetarian chili or lasagna and freeze part of it. You can take it out and reheat it when you don't feel like cooking. Fix a big fresh fruit salad or mixed green salad one day, and eat it over the next three days. Muffins and quick breads freeze well, too.

When you're pregnant, you don't really have to eat different foods than when you're not pregnant — you just need about 300 calories per day *more*. Give yourself permission to take the easy way out. Postpone making gourmet meals until a time when you have more energy. For now, eat according to your appetite, and pay attention to the overall quality of your food choices. See Chapter 15 for guidance in choosing foods and planning meals.

Fighting Nausea and Feeding Cravings

Pregnancy is a time for some strange food aversions and even stranger cravings. They're usually harmless and pass by the end of the first three months of pregnancy. Not always, but usually. The same is true of that infamous bane of the pregnant set — nausea, better known as morning sickness, and known by some as morning, noon, and nighttime sickness.

These aspects of pregnancy are no different for vegetarians than they are for nonvegetarian women.

Quelling the queasies

Morning sickness may be the most uncomfortable symptom of pregnancy, whether you're a vegetarian or not, and for many women, overcoming it is a matter of waiting it out. In the meantime, there are some things that you can do to minimize its effects.

- ✔ Eat small, frequent meals or snacks. Don't give yourself a chance to get hungry between meals because hunger can sometimes accentuate feelings of nausea.

- ✔ Eat foods that are easy to digest, such as fruits, toast, cereal, bagels, and other starchy foods. Foods that are high in carbohydrates such as these take less time to digest. In contrast, fatty or greasy foods such as chips, pastries, cheese, heavy entrees, and rich desserts take longer to digest and may be likely to give you more trouble.

- ✔ If nausea keeps you from eating or drinking for more than one day and night, check with your health care provider for guidance.

- ✔ If vitamin or mineral supplements make you nauseous, try varying the time of day that you take them or try taking them with a substantial meal. If the smell of the supplement is offensive, try coating it with peanut butter before swallowing.

Minding the munchies

If you're having cravings for something outlandish, like, say, tofu cheesecake with chocolate sauce or a hummus and green tomato sandwich, the best thing to do is . . . go for it! This phase isn't going to last forever, and let's face it, pregnancy is a time when all sorts of hormonal changes are taking place and things can be topsy-turvy for a while. There's not much you can do about it, it's not necessary to control it, and it's probably not going to hurt you. As long as you aren't chewing on radial tires or the clay in your backyard, you should be just fine.

Feeding your baby naturally

You might be surprised to learn that you need even more calories when you're breast-feeding — about 200 more calories per day — than you did when you're pregnant. So, most women need an additional 500 calories a day when they are breast-feeding than they did before they were pregnant. No wonder many women find that during the time that they're breast-feeding, they begin losing some of the extra weight they gained while they were pregnant.

Your nutrient needs are just a little higher when you are breast-feeding than when you were pregnant. For instance, you need about 5 grams more protein. You'll easily get the extra nutrients in the additional calories that you'll be eating. Be sure to include plenty of fluids, too. Water is always the best choice. And remember that vegans need to be sure to get a reliable source of vitamin B12.

Chapter 22

Bringing Up Baby

*E*nter a world in which the little people wear mashed potatoes in their hair and toss more of their food onto the floor than into their mouths. Hey, when was the last time you smeared smashed peas up and down your arms and hid cracker bits behind your ears? You were probably two feet tall and had three chins. Me, too.

This scenario is pretty much the same, whether your child is a vegetarian or not. This chapter will help guide you in the progression from breast or bottle to baby food and beyond and address special considerations for vegetarians.

Vegetarian Beginnings

We all start out as vegetarians when you get right down to it. There aren't many kids who start out life guzzling fluid fish or hamburger.

Milk is our first food. Humans make milk for human babies. The alternative, infant formula, is as close a replica as can be made in a laboratory. Babies should be breast-fed or bottle-fed exclusively for the first four to six months of life. They need no other food during this time. In fact, if you start solid foods sooner, your child is more likely to become overweight and to develop allergies, so resist the temptation to start solids too early.

Feeding nature's best: Breast milk

Breast milk is the perfect first food for babies, because it's tailor-made for them. At no other time in our lives do most of us have a diet so well suited to our needs.

From birth through at least the first six months — and longer, if possible — breast-feeding your baby is the best choice, bar none. There are several reasons:

- Breast milk is ideally suited to a baby's nutritional needs. The composition of breast milk makes it the perfect food for human babies. Even baby formulas can't compare, because most nutrition scientists acknowledge that there are probably substances present in breast milk that are needed for good health but have not yet been identified and, therefore, are not available in synthetic formulas.

- Breast milk contains protective substances that give your baby added immunity or protection against certain illnesses. Breast-fed babies are also less likely than others to have problems with allergies later in life.

- Breast-fed babies are more likely than others to maintain an ideal weight throughout life.

- Breast milk is convenient and sterile.

- Breast-feeding is good for Mom because it helps the uterus to return to its former size more quickly and aids in taking off excess "baby fat."

The babies of vegetarian women have a leg up on other infants. Vegetarian women have substantially less environmental contaminants in their breast milk than do nonvegetarian women. The diets of vegetarian women contain only a fraction of the amount of pesticide residues and other contaminants that nonvegetarian women consume unknowingly. These contaminants are concentrated in animal tissues and fat, and women who eat the animal products store the contaminants in their own tissues and fat. Consequently, when they produce breast milk, they pass the contaminants on to their babies through their milk.

Some people are sticklers for details. Here's the question: Can babies who drink breast milk be considered vegans, or do they have to drink a synthetic soy formula to be considered vegans? The answer: Oh, come on! Vegans who breast-feed their babies consider their babies vegans, too.

Using vegetarian formula

Women who breast-feed their babies get lots of applause, but women who can't breast-feed shouldn't be chastised. There are many reasons some women can't or don't want to breast-feed. Those who don't will need to feed their babies a synthetic baby formula instead. Just as with breast-fed babies, formula-fed babies need their formula and nothing but their formula for at least the first four to six months, if not longer.

A few more pointers

You should be aware of a few more issues concerning your baby's nutritional needs during the first 12 months:

✔ Remember: If you are a vegan mom, it's critical that you take a vitamin B12 supplement while you're breast-feeding to ensure that your baby has a source of vitamin B12, too.

✔ If you aren't sure if your baby is getting enough vitamin D, consult your health care provider. Babies over the age of three months who have limited exposure to sunlight need a vitamin D supplement of not more than 400 IU per day.

✔ After the first four to six months of age, breast-fed babies are usually started on iron supplements. Your health care provider can advise you on this issue.

There are several brands of baby formula on the market, and your health care provider will probably recommend a few to you. Most are based on cow's milk, altered to be more easily digested and to more closely resemble human milk. Others contain animal fat or other animal by-products. Vegans don't use these formulas. There are other baby formulas that contain no animal products and are soy based. These formulas, including such brands as Isomil, Prosobee, and Soyalac, are acceptable for use by vegans.

Commercial soymilks are not the same thing as infant soy-based formulas, and they are not appropriate for infants. If you do not breast-feed your baby, be sure that you feed her a commercial infant formula, *not* the commercial soymilks that are meant for general use (such as Edensoy and Westsoy). When your child is older, these will be fine, but not in infancy and toddlerhood.

If your baby is bottle fed, don't put anything in the bottle except breast milk, formula, or water for the first six months. Sugar water drinks, soft drinks, and iced tea are inappropriate for babies and small children, and fruit juices and diluted baby cereals should not be introduced until after the six-month point. Nothing is more nutritious or beneficial to your baby for the first six months than breast milk or infant formula.

Starting with Solids

When your baby is about four to six months of age, you can look for a few clues that will tell you that it's time to begin introducing your baby to solid foods:

✔ Your baby reaches about 13 pounds in weight or doubles his birth-weight.

✔ Your baby wants to breast-feed eight times or more during a 24-hour period.

✔ Your baby takes a quart of formula or more in a 24-hour period and acts like she is still hungry and wants more.

When your baby reaches these milestones, it's time to introduce solid foods — gradually.

Introducing new vegetarian foods

What's the nearly universal first solid food for babies, vegetarian or not? Baby cereal. Usually rice cereal, since almost every baby can tolerate it. It's best to give your baby iron-fortified baby rice cereal until he is at least 18 months old.

Rather than abruptly discontinuing breast or bottle feedings, just supplement these by introducing small amounts of solid foods, one at a time. Start gradually, and continue breast or bottle feedings as usual. Begin by mixing baby rice cereal with breast milk or infant formula and offering a few tablespoons. Work up to two feedings a day, totaling about a half cup. From there, you'll gradually add other foods, one at a time, a little at a time, and your baby will increase the amounts at her own pace.

There aren't any hard-and-fast rules about how to introduce solid foods to babies — just some general guidelines. For instance, all babies — whether their families are vegetarians or not — start out eating the foods that are the easiest to digest and least likely to cause problems such as allergic reactions or choking. These foods are cooked cereals and mashed or pureed fruits and vegetables and their juices. Protein-rich foods and foods that are high in fat are introduced later. It's a good idea to introduce foods one at a time, so that if a baby does have a sensitivity to a food, you can more easily pinpoint the culprit. Once your baby becomes accustomed to cooked cereals and mashed and pureed fruits and vegetables, he can move on to table foods.

Cows' milk should not be given to infants under the age of one year. Cows' milk can cause bleeding in the gastrointestinal tract of human babies and lead to anemia. Studies have also linked cow's milk given to infants with an increased risk for insulin-dependent diabetes.

Knowing what and when to feed your infant

Table 22-1 suggests schedules for feeding vegan babies from 4 through 12 months of age. You'll notice that the guide excludes all animal products. If you prefer to include dairy products and/or eggs, you can substitute them for soy products where indicated.

Table 22-1		Feeding Vegan Babies Ages 4 to 12 Months		
Food	*4 – 7 Months*	*6 – 8 Months*	*7 – 10 Months*	*10 – 12 Months*
Milk	Breast milk or soy formula	Breast milk or soy formula	Breast milk or soy formula	Breast milk or soy formula (24 – 32 ounces)
Cereal and bread	Begin iron-fortified baby cereal mixed with breast milk or soy formula	Continue baby cereal; begin other breads and cereals	Baby cereal; other breads and cereals	Baby cereal until 18 months of age; total of four or more servings (1 serving = ¼ slice bread or 2 to 4 tablespoons cereal)
Fruits and veg-etables	None	Begin juice from cup; 2 to 4 ounces vitamin C source; begin mashed veg-etables and fruits	4 ounces juice; pieces of soft/cooked fruits and vegetables	Table-food diet; allow four servings per day (one serving = 2 to 4 tablespoons fruit and vegetable, 4 ounces juice)
Legumes and nut butters	None	None	Gradually introduce tofu; begin casseroles, pureed legumes, soy cheese, and soy yogurt	Two servings daily, each about ½ ounce; nut butters should not be started before 12 months

Note: Overlap of age ranges occurs due to varying rates of development.

Adapted from Simply Vegan, Third Edition, by Debra Wasserman and Reed Mangels, Ph.D., R.D., 1999. Reprinted with permission from The Vegetarian Resource Group, PO Box 1463, Baltimore, MD 21203; phone 410-366-8343; Web site www.vrg.org.

There is no real trick to feeding most children a healthful vegetarian diet. The main thing is to offer a variety of foods and encourage children to explore new tastes. Table 22-2 presents a daily feeding guide for toddlers and preschoolers ages one through four years. If you need assistance adapting the food guide for your individual child or need more help with menu planning, contact a registered dietitian who is familiar with vegetarian diets and working with families. (A feeding guide for school-aged children is provided in Chapter 23.)

Table 22-2	Meal Planning Guide for Toddlers and Preschoolers Ages 1 to 4
Food Group	*Number of Servings*
Grains	6 or more (1 serving = ½ to 1 slice bread; or ¼ to ½ cup cooked cereal, grain, or pasta; or ½ to 1 cup ready-to-eat cereal)
Legumes, nuts, seeds	2 or more (1 serving = ¼ to ½ cup cooked beans, tofu, tempeh, or textured vegetable protein; or 1½ to 3 ounces meat substitute; or 1 to 2 tablespoons nuts, seeds, or nut or seed butter)
Fortified soymilk, infant formula, or breast milk	3 (1 serving = 1 cup)
Vegetables	2 or more (1 serving = ¼ to ½ cup cooked or ½ to 1 cup raw vegetables)
Fruits	3 or more (1 serving = ¼ to ½ cup canned fruit; or ½ cup juice; or 1 medium fruit)
Fats	3 to 4 (1 serving = 1 teaspoon margarine or oil)

Adapted from Simply Vegan, Third Edition, by Debra Wasserman and Reed Mangels, Ph.D., R.D., 1999. Adapted with permission from The Vegetarian Resource Group, PO Box 1463, Baltimore, MD 21203; phone 410-366-8343; Web site www.vrg.org.

Health care providers may be behind the curve

Many health care providers are neither familiar nor comfortable with the concept of vegetarian diets for children. Be assured that vegetarian diets are perfectly safe and adequate for children and that they have numerous advantages over nonvegetarian diets. They are outside U.S. culture at this time, and that is the primary reason you will meet with resistance from health care providers. You may also find a lack of support for vegetarian diets in baby and child-care books that you read. Again, be assured that these opinions are not consistent with scientific knowledge.

Keeping Your Vegetarian Toddler on Track

Vegetarian diets are associated with numerous health advantages, so starting children out on the right foot helps to cement good eating habits that will follow them into adulthood. Even so, once young vegetarian children begin eating table foods, there are a few issues about which you should be aware.

The backlash of bulky foods

Vegetarian diets — particularly low-fat or vegan diets — can be bulky. Many plant foods are high in fiber and relatively low in calories. Because young children have small stomachs, they may become full before they've had a chance to take in enough calories to meet their energy needs. For this reason, it's important to be sure to include plenty of calorie-dense foods in the diets of young vegetarian children.

Fighting back with plant fats

When diets are based on bulky plant products, one of the ways in which young children can be assured of getting enough calories is by not overly restricting dietary fat. Some adults may want to keep their fat intakes to a minimum, especially to control their weight, but this very aspect of plant-based diets that helps adults control their weight can backfire for young children if their fat intake is too controlled.

Liberally using plant sources of fat can help provide young children with the extra calories they need during a period of their lives in which they are growing and developing rapidly. So, for instance, adding a slice of avocado (nearly all fat) to a sandwich is fine, or using nut and seed butters on sandwiches and vegetable sticks is also a good idea.

Children under the age of one year should not be given honey or corn syrup. These foods, which can carry Clostridium spores that cause botulism, can cause food poisoning in young children.

Serving snacks to fill the gaps

Another way to ensure that vegetarian kids get enough calories is to include between-meals snacks in their diets. In the case of toddlers, you'll need to make sure that you don't give them things that they can choke on. For instance, grapes and whole tofu hotdogs are dangerous, because they can easily get stuck in the esophagus. If you want to offer these foods to a small child, be sure to slice them in half or into quarters. Be careful with chips, nuts, and other small items that can also lodge in a small child's throat. Young children should be supervised when they are eating.

A few nutritious snack ideas for vegetarian toddlers include

- ✔ Soy yogurt
- ✔ Small pieces of fresh fruit
- ✔ Single-serving aseptic boxes of fruit juice or soymilk
- ✔ Graham crackers
- ✔ Tofu processed with calcium, served as cubes or made into smoothies or pudding
- ✔ Whole-grain cereal "O's"
- ✔ Cooked or dry cereal with soymilk
- ✔ A dab of smooth peanut or almond butter on a cracker

Chapter 23

Vegetarian Diets for Children and Teens

● ●

In This Chapter

▶ Evaluating growth rates of vegetarian kids

▶ Ensuring that kids and teens get the nutrition they need

▶ Getting kids to eat their vegetables

▶ Handling school meals, weight concerns, and other challenges

● ●

A 1995 Roper Poll conducted for the nonprofit Vegetarian Resource Group found that children from 8 to 12 years of age are becoming vegetarians at twice the rate of adults. They're doing it because they have compassion for animals and an interest in saving the planet from environmental destruction caused by raising animals for food. Many of these kids are "going it alone" and are the only vegetarians in their households. You've got to admire that kind of courage. But when Mom and Dad aren't vegetarians themselves, there can be some hand wringing and concern about whether vegetarian diets are adequate for kids.

But even in homes where vegetarianism is the norm, people have questions about vegetarian nutrition for kids. So, here's the first piece of insight: Feeding any child — vegetarian or not — takes time, patience, and care. A diet that is haphazard, heavy on chips and soft drinks and light on fruits and vegetables, or otherwise poorly planned, is not likely to meet the needs of any growing child. On the other hand, a well-planned vegetarian diet offers health advantages over nonvegetarian diets for kids, and it helps to put into motion a lifestyle of healthful eating that, with any luck, will become a pattern for a lifetime.

This chapter explores the most common questions and concerns that care-givers have about vegetarian diets for children and teenagers.

Dismissing Concerns about Children's Growth Rates

Some people worry about growth rates in children who don't eat meat. They have concerns that children raised on vegetarian diets will suffer from growth retardation. There have been reports in the scientific literature over the years about poor growth in vegetarian children, but a closer look at the studies settles that concern for most of us. The growth problems occurred in a couple of circumstances:

✔ The children lived in poverty in developing countries and didn't have enough to eat.

✔ The children did not live in poverty but were being fed bizarre, inadequate diets that were severely limited in variety and calories.

Of course, malnutrition, not vegetarianism, causes growth retardation. Any child, vegetarian or not, who doesn't have enough to eat will suffer from nutritional deficiencies and may have difficulties developing properly.

In this book, we're talking about vegetarian — including vegan — diets that contain adequate calories and varieties of foods to ensure that nutritional needs are met. As stated throughout this book, not only do reasonable vegetarian diets meet nutritional needs, but they are associated with health advantages as well.

Gauging growth rates

Questioning growth rates in vegetarian children begs the question, "What's a normal rate of growth for a child, anyway?"

Your pediatrician has growth charts on which she plots your child's height and weight at regular intervals and compares them to population norms. You may even be doing this yourself at home. Growth rates are usually reported in percentiles. For instance, one child may be growing at the 50th percentile for height and weight, while another child of the same age may be growing at the 90th percentile. Still another same-aged child may be growing at the 25th percentile. Is one child healthier than the other? Not necessarily.

Within any group of people, we'd expect to see 50 percent growing at the 50th percentile, 25 percent growing at the 25th percentile, and so on. That's called *normal distribution*. In other words, variation is normal within population groups. A child growing at the 25th percentile isn't necessarily healthier or less healthy than a child growing at the 90th percentile.

What's important is for a child growing at a particular rate to continue to grow at that same rate. A decline in a child's growth rate would be a signal to investigate the reason for the decline. So, a child growing at the 35th percentile who continues to grow at the 35th percentile is probably fine. But if that child's rate of growth fell to the 25th percentile, then the parent or health care provider should look into possible causes.

Monitoring your expectations

Kids fed on a meat-and-potatoes diet are expected to go through growth spurts at certain ages. Most of us hope that our children grow up to be "big and strong." We aim for football-player-sized kids and worry that the playground bully is going to pick on our child if he's too small. As a culture, we value big and tall.

The growth rates of lacto and lacto ovo vegetarian children are similar to the growth rates of nonvegetarian children. But there is very little information about growth rates of vegan children in the United States. A peek at the growth rates of children in China eating a near-vegan diet has given scientists some idea of what we might expect to see, however.

In a population study called the China Project, which began in 1983, scientists found that the children eating a near-vegan diet grew more slowly than U.S. children eating a standard, Western-style diet containing meat and milk. The Chinese children attained full adult stature eventually, but they took longer to get there. They grew over a period of about 21 years, as compared to American children, who stop growing at about the age of 18 years. Chinese girls reach menarche, or had their first menstrual cycle at an average age of 17 years, compared to 12 years for U.S. girls. In the Chinese, this later age of menarche was associated with lower rates of breast cancer in Chinese women, theoretically because they were exposed to high levels of circulating estrogen hormones for a shorter period of time.

So, it's possible that U.S. vegan children may grow more slowly than other children, but we don't know if that's good, bad, or indifferent. It's likely that if there is a difference, the difference may be associated with health benefits in children eating a healthful vegan diet.

The most important thing for parents of vegetarian children to know is that their child's growth rate should be constant or increase. If it takes a nosedive, that's the time to investigate and intervene. In the meantime, if a child is growing and is otherwise healthy, there's no need to worry.

Ask your health care provider for a growth record form so that you can follow your child's rate of growth at home. Your health care provider can show you how simple it is to plot your child's height and weight monthly or quarterly. That way, you can rest assured that your child is making satisfactory progress, and you'll be the first to know if there's a problem.

Fighting childhood obesity

The percentage of U.S. children who are overweight has risen to the point where public health nutritionists now consider childhood obesity to be a major public health problem. The problem is attributed to diets that are too rich in fat and too low in fiber, as well as to declining levels of physical activity among children, who now spend more time than ever in front of the television and computer. Vegetarian children are more likely than other children to be at their ideal body weights because their diets contain substantially more fiber and less total fat, saturated fat, and cholesterol.

Giving Your Child Enough to Grow On

Vegetarian diets have health advantages for everyone, but a few of the characteristics that make vegetarian diets so healthful can also be pitfalls for children if you aren't aware of them and don't take precautions. The primary issue is the bulkiness of a vegetarian diet and the fact that some children can fill up before they have taken in enough calories.

Filling that belly

It's important to be aware of the potential bulkiness of a vegetarian diet and be sure to include plenty of calorie-dense foods in a child's diet. That means emphasizing starchy, high-calorie foods such as breads, cereals, and starchy vegetables such as beans, peas, and potatoes, and minimizing low-calorie, bulky foods such as large lettuce salads and low-calorie raw vegetables. It's okay to include those foods in your child's diet, but don't let them displace too much of the higher-calorie foods.

Feel free to use some vegetable sources of fat in your child's diet, such as seed and nut butters, olive oil, and avocado slices. These fats are a concentrated source of calories and, while some adults may want to limit fatty foods themselves to control their weight, kids need the extra calories for growth.

Like other types of vegetarian diets, vegan diets can be healthful for children. If you have recently switched to a vegan diet and your child loses weight or does not seem to be growing as quickly as before the switch, add sources of concentrated calories, such as vegetable sources of fat, and substitute more starchy foods for lower-calorie, bulkier foods.

Supplementing with snacks

Give your kids nutritious snacks between meals. In Chapter 22, you can find a list of some snacks that are good choices for younger children. For older children and teens, this list can be expanded to also include the following:

- Muffins
- Whole-grain cookies
- Whole-grain crackers
- Dried fruit
- Popcorn
- Cereal and soymilk or skim cows' milk
- Fresh vegetable sticks with hummus or black bean dip
- Frozen fruit bars
- Bean burritos and tacos
- Bagels
- Sandwiches
- Fresh fruit
- Smoothies made with soymilk and fresh fruit, ice cream substitute, or nonfat dairy products
- Veggie burgers
- Individual frozen vegetarian pizzas
- Frozen waffles with maple syrup or jam or jelly
- Whole-grain toast with jam or jelly

Remembering Basic Nutrition for Kids

When it comes to designing a vegetarian diet for kids and teens, a few key nutrients deserve special attention.

Providing protein

The most foolproof way of ensuring that your child gets enough protein is to make sure she gets enough calories to meet her energy needs. When a child's diet is too low in calories, the body will burn protein for energy. Protein and calorie malnutrition go hand-in-hand. When there are enough calories in the diet, protein can be used for building new tissues instead of being burned for energy. (See Chapter 6 for information on the relationship between calcium and protein.)

So, the best ways to ensure that your child has enough protein are to be sure that she has enough calories to meet her energy needs and that she's getting a reasonable variety of foods, including fruits, vegetables, grains, legumes, nuts, and seeds. Some of the foods that are especially good sources of protein and are also likely to be hits with children are

- ✔ Bean burritos and tacos
- ✔ Veggie burgers
- ✔ Veggie hotdogs
- ✔ Hummus or other bean dip with vegetable sticks or tortilla chips
- ✔ Peanut butter on apple chunks or celery sticks
- ✔ Peanut butter sandwiches made with whole-grain bread or crackers
- ✔ Tofu salad sandwiches
- ✔ Soymilk and fruit smoothies
- ✔ Tofu or nonfat ricotta cheese and vegetable lasagna
- ✔ Vegetarian pizza
- ✔ Nonfat or soy yogurt
- ✔ Nonfat or soy cheese on crackers
- ✔ Tempeh sloppy joes

Catching calcium

Because children and teens are in a period of rapid growth, they need plenty of calcium in their diets to accommodate the development of their teeth and bones. Several factors, including the presence of vitamin D and absorption and retention of calcium, are at least as important to maintaining a healthy body as having adequate amounts of calcium in the diet. Nevertheless, it's a good idea to encourage children and teens to get three servings of calcium-rich foods each day. Calcium-rich foods include dark green, leafy vegetables, broccoli, legumes, almonds and sesame seeds, and calcium-fortified orange juice. See Chapter 6 for a list of suggestions. Aim for big servings — at least a cup at a time. Your kids won't eat their vegetables? Keep reading — that discussion comes later in this chapter.

Calcium-fortified orange juice and fortified soymilk are easy ways to add calcium to the hit-or-miss diets of older kids and teens.

Including iron

Many of the foods that are high in calcium also happen to be high in iron, so if you can fix these foods for your family or have quick-and-easy sources on hand for your kids to serve themselves, you'll get a double benefit. Some good plant sources of iron include dark green, leafy vegetables, soybeans and other legumes, bran flakes, and blackstrap molasses. (See Chapter 7 for more on iron.)

Remember, too, that it's important for vegetarians to have good food sources of vitamin C present at meals to increase the body's absorption of the iron present in that meal. So, make fruits and vegetables readily available to your kids. With plenty of fruits and vegetables on the menu, you'll help ensure that your kids get enough calcium, iron, and vitamin C. Strategies for increasing the likelihood that your child will eat these foods are coming right up.

Incidentally, if you're thinking that getting kids to eat fruits and vegetables is an insurmountable challenge and a reason to nix the idea of a vegetarian diet, think again. All kids need plenty of fruits and vegetables, regardless of whether they eat meat or drink cows' milk, and adding meat or milk to your child's diet would displace even more plant matter. So, the answer to getting kids to eat well goes beyond whether they are vegetarians.

Remembering the vitamins

Vitamins play a big role in maintaining optimal health. Make sure your kids get what they need.

Vitamin B12

Everyone, including children and teens, needs a reliable source of vitamin B12. If your kids are eating a vegan or near-vegan diet, they should be eating vitamin B12 – fortified foods regularly or taking a vitamin B12 supplement. If there's any doubt about whether fortified foods are providing enough vitamin B12, the safest bet is to have your kids take a supplement. See Chapter 8 for more on vitamin B12.

Vitamin D

The important thing to remember about vitamin D and children is that vitamin D, in concert with calcium, is critical for the normal growth and development of bones and teeth. If you have any doubts about whether your child is at risk of not getting enough vitamin D, ask a registered dietitian or your health care provider for an assessment and recommendations. (For more on vitamin D, see Chapter 9.)

Getting kids to eat good foods

Kids will eat foods that are presented appealingly and are convenient to eat. If you want them to eat fruits and vegetables, consider keeping a bowl of seasonal fresh fruit on the kitchen counter or table, fresh fruit salad in the refrigerator, and cut-up fresh vegetables in a container on the top shelf of the refrigerator — in plain sight of hungry scavengers. Bags of baby carrots that are already peeled are a favorite. Keep hummus, salsa, and black bean dip on hand for dipping fresh vegetable sticks.

Aiming for the basics

Of course, we could keep right on going from there and list numerous other nutrients, their roles in the growth and development of children, and the importance of including good food sources in the diet. When it gets right down to it, however, the real issues are ensuring that your child gets

- ✔ Adequate calories
- ✔ A reasonable variety of foods
- ✔ A reliable source of vitamin B12 for vegan and near-vegan children and adequate vitamin D
- ✔ A limited amount of junk foods, so that these foods don't displace more nutritious foods

Helping Your Child Learn to Love Fruits and Vegetables

Now, the real challenge is how to get Johnny to eat his vegetables. If you haven't learned by now, it's usually a losing battle to try to force people to do things they don't want to do. Kids are no exception.

There are some strategies, however, that may increase the likelihood that Johnny will eat his vegetables. More importantly, there are some things you can do to increase the likelihood that your children will grow up enjoying healthful foods and will make them a part of their adult lifestyles.

Table 23-1 suggests meals that are suitable for school-aged children up to 12 years of age. This list excludes all animal products. If you prefer to include dairy products and/or eggs, you can substitute them for soy products where indicated.

All in the family — vegetarian pets

When some people say that their whole family is vegetarian, they mean their cat and dog, too. Dogs are naturally omnivorous and can fare well on a diet that excludes meat. Cats, on the other hand, are carnivorous and need the nutrients found in meat. Specifically, cats must have a source of the amino acid taurine in their diets, and there is no taurine in the plant world. If you don't feed your cat meat, you must provide a taurine supplement. Your veterinarian may or may not be receptive to the idea of a vegetarian diet for cats and dogs, just as many human health care providers are not familiar with vegetarian diets for people.

Table 23-1	Meal Planning Guide for School-Aged Children
Food Group	*Number of Servings*
Grains	6 or more for 5- to 6-year olds; 7 or more for 7- to 12-year olds (1 serving = 1 slice of bread; or ½ cup cooked cereal, grain, or pasta; or ¾ cup to 1 cup ready-to-eat cereal)
Legumes, nuts, seeds	½ to 3 for 5- to 6-year olds; 3 or more for 7- to 12-year olds (1 serving = ½ cup cooked beans, tofu, tempeh, or textured vegetable protein; or 3 ounces of meat substitute; or 2 tablespoons nuts, seeds, or nut or seed butter)
Fortified soymilk	3 (1 serving = 1 cup)
Vegetables	2 or more for 5- to 6-year olds; 3 or more for 7- to 12-year olds (1 serving = ½ cup cooked or 1 cup raw vegetables)
Fruits	2 to 4 for 5- to 6-year olds; 3 or more for 7- to 12-year olds (1 serving = ½ cup canned fruit; or ¾ cup juice; or 1 medium fruit)
Fats	4 for 5- to 6-year olds; 5 for 7- to 12-year olds (1 serving = 1 teaspoon margarine or oil)

Adapted from Simply Vegan, Third Edition, by Debra Wasserman and Reed Mangels, Ph.D., R.D., 1999. Adapted with permission from The Vegetarian Resource Group, PO Box 1463, Baltimore, MD 21203; phone 410-366-8343; Web site www.vrg.org.

What can you do to help ensure that your children will grow up to love healthful foods, such as fruits and vegetables? A lot, and it's not that difficult to do. Consider the suggestions that follow.

Setting an example

You should model the behavior that you want your children to adopt. If you want your children to like broccoli and sweet potatoes, let them see you enjoying these foods yourself.

What if you don't like broccoli? There's no need to pretend to like something that you don't. Children can spot a fake. But you don't have to sneer at it, either. If you don't care for a food, fix it for the others in your household, and don't make a big show out of the fact that there isn't any on your plate.

Present foods with a positive attitude. It will make all the difference in the world. At the same time, don't push. You also don't have to be obvious — a wide grin and "Aren't these lovely Brussels sprouts?" isn't necessary, but present the food with an air that says that you have every reason to expect that your family is going to be pleased with this food.

It's no use trying to be the diet police. You don't have to eat foods that you don't like, and you can let your children express food preferences, too. We don't all like the same foods. If your child expresses dislike for a food that you'd like to see her eat, play it low key. She may come around in time. If not, there's no need to fret. There are hundreds of different vegetables, fruits, and grains. If your child doesn't like one or another, there are plenty of others to take its place.

Encouraging freedom of choice

Children, like everyone else, prefer a measure of freedom. If your child turns up his nose at a particular food, offer one or two other choices. For instance, if your child says no to cooked carrots, offer a few raw carrots with dip or some steamed, mixed vegetables instead. If your child refuses these, let it go. The next meal will bring new choices.

Growing to like new foods

Antonia Demas, PhD, Director of the Food Studies Institute in Trumansburg, New York, has developed an innovative elementary school curriculum that teaches children about foods by using a hands-on, experiential approach that combines nutrition, anthropology, and the arts. Using her method, children learn about and prepare foods from other cultures, drawing from the healthiest traditions of those cuisines. In her studies, Demas has found that children who have classroom exposure to new foods are 5 to 20 times more likely to choose those foods when they are subsequently served in the school cafeteria than are children who had no previous exposure to the same foods.

Get your children involved in meal planning. Ask about their ideas and preferences. Then take your children shopping for food. Children are more likely to eat what they've had a hand in choosing. If you are buying apples or pears from a bin, let your child pick out two or three and put them into the bag. Let older children have even more responsibility. Send your teen to the opposite side of the produce department to pick out a head of cauliflower. Who cares if it's the best one? It's more important that your kids become involved.

Nurturing a spirit of adventure

Have some fun experimenting with new fruits and vegetables. You and your child are on even ground when you pick up a food at the supermarket that's totally new to both of you. Try something challenging, such as a really strange-looking piece of exotic fruit or a spaghetti squash.

If you get something new home and taste it and find that you don't like it, that's okay. It's part of the process of trying new things. Sometimes you hit on a new favorite, and sometimes you turn up a dud. At least you tried, and finding those new favorites makes it all worthwhile.

Preparing meals together

Your kids will be very likely to eat food that they've had a hand in fixing. Supervise young children and let them help with simple tasks like retrieving canned goods from the pantry or dumping prepared ingredients into a pot. Older kids can help wash and peel fruits and vegetables for salads and assemble other ingredients for casseroles and stir-fries.

Growing your own food

Let your kids learn how their foods grow and help them gain an interest in and appreciation for fresh foods. Plant a window-sill herb garden, grow a pot of tomatoes on your back porch or apartment balcony, or plant a small kitchen garden or a full-sized backyard garden — whatever makes sense for your lifestyle, on a small scale or large.

Managing Special Child/Teen Challenges

Sooner or later, all vegetarians, and those who love them, will stumble upon the many challenges — some big, some small — that occur when meat-and-potatoes folks converge with veggie-burger-hold-the-cheese types. There are a few special cases that pertain to older children and teens who might be dealing with issues of social acceptance.

Eating in the school cafeteria

There's no getting around it — it's tough to find a healthy school lunch, and it's tougher to find a healthy vegetarian school meal. Even the U.S. Department of Agriculture's surveys of its own program have found that most, if not all, school meals are too high in fat and too low in fiber and do not meet the department's Dietary Guidelines for Americans.

Over the past several years, lots of time, energy, and money have been poured into revamping school meals programs and bringing them into compliance with current dietary recommendations. The fact is, however, that they aren't anywhere close to being there. Steps have been taken in the right direction, though, and some of the changes in regulations that have taken place over the past few years have made more vegetarian options feasible. (But *feasible* doesn't necessarily mean *available*.)

For instance, yogurt can be served and credited to schools as a meat replacement, and nondairy cheeses can be served in lieu of dairy cheeses if they are nutritionally similar. Schools also have the option of using a nutrient-based menu planning system if they so choose. A nutrient-based menu planning system allows the school to evaluate meals based on overall nutritional composition, rather than on whether a meal consists of a specified number of servings from various food groups. Theoretically, a nutrient-based system would make it easier to offer meatless menus because servings from the "meat group" wouldn't be mandatory. In reality, a rare few schools in the United States are using this system because changing to the new system from the old food groups system would take more time and energy than most schools are willing to devote. Why bother, when the regulations permit them to continue using the old system?

To be fair to the schools, I should point out that the issue is complex. The system has limitations, and radical changes can't be expected to take place overnight. School food-service personnel certainly have the kids' best interests at heart. It's just that kids who want vegetarian options at school aren't going to find many, and kids who want vegan options are going to find even fewer. What to do? Here are some ideas:

 ✔ Take a bag lunch. If it's not too uncool, your child might want to consider packing a lunch from home. Neither hummus nor peanut butter need refrigeration for the few hours that they're in a locker before lunch. A bagel, a muffin, some carrot sticks with some hummus or salsa for dip, and some fresh fruit are also portable and practical. If a microwave oven is available at school, soup cups are convenient and add variety. Just add hot water, stir, and it's a meal. You can also buy vegetarian chili and rice or pasta dishes that only require hot water to become a hot lunch. Natural foods stores usually have the biggest selection.

✔ If your child wouldn't be caught dead with a bag lunch, then there are a couple of other options. Ask the school for a copy of the cafeteria menu. You and your child can sit down together and peruse the menu for the best choices each day. Think about whether an entrée could be easily modified by the school to make it vegetarian. For instance, if macaroni and cheese with ham is on the menu, could the school set aside one serving without ham for your child? If spaghetti with meat sauce is scheduled, with a day's or two days' notice, could the school provide a meatless sauce for your child? If there's not going to be an appropriate vegetarian entrée, could your child take one or two side dishes from the cafeteria line and supplement them with something brought from home, such as a sandwich?

If it hasn't occurred to you that your child may not share your enthusiasm for eating a vegan or vegetarian diet at school, give it some thought. Though surveys show that kids are adopting vegetarian diets at twice the rate of adults, your child may or may not want to comply away from home. Most experienced vegetarians find that strong-arm tactics do little good in getting kids to eat what parents want them to eat. Set a good example at home, encourage your child to eat well while away, then let your child choose. See Chapter 11 for more on getting (and keeping) your children on a vegetarian diet.

Finding satisfactory vegetarian meal options at school can be a frustrating experience, but it's not impossible. Because the circumstances are different for each student and each school, you might also want to consider sitting down with school food service personnel and discussing practical solutions that both your child and the school can live with.

Weighing the weight issue

Older children and teens are body conscious. More likely than not, the girls want to lose weight and the boys want to gain it.

If diet is the cause of too much pudge, the culprits are probably chips, candy bars, fast foods, and other sweets and fatty foods. Clean up your child's diet. Replace the junk foods with more fresh fruits and bigger helpings of vegetables, whole grains, and legumes. Offer a lentil soup cup instead of a large order of fries. Give your child a big apple instead of a bag of nacho chips.

Dissecting your school's biology curriculum

The biology curriculum in many schools calls for the dissection of animals. There may be options for kids who have an ethical objection to learning about anatomy this way. Some cities and states have policies that give students alternatives, such as plastic models and computer simulations of dissections. At least three states — California, Florida, and Pennsylvania — have laws giving students the right to use an alternative method. Students who want to learn more about alternatives to dissection can contact the National Antivivisection Society's toll-free hotline for more information — 800-922-FROG or call 312-427-6065.

If the diet is already up to snuff, then the answer is probably exercise — lack thereof. Encourage your child to get moving. For teens, aerobics classes, school sports, and weight lifting are excellent ways of increasing cardiovascular fitness as well as overall strength, and burning more calories will help with weight loss. Suggest that your child take up biking, hiking, or canoeing. Switch activities depending on the season. Snow ski in the winter and swim in the summer. Mix it up to avoid getting into a rut. Go in-line skating with your child on cool, sunny days and play racquetball at the gym when the weather is poor. Make physical activity a permanent part of your family's lifestyle now so that you can keep your weight down as both you and your children age. Weight lifting at the gym may not be appropriate for younger kids, but you can get them involved in swimming lessons, tennis, figure skating, gymnastics, and other age-appropriate activities.

Eating disorders are more common in teens — especially girls — than in adults. There's no cause-and-effect relationship between vegetarian diets and eating disorders, such as anorexia nervosa (self-starvation) and bulimia (bingeing and purging). Some anorexics do stop eating meat, but it's likely to be because to the effects of the anorexia cause a loss of the taste for meat. Being vegetarian in itself does not induce an eating disorder. Eating disorders have psychological origins, and people with eating disorders need psychiatric or psychological intervention.

Teen boys are more likely than teen girls to feel that they are too skinny. Nature will probably take its course, and today's string bean will be tomorrow's 40 regular. It just happens sooner for some beans than for others, and the waiting and comparing of physiques can get a little nerve-wracking.

So, if your teen wants to gain weight, the way to do it is simply to eat more of "the good stuff." Increase serving sizes at meals, and add healthful snacks between meals. Smoothies and juice blends add easy, quick calories. Increasing weight-bearing exercise — within limits, of course — will also help the body to add more muscle tissue.

Feeding your vegetarian teen athlete

If your teen is active in sports, you may wonder if he or she is getting enough protein, other nutrients, and calories on a vegetarian diet. The quick answer is this: Teens have greater needs for some nutrients than adults do to begin with because they are in a period of rapid growth and development, and being vigorously physically active increases those needs slightly. However, teens who are physically active usually also take in more calories to accommodate their higher activity levels. Assuming that those extra calories are coming from wholesome foods and not junk, teens will get the additional nutrients they need in the extra calories they'll be consuming.

The increase in nutritional needs resulting from physical activity is really very small for most "non-elite" athletes and is essentially inconsequential. Nutrient recommendations have a generous margin of safety worked in. Professional and Olympic-level athletes are the people who may truly have substantially increased needs for certain nutrients and may have to be more careful in planning their diets. (See Chapter 25 for more on vegetarian diets for serious athletes.)

The Vegetarian Resource Group publishes the brochure "Vegetarian Nutrition for Teenagers!" For a free copy, send a self-addressed, stamped business-sized envelope to VRG, PO Box 1463, Baltimore, MD 21203, or call 410-366-8343.

Chapter 24

Aging Healthfully: Vegetarianism for Older Adults

....

In This Chapter

▶ Exploring the nutritional needs of aging adults

▶ Reducing common age-related problems through diet

▶ Combining vegetarian and therapeutic diets to combat illness

▶ Simplifying meal preparation

....

*H*ave you hit the age of 40 yet? If so, have you noticed how much younger you seem (in your own eyes) as compared to your parents at the same age? True, your perspective is different now. But your parents at 70 years of age seem so much younger than your grandparents did at the same age. It's not just a matter of fashion. People are staying healthy longer these days. It's not completely uncommon to meet someone who is 100 years old.

More people are enjoying a generally healthy and vital old age, but age-related health problems *do* increase as we age. We consider conditions such as constipation, hemorrhoids, and weight gain to be normal parts of the aging process. We figure that diabetes and high blood pressure are bound to crop up eventually. After all, other elderly family members have had the same ailments.

The science of *gerontology*, the study of normal aging, is still young, but scientists are gaining insights into some of the aspects of aging that most of us take for granted as being part of growing old. A similar pattern of changes takes place among all humans as we age, but these changes occur at different times for different individuals. Some people never develop certain conditions. These differences among people can be due to genetics as well as lifestyle factors.

Diet is one lifestyle factor that makes an undeniable difference in the way people age. Vegetarians have lower rates of coronary artery disease, high blood pressure, diabetes, some forms of cancer, obesity, gallstones, and kidney stones than do nonvegetarians. Vegetarians generally also live longer than nonvegetarians. Granted, some of the health and longevity differences may be due to lifestyle factors such as a higher level of physical activity and not smoking, which are more typical of vegetarians than of nonvegetarians. But a vegetarian diet confers nutritional advantages, too, and these translate into improved quality of life for many older adults.

This chapter examines some of the ways in which a vegetarian diet affects older adults and presents strategies for minimizing many age-related discomforts.

Monitoring Your Nutritional Needs as You Age

Older folks have been at the back of the line when it comes to research on the body's nutritional needs throughout the lifecycle. Nutrition scientists are getting there, but we still know very little about how the aging process affects the body's ability to digest, absorb, and retain nutrients. Until we know more, recommended intakes for most nutrients for older adults are simply extrapolated from the recommendations for younger people. However, we do know a few things, such as how metabolism and the body's need for certain nutrients change with age.

Declining metabolism and its effects

Yes, what you've always heard is true: Your metabolism declines as you age. Unfair! Unfair! But the sad hard fact is that you need fewer calories the older you get, assuming that your physical activity level stays the same. In fact, if your activity level decreases, then your calorie needs decline even further. Oh, woe!

It gets worse. If you consume fewer calories, your intakes of protein, vitamins, minerals, and other nutrients also decrease. Unfortunately, as far as anyone knows right now, your nutritional needs do not diminish. Your needs for certain nutrients may actually rise. So, that means that you have to be extra careful to eat well. You have to get the same amount of nutrition that you got when you were younger (and eating more calories), but you have to get it in less food. If you haven't caught my drift, that means that you have to eat fewer *empty-calorie foods*. Less junk. Fewer sweets, snack chips, cakes, cookies, candy, soft drinks, and alcohol. Empty-calorie foods are nutritional freeloaders — they displace more nutrient-dense foods and provide little nutrition in exchange for the calories.

Increasing needs for certain nutrients

A great deal of research is still needed on how nutritional needs change for older people, but scientists are reasonably sure that needs do change. That may be due, in part, to the fact that absorption of certain nutrients declines with age. For example, older people are thought to produce less stomach acid, which is vital in helping the body absorb vitamin B12. That's why the recently revised federal recommendations for vitamin B12 intake for older adults were raised to 3 micrograms per day, whereas the vitamin B12 recommendation for younger people is 2 micrograms. This is especially noteworthy for older vegans, who need to be careful to have a reliable source of vitamin B12 in their diets.

Calorie and protein needs

Here's more food for thought: If you are an elderly couch potato, your calorie needs may be very low. In that case, your intake of many nutrients may be marginal or inadequate because you may not be eating very much. If you're a vegetarian and your calorie intake is low, your protein intake may actually be an issue.

Some scientists think that protein needs are somewhat higher for older people than for younger adults. Because vegetarians already get less protein than nonvegetarians — which is usually an advantage — intakes for elderly people who have low calorie intakes may dip *too* low. If this is the case with you, be sure to add plenty of protein-rich foods to your diet.

Vitamin D and calcium needs

Current research also indicates that older people don't manufacture as much vitamin D, and some scientists think that vitamin D needs for older people may be as high as twice the current recommendations. On the other hand, if vitamin D production naturally decreases with age, maybe that's the way nature intended it to be. In either case, older adults need to have a source of vitamin D in their diets or have enough sunlight exposure to allow them to produce it. If you are an elderly vegetarian who doesn't drink milk or eat other dairy products, be aware of this because you can't count on getting your vitamin D from fortified dairy products as other people do. If your exposure to sunlight is limited, use vitamin D – fortified foods such as some brands of soymilk, or get your vitamin D from a supplement.

Vitamin D and calcium work hand-in-hand to keep your bones strong. Bone loss accelerates with age, so recommendations for calcium intake are higher for older people than for people in middle age. All the more reason for older folks to be frugal with their calories and save them for nutritious foods, rather than filling up on sweets and junk.

Making Your Diet Work for You

You knew you were getting old when your eyebrows started turning gray. Or when that stray hair sprouted on your chin. Yeah, things were changing.

Besides the obvious outward signs of aging — wrinkles, lines, and gray hair — there are other common complaints of people when they get older. Most have to do in some way with the digestive tract. People start getting constipated, or they have more trouble with heartburn and indigestion. Some of these problems are a result of a decrease in the production of the stomach secretions that aid digestion, or they're in some other way a result of the body not functioning as efficiently as it once did.

On the other hand, many of these problems are the result of lifelong assaults on the body via a poor diet or lack of regular exercise or any of a host of other destructive habits, such as smoking or abusing alcohol. For instance, if you've been exercising, eating plenty of fiber, and drinking enough water for the past 20 years, you're much less likely than other people to have hemorrhoids or varicose veins.

The general dietary recommendations for older adults are actually not dissimilar to those for younger people. Get enough calories to meet your energy needs and maintain an ideal weight, eat a variety of wholesome foods, including fruits, vegetables, whole grains, legumes, and a limited number of seeds and nuts. Drink plenty of fluids, and limit the sweets, junk, and other empty-calorie foods.

Eating a vegetarian diet can help prevent or delay many of the common problems associated with getting older, and a vegetarian diet can also help alleviate some of the problems once they've developed.

Controlling constipation

Constipation is nearly always due to dietary factors. Regardless of your age, you need plenty of fiber in your diet from fruits, whole grains, vegetables, and legumes, plus plenty of fluids. (See Chapter 2 for more on fiber.) Regular exercise also helps to promote normal laxation.

Older adults develop problems with constipation when their calorie intakes dip too low. They're eating less, so they take in less fiber. If they're eating too many desserts and junk foods, they may be getting even less fiber. Older people are also notorious for being physically inactive. Both of these factors — low fiber intake and low activity level — can cause you to become constipated.

Constipation can be made worse if you are taking certain medications, including antacids made with aluminum hydroxide or calcium carbonate, or if you are a habitual laxative user.

You can take steps to get yourself "moving" again. Keep the following points in mind:

✔ You can't have too much fiber in your diet. Be sure to eat plenty of fresh fruit, vegetables, whole-grain breads and cereal products, and legumes. Review Chapter 2 for more information about dietary fiber.

✔ Make it a habit to drink fluids frequently. Water is best. You don't necessarily have to count eight glasses per day, but keep a pitcher of water on your desk and a bottle of water in your car, and drink them regularly. Stopping for a sip every time you pass a water fountain is a good idea.

✔ Prunes and prune juice have a laxative effect for many people.

✔ Keeping fatty foods and junk foods to a minimum is smart because these foods are usually low in fiber and will displace other foods that might contribute fiber to your diet.

✔ You won't be as likely to need antacids if you keep your fat intake low. Fat takes longer to digest than other nutrients, so it stays in the stomach longer and can promote indigestion and heartburn.

✔ Regular physical activity keeps your muscles (including those in your abdomen) toned and helps to prevent constipation.

Because vegetarian diets tend to be lower in fat and higher in fiber than non-vegetarian diets, elderly vegetarians are less likely to have problems with constipation than elderly nonvegetarians.

Healing heartburn

Vegetarians have less heartburn than nonvegetarians because they tend to have less fat in their diets. If you are a vegetarian and do have trouble with heartburn, examine your diet. You may be eating too many high-fat dairy products or greasy junk foods such as chips, donuts, and french fries.

Staying physically active and healthy

Regular exercise is an important component of a healthy lifestyle, and it's just as important for older adults as it is for younger people. When you're regularly and vigorously physically active, you burn more calories. Therefore, you can eat more. The more food you consume, the more likely it is that you'll get the nutrients you need. You're likely to preserve more bone and muscle tissues, too, when you exercise regularly, especially when the activity is weight-bearing exercise, such as walking or using weight sets. If you stay physically active, you'll also be more likely to keep your weight at an ideal level.

In addition to cutting the fat in your diet, you can help prevent heartburn by avoiding reclining immediately after a meal. If you do lie down for a nap after lunch, put a couple pillows under your back so that you're elevated at least 30 degrees and aren't lying flat. Avoid overeating, and try eating smaller, more frequent meals.

Getting a grip on gas

You may prefer to call it "flatulence." By any name, it's intestinal gas, which can be caused by a number of things, including the higher fiber content of a vegetarian diet. More than just a social problem, gas can cause discomfort in your abdomen, and it can cause you to belch or feel bloated. Before you incriminate your beans and cabbage, though, a few other causes of gas could be exacerbating your problem, including carbonated beverages, swallowing too much air when you're eating, and certain medications.

If you do think your diet is the problem, though, you've got a few options. Consider these gas-busters:

- Single out the foods that are the culprits. Beans? Cabbage? Onions? Eliminate one at a time until you reduce your gas production to a level you can live with. The foods that cause gas in one individual don't necessarily cause gas in everyone else and, unfortunately, the foods that do cause gas are among the most nutritious.

- Try using a product such as Beano, which uses enzymes to break down some of the carbohydrate that causes gas. Products such as these come in liquid form — you squeeze a few drops on the food before you eat it. Its effectiveness varies from person to person.

- Get active. People who exercise regularly have fewer problems with gas.

- Give it time. If you're new to a vegetarian diet, your body will adjust to the increased fiber load over several weeks, and your problem with gas should subside.

- Avoid carbonated beverages.

- Eat slowly and chew your food thoroughly to minimize the amount of air that you take in with each bite.

Fighting Disease on a Vegetarian Diet

You're diabetic and you follow a special diet? Maybe you're on a special diet for high blood pressure or heart disease? It doesn't matter. A vegetarian diet is compatible with restrictions for any diet and, in many cases, a vegetarian diet is the ideal for people with medical conditions.

For instance, if you have diabetes, you may be able to reduce the amount of medication or insulin you presently take if you switch to a vegetarian diet. The fiber content of vegetarian diets helps to control blood sugar levels. If your health care provider has told you to switch to chicken and fish instead of red meat to protect your heart, a vegetarian diet that limits high-fat dairy products and eggs would be even better.

Vegetarian diets are usually low in fat and high in fiber, so they can help you control your weight. Weight control is an important component of the dietary management of diabetes, heart disease, high blood pressure, arthritis, and many other conditions.

There's no reason that you can't eat a vegetarian diet, whatever your ailment. If you need help adapting a vegetarian diet to your special needs, contact a registered dietitian with expertise in vegetarian nutrition. The American Dietetic Association's referral service, 800-366-1655 or 312-899-0040, can help you find a dietitian in your area.

Making It Easy on Yourself

Do you have little time for shopping and preparing meals from scratch? Does arthritis make it difficult to open bottles and packages, or does poor eyesight make it difficult for you to read package instructions or drive to the grocery store? Do you live alone and find it difficult to cook for one?

You don't have to be old to want to make meal planning easier on yourself. There are lots of reasons for wanting your meals to be quick and convenient to prepare. There are also lots of ways to save yourself time and energy planning meals.

Cooking ahead

If you do cook meals from scratch — even occasionally — it's a great idea to make enough of a recipe that you can freeze part of it for later, when you don't feel like cooking. Foods that freeze especially well include vegetarian chili, lasagna, casseroles, cookies, muffins, quick breads, and soups. If you freeze them in small batches or single servings, they're even more convenient. Muffins and cookies can be taken out of the freezer one or two at a time. Other foods can be heated as needed.

When you make rice, make more than you'll need for one meal. Leftover rice will keep in the refrigerator in an airtight container or covered dish for a week or more. Reheat it and top it with vegetarian chili, black beans, or sautéed vegetables. You can even use leftover rice to make rice pudding. Just be careful not to let it sit too long!

Going natural

There's no legal definition for the term *natural foods,* but within the food industry it's generally understood to mean foods that have been minimally processed and are as close to their natural state as possible. They may have been altered by grinding, chopping, drying, freezing, heating, fermenting, or separating, but they have not been altered through a chemical process (such as the hydrogenation of oils). They are free of artificial flavorings and colorings, preservatives, and any other additives that do not occur naturally in the food. The term *natural* doesn't necessarily apply to hormone use, organic feed for animals, or environmental practices used to grow the food.

Eating prepared foods

Just because you don't cook doesn't mean you can't eat well. There's nothing wrong with occasionally having a bowl of whole-grain cereal with soymilk for lunch or dinner. Some commercial vegetarian frozen entrées are also good choices. Natural foods brands that you find in natural foods stores (and increasingly in the regular neighborhood supermarket, too) can be particularly good choices. They tend to be lower in sodium and higher in fiber than mainstream brands.

Try frozen bean burritos and dishes such as Indian curried vegetables, Chinese stir-fries, and others. Vegetarian burger patties are also quick and convenient. Some other good choices for quick meals or snacks include

- Flavored soy yogurt
- Soup cups (just add hot water)
- Packets of instant hot cereal
- Individual servings of canned fruit or soy pudding
- Boil-and-serve bags of frozen vegetable combinations
- Instant rice
- Bagels
- Vegetarian baked beans
- Fresh fruit
- Potatoes and sweet potatoes (microwave them or bake in the oven)
- Canned fruits packed in their own juice

✔ Whole-grain crackers

✔ Nut butters such as peanut butter and almond butter

✔ Fresh vegetables, precut and packaged, such as celery and carrot sticks and broccoli and cauliflower florets

✔ Canned refried beans or canned whole beans

✔ Flour tortillas

Banishing the blues

Many older people live alone. Some have lost a spouse or companion, and some feel depressed due to medications they're taking, physical disabilities, or complications related to preparing meals for and otherwise taking care of themselves. All these factors can make a person lose interest in taking care of himself or herself by eating well.

There are a number of ways of coping. Sometimes it's easier to eat smaller, more frequent meals or snacks than to try to keep up with a three-meals-a-day schedule. Relying on some of the quickie foods listed earlier can also be helpful. It may also help some people to eat in a group with others. Just being with other people is a good way to lift your spirits. Many local vegetarian organizations hold regular potluck dinner meetings, and some organize regular restaurant gatherings and special holiday meals. Getting active with a local vegetarian society can be a good way to meet others and to enjoy a meal in the company of others.

The National Meals on Wheels Foundation and the Vegetarian Resource Group (VRG) have created a four-week vegetarian menu for use in Meals on Wheels programs nationwide. The menus can also be used in other congregate meal settings or senior centers. The menus are lacto ovo vegetarian, but instructions are provided for adapting the menus for vegans, as well. The menu set is available, free of charge, by contacting VRG at PO Box 1463, Baltimore, MD 21203; phone 410-366-8343; e-mail vrg@vrg.org, Web site www.vrg.org.

Chapter 25

Maintaining Your Competitive Edge: Vegetarian Diets for Athletes

*E*veryone has a unique reason for going vegetarian. When I was 16 years old and a competitive swimmer, a book by Murray Rose caught my eye and inspired me to change my lifestyle forever. Murray Rose was an Australian swimmer who attributed his athletic endurance to his vegetarian diet. Rose was a three-time Olympic gold medalist and world record holder in swimming in Melbourne in 1956. He won a gold medal, a silver medal, and another world record at the 1960 Olympic Games in Rome. I'm not sure that the switch to a vegetarian diet improved my own athletic performance, but it didn't hurt, and the diet stuck.

In this chapter, the term *athlete* applies to a person who is vigorously physically active most days of the week for extended periods of time. Swimmers or runners or triathletes who are training hard are considered athletes. Going to the gym three times a week to work out on the stair climber and lift weights is great, but it's not enough activity to make any appreciable difference in your nutritional needs. Ditto for golfers and weekend warriors.

Sharpening Your Edge

Today, we know that vegetarian diets can be advantageous for athletes. Some, but not all, studies have shown that vegetarian athletes have greater endurance than those who are not vegetarian. What seems to make the most difference in athletic performance is the overall makeup of the diet. It is crucial that an athlete's diet consist primarily of carbohydrates, with adequate amounts of protein and fat. That describes most vegetarian diets to a tee.

Athletes who eat a typical U.S.-style diet that emphasizes meat have a much harder time getting the optimal mix of nutrients in their diets.

Can athletes do well on a vegetarian diet? You bet. A vegetarian diet is tailor-made for helping athletes achieve optimal performance. Table 25-1 presents a list of famous vegetarian athletes.

Table 25-1	Famous Vegetarian Athletes
Athlete (Country)	*Athletic Achievement*
Surya Bonaly (France)	Olympic figure skater
Andreas Cahling (Sweden)	Champion body builder and Olympic gold medalist in ski jump
Chris Campbell (USA)	Olympic wrestler
Desmond Howard (USA)	Professional football player and Heisman trophy winner
Peter Hussing (Germany)	European super-heavyweight amateur boxing champion
Billie Jean King (USA)	Champion tennis player
Carl Lewis (USA)	Olympic runner
Ingra Manecke (Germany)	Champion discus thrower
Bill Manetti (USA)	Power-lifting champion
Edwin Moses (USA)	Olympic gold medalist and world record holder in track
Martina Navratilova (USA)	Champion tennis player
Paavo Nurmi (Finland)	Long-distance runner, Olympic gold medalist and holder of 20 world records
Bill Pearl (USA)	Weight lifter and four-time Mr. Universe
Dave Scott (USA)	Six-time winner of the Ironman triathlon

Thinking again about packing in protein

Experts have different opinions about how much protein athletes need. Some question whether physical activity level affects the body's need for protein at all. Others feel that increased physical activity level does necessitate higher levels of protein, depending on the kind of activity.

Both the American and the Canadian Dietetic Associations recommend that athletes aim for 1.5 grams of protein per kilogram of body weight, or almost double the amount recommended for nonathletes. Some scientists differentiate and say that endurance athletes need a little less than that and strength athletes need a little more. The extra protein isn't needed primarily for muscle development, though, as you might think. Instead, it's needed to compensate for the protein that athletes burn up as fuel. Some athletes need a tremendous number of calories to meet their energy needs, and if they don't have enough fuel from carbohydrates and fats, their bodies turn to protein for energy. When that happens, they need extra protein in their diets so that enough will be available for building and repairing tissues. For more on protein, see Chapter 5.

Studies on the protein requirements of athletes have focused on young males. Female athletes and older adult athletes may have different needs. It's likely that the protein needs of female athletes are lower than those of male athletes, and the needs of older adult athletes may be higher.

Ensuring adequate protein intake

Because athletes need more calories than people who are less active, they tend to consume more protein via the extra food they eat. If you're one of these people, usually, just getting enough calories to meet your energy needs and eating a reasonable variety of foods is enough to ensure that you get the protein you need. This is especially true for endurance athletes, such as swimmers, cyclists, runners, and triathletes. If you are into strength training (weight lifting, wrestling, or football, for example), you need to be more aware of getting enough protein-rich foods in your diet, especially if your calorie intake is low. Any athlete who is restricting calories to lose weight while training should also be more careful to get enough protein.

Identifying foods that boost your protein

It's easy for athletes to add protein to a vegetarian diet. Each of the following foods would add at least 10 grams of protein (as well as other nutrients) to your diet:

- A large bowl of whole-grain cereal with soymilk
- A bagel with peanut butter
- A 12-ounce soymilk smoothie with wheat germ and strawberries
- 1 cup vegetarian chili over 1 cup rice
- A tempeh sloppy joe
- 1 cup soy yogurt with ½ cup Grape-Nuts
- A pita pocket with hummus and grated carrots
- A large baked potato topped with 1 cup lentil soup

✔ Two bean burritos

✔ A bean taco and a bean burrito

✔ A large plate of pasta tossed with olive oil and vegetables

Don't forget that there are advantages to getting your protein from plant sources. Plant sources of protein are associated with better kidney function and lower rates of some types of cancer and heart disease.

A little protein is a good thing, but too much isn't. In times past, it was a tradition for coaches to serve their football players big steaks at the training table before games. A baked potato with butter and sour cream and a tossed salad with gobs of high-fat dressing rounded out the meal. High-protein, high-fat meals like that actually make players sluggish and are generally bad for your health. Instead of a steak, athletes are better off with a big plate of spaghetti with tomato sauce, a heaping helping of stir-fry with vegetables and tofu, or bean burritos with rice and vegetables.

Cashing in with carbohydrates

It's well known that a diet that consists primarily of carbohydrates — vegetables, pasta, rice and other grains and grain products, fruits, and legumes — improves an athlete's stamina and results in better performance. Athletes who restrict their carbohydrate intake show poorer performance levels. It isn't surprising, then, that vegetarian diets have advantages for athletes, because vegetarian diets tend to consist primarily of carbohydrate-rich foods.

Fueling your muscles

When you eat a diet that is high in carbohydrates, your body stores some of the carbohydrates in the form of *glycogen,* a form of sugar that is stored in your muscles and liver. Your body calls on its stockpile of glycogen for energy during athletic events. Whether you engage in endurance events — such as swimming, cycling, or running — or in shorter, high-intensity activities — such as a ski jump or running a sprint or the high hurdles — your muscle and liver glycogen stores are a vital energy supply and a critical determinant of your ability to perform your best.

Getting the right kind of carbs

Getting enough calories and carbohydrate in your diet helps to ensure that the protein in your diet is available for the growth and repair of tissues and that it doesn't have to be sacrificed and burned for fuel. But not just any carbohydrates will do.

Old assumptions about carb loading

Athletes used to "carb load" before an event. They would restrict their carbohydrate intake and load up on fat and protein for a few days, and then they would then gorge on carbohydrate-rich foods for a couple days just before the event. The idea was that this method would maximize their muscles' storage of fuel and result in better performance. Now we know that it's more effective just to eat a high-carbohydrate diet all the time. Most vegetarians are, in effect, in a constant state of carbohydrate loading.

Soft drinks, candy, snack cakes, and other junk foods consist mainly of carbohydrates, but these are empty-calorie foods. Anyone who depends on their diet to help them feel and perform their best needs to take pains not to let the junk displace the more nutrient-dense foods from their diet. Junk-food forms of carbohydrates do provide calories, so they can help keep your body from needing to burn protein for fuel. But you need the nutrients in the more wholesome foods, too. You've got to look at the big picture, not just a little piece of it.

Good choices for carbohydrate include

- ✔ Pasta
- ✔ Beans
- ✔ Rice
- ✔ Potatoes
- ✔ Lentils
- ✔ Breads
- ✔ Cold and hot cereals
- ✔ Soymilk
- ✔ All vegetables
- ✔ All fruits

Actually, any combination of all of the items listed here can provide you with an excellent source of carbohydrates.

Some athletes have tremendously high calorie needs, and many carbohydrate-rich foods are bulky. They can be so filling that some athletes can get full at meals before taking in enough calories. If this is your experience, go ahead and include some low fiber, refined foods in your diet, despite the fact that most other people need more fiber. For instance, you may choose to eat refined breakfast cereals or white bread instead of whole-grain products.

Getting the skinny on fat

Everyone — athletes included — should limit their intake of saturated fat, and people who are overweight should limit their total intake of fat. But there are some situations in which a little extra fat added to the diet can be just the right move, particularly when the fat that's being eaten is from a plant source.

If you are having trouble getting enough calories on a vegetarian diet, it's fine to use a little extra peanut butter, almond butter, or olive oil on your toast, bread, or crackers. Avocado slices on a sandwich, guacamole dip, tahini, olives, seeds, and nuts are also nutritious and versatile. Just a little bit of any of these can boost your calorie intake by hundreds of calories. This is a little on the scary side for anyone who wants to lose weight, but useful information for the skinnies looking for a convenient source of extra calories.

Meeting Your Vitamin and Mineral Needs

Generally speaking, a well-planned vegetarian diet that emphasizes adequate calories and variety and limits the junk should provide athletes with all the nutrients they need. Under certain circumstances, though, a few nutrients may deserve some special attention.

Calcium

Athletes have the same needs for calcium as nonathletes, but some female athletes who train intensely may be at risk if their level of training causes *amenorrhea,* the cessation of regular menstrual cycles. Amenorrhea isn't caused by vegetarian diets; any female athlete may stop having periods when training too intensely. Like postmenopausal women, amenorrheal women have reduced levels of estrogen, and that can lead to accelerated loss of calcium from the bones. Of course, you already know that several factors affect bone health and that the amount of calcium you absorb and retain from your diet is more significant than how much calcium your diet contains in the first place. Nevertheless, if you are a female athlete who has stopped having periods or who skips periods, the recommendations for calcium intake are higher for you. That means you need to push the calcium-rich foods and make less room in your diet for junk. (See Chapter 6 for more information about calcium.)

Getting creatine from supplements

Many vegetarian athletes have questions about creatine supplements, which come in the form of creatine monohydrate. Some studies have shown that creatine supplements improve the performance of athletes engaged in high-intensity (as opposed to endurance) activities. Vegetarians get virtually no creatine naturally in their diets because it's found in animal muscles.

Companies that produce creatine supplements assure vegetarians that the supplements are not made from animal sources. Nevertheless, more research is needed before nutritionists can recommend creatine supplements to athletes, and the prudent choice is to avoid them for now. Rarely can any supplement beat the benefits of simply eating a healthful diet.

Iron

All athletes — vegetarian or not — are at an increased risk of iron deficiency due to iron losses in the body that occur with prolonged, vigorous activity. Female endurance athletes are at the greatest risk, as are athletes who have low iron stores. (See Chapter 7 for a refresher on iron.) There's no need to take a supplement unless blood tests show that you need one. Men, in particular, should avoid taking unnecessary iron supplements due to the connection between high intakes of iron and coronary artery disease.

Other vitamins and minerals

Vegans especially need to remember to have a reliable source of vitamin B12 in their diets. Some studies also show that exercise raises the need for riboflavin and zinc. Other research is pointing to advantages for athletes who get plenty of antioxidant nutrients (vitamins C and E, and the carotenoids) in their diets. But now we're speculating. Don't pull out your hair. At this point, the most practical advice for anyone is simply to do your best to eat well.

Planning Meals for Peak Performance

Whether you are in training or getting ready for an athletic event, what you eat and when you eat it can make a difference in your level of performance.

Before an athletic event

If you generally eat a high carbohydrate, vegetarian diet, you're ahead of the game already. When it gets closer to the time of the event in which you'll be competing, it's time to pull a few more tricks out of your sleeve.

In the hours before the event, you want to eat foods that are easy to digest and will keep your energy level up. High-carbohydrate foods are good choices, but now's the time to minimize your fat and protein intakes. Fat, in particular, takes longer to digest than other nutrients. You want your stomach to empty quickly to give your food time to get to the intestines, where it can be absorbed before you burst into action. That's the reason to keep your fat intake low at this point. Avoiding foods that are concentrated in protein is also a good idea immediately before an event because protein also takes a bit longer to digest than carbohydrate. That leaves fruits, vegetables, and grains as the best choices in the hours before an event.

It's also a good idea to avoid foods that are excessively high in sodium or salt because these foods can make you retain fluids, which may impair your performance or make you feel less than your best. Foods that are especially high in fiber are probably best saved for after the event, too, because you'll probably want your large intestine to be as empty as possible during the event. High-fiber foods can cause some people to have diarrhea and others to become constipated before athletic events, especially when they're anxious.

The best rule is to give yourself one hour before the event for every 200 calories of food you eat, up to about 800 calories. In other words, if you eat a meal that contains 400 calories, it's best to eat it two hours before the event.

Here are some good pre-event light meal and snack ideas:

- A bowl of cereal with soymilk
- A soymilk and fruit smoothie
- A bagel with jam
- A banana and several graham crackers
- Pancakes or waffles with syrup
- Toast or English muffins and 1 cup soy yogurt
- A tomato sandwich and a glass of fruit juice
- Cooked vegetables over steamed rice
- Pasta tossed with cooked vegetables or topped with marinara sauce

During an athletic event

Have you ever played a set of tennis in the blazing sun on a hot summer day or paddled a canoe or kayak for several hours on a river in the middle of August? If so, you might have needed as much as 2 cups of water every 15 minutes in order to replace the fluids your body lost during heavy exercise in the extreme heat. Many athletes don't pay enough attention to fluid replacement, yet it's critical to your health and optimal performance.

It's important to drink ½ to 1 cup of water every 10 to 20 minutes while you are exercising and, when possible, when you are competing. If you are working out in a gym, make it a point to take frequent breaks to visit the water fountain. One good gulp or several sips can equal ½ to 1 cup of water. In other settings, keep a water bottle with you on a nearby bench, in your boat, or strapped to your bike.

Water is the best choice for exercise sessions or athletic events that last up to 90 minutes. After that, there's a benefit to getting some carbohydrates in addition to the water to help boost your blood sugar and prolong the period of time before your muscles tire out. There may also be some benefit to eating or drinking carbohydrates sooner when the activity is of very high intensity, such as racquetball or weight training.

In these situations, it's a good idea to aim for about 30 to 80 grams of carbohydrates per hour. Sports drinks are fine for this purpose and may be more convenient than eating solid food. An added advantage is that they provide fluid as well as carbohydrates. For most brands of commercial sports drinks, that means aiming for ½ to 1 cup every 15 minutes, or twice as much every ½ hour. In lieu of commercial sports drinks, you might prefer to drink fruit juice diluted 1:1 with water. For example, mix 2 cups of apple juice or cranberry juice with 2 cups of water, and drink it over a 1-hour period.

Fruit is also a good choice for a carbohydrate boost. A large banana contains at least 30 grams of carbohydrates, and so do two small oranges.

After an athletic event

After the event or exercise session, protein can come back to your table. You need protein for the repair of any damaged muscles. Your body also needs to replenish its stores of muscle and liver glycogen, amino acids, and fluids. So, calories, protein, carbohydrate, and fluids are all very important immediately after an athletic event. The sooner you begin to replace these nutrients, the better. In fact, studies have shown that your body is more efficient at socking away glycogen in the minutes and hours immediately following the event than it is if you wait several hours before eating.

Staying at Top Speed with Practical Tips

REMEMBER

Here are a few final pointers for vegetarian athletes — or any athlete wanting to maximize athletic performance:

✔ If your calorie needs are high, add snacks between meals. Dried fruit mixtures, bagels, fresh fruit, soup and crackers, hot or cold cereal with soymilk, a half sandwich, soy yogurt or a smoothie, a bean burrito, or baked beans with toast are all excellent choices.

✔ If you have trouble getting enough calories with meals and snacks, reduce your intake of the bulkiest foods, such as salad greens and low-calorie vegetables, and eat more starchy vegetables such as potatoes, sweet potatoes, peas, beans, and lentils. Liquids can be an especially efficient way to add extra calories — try fruit or soy yogurt shakes and smoothies. Make your own blends, using wheat germ, soy yogurt and soymilk, and frozen or fresh fruit. Remember, too, that some added vegetable fats can be fine for athletes who need a compact source of extra calories.

✔ Take a portable snack in your gym bag, backpack, or bike pack for immediately after your workout to replace carbohydrates and protein and provide calories. Fresh fruit, a sports bar, a bagel, or a package of crackers and bottle of fruit juice are good choices.

✔ Keep fluids with you when you work out — fruit juice, sports drinks, or bottled water.

✔ Don't work out when you're hungry. Your session will suffer. Take a break and have a light snack first.

✔ If you get the pre-event jitters, eat only foods that are easy to digest and low in fiber. Some athletes who get too nervous to eat any solid food before an event may find that it's possible to drink a smoothie or eat some yogurt.

Part VII
The Part of Tens

The 5th Wave   By Rich Tennant

@RICHTENNANT

VEGETARIAN BUFFET

ZINC   B12   IRON   RIBOFLAVIN   CALCIUM

In this part . . .

*L*ike every other *...For Dummies* book, this one ends
with tidy tidbits of information presented in nifty lists
to make it easy for you to grab at a glance.

These final chapters offer some important parting shots of
advice on getting involved with vegetarian groups and jus-
tifying your switch to a vegetarian lifestyle.

Chapter 26

Ten Great Ways to Get Involved

In This Chapter

▶ Getting to know local and U.S. vegetarian groups

▶ Identifying compatible community resources

▶ Learning about other opportunities for action

*N*ow comes the fun part — putting your newfound knowledge into practice and reaching out to interact with other vegetarians. Not that you *have* to reach out to anyone, of course. You may be quite content to do your own thing, all by yourself. But if you are curious and inclined to investigate some of the resources that are available out there, you'll find some good sources of additional support and information.

This chapter introduces you to linkages with the wider vegetarian world that you might find particularly valuable or interesting. You'll find that there's a wide range of individuals and groups who practice a vegetarian lifestyle. They all have different reasons for their vegetarianism; different outlooks, approaches, and interests; and different things to offer you.

As you explore these resources, don't be surprised to find some of them weird and others wonderful. It's similar to experimenting with new foods — you'll find some duds and some new favorites. Likewise, what appeals to you may not be the same as what appeals to someone else. Investigate, stick with what you like, or move on to something else.

Connecting with Local Vegetarian Groups

If you live in a large metropolitan area, it's very likely that a local vegetarian organization is operating close by. If you live in a midsize city, it's also quite possible that there's a vegetarian group in your area. If you live in a small town, don't give up hope until you've checked around. It takes just one interested person to get a group started, and you may be surprised to learn that there's a vegetarian group alive and well in your little town. Local vegetarian organizations are thriving in some of the most unlikely places.

Local vegetarian organizations come in all shapes and sizes. Some are affiliated with churches such as the Seventh-Day Adventist Church, and some are affiliated with other philosophical, environmental, or political movements or groups. However, the vast majority are simply organized and run by people drawn together by nothing more than their desire to follow a vegetarian lifestyle.

You don't necessarily have to be a vegetarian to join a local vegetarian organization or to attend meetings. Some people attend just because they're interested in vegetarianism and want to learn more.

Local vegetarian organizations usually meet once a month or every other month in a particular location that can range from someone's house to a church community room or a room in the local library or other public place. Some groups even meet at restaurants.

Groups vary in what they do when they meet. Most groups' meetings are strictly social events and revolve around a potluck or covered-dish dinner. Every member brings a dish or beverage to share with the others. Many groups ask that members bring a note that describes the dish and labels it vegan, lacto vegetarian, or lacto ovo vegetarian. Nonmembers (and nonvegetarians) can usually attend, but some groups ask that people who attend without bringing a dish to share pay a nominal fee — typically $3 to $5 per person.

At some meetings, groups sponsor a speaker. The speaker may be a nutritionist or physician who discusses the health and nutrition aspects of vegetarian diets, or might be an environmentalist or local activist who speaks on a relevant issue.

Most meetings have an informal agenda of some sort. The president or presiding member may update the group about the status of the group's activities, such as hosting a booth at a local health fair, compiling a cookbook as a fundraiser, or providing local news of interest to members.

Some groups publish newsletters, and many sponsor special meetings or events around particular holidays or observances, such as Thanksgiving, the Fourth of July, or World Vegetarian Day, on October 1st. Restaurant gatherings are also popular events.

Attending meetings of a local vegetarian society can be a nice way to sample a variety of vegetarian foods and to discuss vegetarian issues with like-minded and sympathetic individuals. Many people form long-term friendships with other members, some of whom they may never have met otherwise.

There are several ways to locate a vegetarian organization in your area.

✔ Ask the manager of a local natural foods store. Vegetarian organizations often do business of one sort or another with local natural foods stores, so check with the manager to see if he or she can give you the name and phone number of a contact person. News of meetings may even be posted in the store's in-store newsletter, if there is one.

✔ Call a local Seventh-Day Adventist Church. If a vegetarian group is active in your area, the chances are good that the church knows about it. The meetings may even be held in the church community room, although the group may not have any other connection with the church. Another good bet is to call a Unitarian Universalist Church — another likely spot for vegetarian society meetings.

✔ Call a U.S. national organization such as the Vegetarian Resource Group (whose phone number is 410-366-8343) to see if they know of a group in your area.

✔ Check a local newspaper or an alternative-press paper for a mention of a vegetarian society meeting.

✔ Ask your friends. If your friends don't know of a local organization, maybe they know someone who does.

✔ If there is a college or university in your area, check with student affairs to see if there is a student vegetarian group on campus.

If there is no vegetarian organization where you live, why not start one yourself? You may be surprised at how many people will want to join. The Vegetarian Resource Group can provide you with materials to help you organize your own local group (for contact information, see Appendix A).

Joining U.S. National Vegetarian Groups

Several U.S. national groups promote a vegetarian lifestyle (see Appendix A for contact information). National vegetarian organizations serve a different function than local groups, although they can also be a good source of support for anyone adopting a vegetarian lifestyle.

Like local groups, national vegetarian organizations vary in many ways. However, they all tend to be more involved in advocacy issues on the national level than are local groups, which are more active in the local area in which they are located. They may publish a newsletter or magazine that is distributed to a wide national audience, and they may sponsor conferences or other events that draw participants from around the country and even internationally. They tend to address issues of general concern and interest to vegetarians everywhere and to report on events that happen nationally.

The differences between national and local vegetarian organizations are like the differences between the national and local news on television. It's nice to have both. One gives a bigger picture; the other keeps you up on what's happening close to home.

For an international perspective, visit the following Web sites:

✔ Vegetarian Society of the U.K. (VSUK) http://www.vegsoc.org/

✔ International Vegetarian Union (IVU) http://www.ivu.org/

Participating in Programs at Alternative Health Care Centers

If your community doesn't have a local vegetarian society or if it's not your style, there may be some other places where you can get support locally, such as at some alternative health care centers. These may be billed as mind/body centers, complementary or integrative medicine centers, or holistic health centers. Some are affiliated with hospitals, and others are independent. If they have a nutrition component, with nutrition counseling, cooking classes, or tours of a local natural foods store, they may be helpful to you.

Hospitals are jumping on the alternative health bandwagon and are setting up mind/body centers, complementary or integrative medicine centers, and holistic health centers. If you seek out information about vegetarian diets from a nutritionist or other health care provider at one of these centers, be sure that the person is knowledgeable and qualified to discuss vegetarian nutrition with you. Most dietitians and other health care providers have little, if any, experience or knowledge about vegetarian diets and may not be in a position to counsel you properly. Be cautious. Ask about the practitioner's experience with vegetarian diets. If he or she begins talking about concerns about protein, a need for lots of supplements, or in other ways appears unsupportive, say "thanks, but no thanks" and look elsewhere for guidance. Traditionally trained health care personnel are often still learning when it comes to alternative health matters.

Taking Cooking Classes

If your local community college, cooking supply store, or natural foods store offers cooking classes, you may be in luck. If they don't already offer classes on cooking with tofu and tempeh, vegetarian cuisine, Indian or Asian cuisine, or other subjects that interest you, request them. Schools and businesses will often add a course if there's a demonstrated interest in it.

Attending Health Fairs

Health fairs sponsored by the Seventh-Day Adventist Church typically provide a variety of resources concerning vegetarian diets. You don't have to be a church member to attend. In fact, the church typically advertises to the entire community and welcomes nonmembers.

Visiting Jewish Community Centers and YMCAs

Check with area organizations such as Jewish Community Centers and YMCAs to see if they have any events or activities planned that relate to natural foods, cooking (ethnic, vegetarian, or soy foods, for instance), or other topics that may relate to vegetarianism.

Calling Organic Gardening Clubs

Some communities have organic gardening organizations, which may be of interest to some vegetarians and through which you might meet other vegetarians. Inquire at your local gardening shop or natural foods store to see if anyone knows of one in your area. You might also search the Internet for local gardening clubs.

Celebrating World Vegetarian Day

Vegetarians around the globe observe World Vegetarian Day on October 1 each year. Watch newspapers and signs around natural foods stores for community events relating to this special day, such as vegetarian fairs, cooking demos, lectures, and dinners.

Observing the Great American Meatout

March 20 is the Great American Meatout, a nationwide, annual campaign that encourages people to "Choose life: Kick the meat habit." The Meatout is modeled after the successful Great American Smokeout public health campaign. For information about local events that may be planned, contact the event's sponsor, the Farm Animal Reform Movement (FARM), online at www.farmusa.org.

Participating in Earth Day

Many vegetarians also attend another annual observance, Earth Day. Watch for Earth Day events that may be publicized in your community, such as fairs and lectures. Vegetarian organizations are often represented at Earth Day events. There may be tables of literature or books for sale that would be of interest to you as well as tee shirts, bumper stickers, and food samples. Earth Day is April 22, though some communities hold events a day or two before or after that date, so that they can plan weekend activities.

Chapter 27

Ten Sound Reasons for Going Vegetarian

*I*f you need any more convincing to become a vegetarian, this chapter lists the bottom-line reasons for making the switch.

Talk to any veteran vegetarian, and you will probably find that one of these reasons was the thing that compelled that person to kick the meat habit. After that, other reasons gradually became apparent, adding weight to the original decision.

Which of these reasons speaks to you?

Vegetarian Diets Are Low in Fat

Generally speaking, vegetarian diets tend to be lower than nonvegetarian diets in total fat, saturated fat, and cholesterol. Vegetarian diets are associated with reduced rates of some forms of cancer, coronary artery disease, diabetes, high blood pressure, and obesity.

Vegetarian Diets Are Moderate in Protein

Vegetarian diets tend to be protein controlled. That is, they contain enough protein without being too *high* in protein. That's important, because lower protein intakes help your body conserve its calcium stores and lessen the burden on your kidneys.

Vegetarian Diets Are Full of Fiber and Phytochemicals

Unless you are a junk food vegetarian, your diet is likely to be far greater in dietary fiber than are nonvegetarian diets. Diets that are full of bulky fiber foods help to make you full before you fill out. In other words, you stop eating sooner because you feel full sooner. People who eat high-fiber diets tend to be leaner. They also have less trouble than others with constipation, hemorrhoids, varicose veins, and diverticulosis.

Fruit-, grain-, and vegetable-rich vegetarian diets are also high in phytochemicals, such as beta-carotene, vitamins E and C, and selenium, which promote and protect our health.

Vegetarian Diets Protect the Land

Livestock grazing causes *desertification* of the land by causing erosion of the topsoil and drying out of the land. Topsoil is being destroyed faster than it can be created due to people's appetite for meat. All over the world, we are losing irreplaceable trees and forests to make way for cattle grazing. By eating a vegetarian diet, you can contribute to minimizing this devastation.

Vegetarian Diets Conserve Water

Animal agriculture is one of the greatest threats to the world's supply of fresh water. Factory farms suck up tremendous quantities of water from aquifers deep beneath the earth's surface in order to irrigate grazing lands for livestock. Adding insult to injury, animal agriculture pollutes rivers and streams by contaminating water supplies with pesticides, herbicides, and fertilizers used to grow food for the animals. Nitrogenous fecal waste from the animals themselves compounds the problem. By choosing a vegetarian lifestyle, you can do your part *not* to support this contamination.

Vegetarian Diets Conserve Fossil Fuels

The production of meat, eggs, and dairy products makes intensive use of fossil fuels such as petroleum, which is needed to transport animal feed and animals as well as to run the machinery on the factory farms where animals are raised. Vote with your wallet — don't buy these animal products! By opting to avoid them, you can do your part to conserve fossil fuels.

Vegetarian Diets May Ease World Hunger

Vegetarian diets can sustain more people than can diets that center on meat and other animal products. When people eat foods directly from the soil such as fruits, vegetables, grains, legumes, nuts, and seeds, more people can be fed than would be fed if the food were first given to animals to produce meat or milk.

Vegetarian Diets Are the Choice of Compassion

Albert Schweitzer said, "Until he extends his circle of compassion to include all living things, man will not himself find peace."

Leonardo da Vinci said, "I have from an early age abjured the use of meat, and the time will come when men such as I will look on the murder of animals as they now look on the murder of men."

Enough said?

Meat Is a Turn-off

Some people go vegetarian for the simple reason that they don't like meat. They may not like the flavor or the texture. Or they may be turned off by thoughts of *Salmonella, Listeria,* and Mad Cow disease. Or they may not like the idea that they are chewing on someone's femur or thigh.

Vegetarians Are Thinkers

Vegetarians are in good company. Some of the greatest thinkers and philosophers — including Charles Darwin, Thomas Edison, Albert Einstein, Ben Franklin, Mahatma Ghandi, Sir Isaac Newton, and Plato — have advocated following a vegetarian diet.

Appendix A

Helpful Resources for Vegetarians

*W*ith this book, you have a solid introduction to all things vegetarian. The next step? Do it all over again. And again. And again. Not necessarily the same book — just the same topics. The reason? Let's face it, it takes most people several rounds before they absorb and understand a new subject well. Repetition is good. It helps us learn.

Besides, it's helpful to hear (or read, or view) the same subject matter presented differently by a variety of people or media. Sometimes, hearing the same information presented in a slightly different way is all it takes to make it "click."

The resources outlined in this appendix are not an exhaustive listing of everything that is available. They're a sampling of some of those that I have found to be the best. There's no need to rush out and read or see or contact every one of them immediately. Move along at whatever pace seems appropriate for you, and choose those resources that sound the most interesting. You may prefer books to videos, or you might have an itch to dive right in to cookbooks and experiment with new recipes.

Groups and Organizations

It's important to know where to go for great resources. The ones that follow will get you started.

The Vegetarian Resource Group

The Vegetarian Resource Group (VRG) is a U.S. nonprofit organization that educates the public about the interrelated issues of health, nutrition, ecology, ethics, and world hunger. The group publishes the bimonthly *Vegetarian Journal* and provides numerous other printed materials for consumers and health professionals. Materials are provided free of charge or at a modest cost in bulk, and many are available in Spanish. VRG's health and nutrition materials are peer reviewed by registered dietitians and physicians. VRG also advocates for progressive changes in U.S. food and nutrition policy.

You can reach VRG at PO Box 1463; Baltimore, MD 21203; phone 410-366-8343, fax 410-366-8803; e-mail vrg@vrg.org, Web site www.vrg.org. From VRG's Web site you can download and order materials, including handouts, reprints of articles, recipes, and more.

The American Dietetic Association

The American Dietetic Association (ADA) has two primary resources for vegetarians. One is contained within the public education arm of the organization, the National Center for Nutrition and Dietetics (NCND). You can call NCND at 800-366-1655 or 312-899-0040 and request one free copy of the brochure "Eating Well, the Vegetarian Way" or visit their Web site at www.eatright.org/ncnd.html. You can also request a copy of the ADA's position paper on vegetarian diets. Note that prerecorded messages on the ADA's consumer nutrition hotline (also 800-366-1655 or 312-899-0040) are funded by the food industry. It's common to hear messages with tips from such food industry groups as beef and pork producers, egg producers, cheese manufacturers, and the sugar industry, either directly or indirectly promoting their products.

The ADA offers a referral service for people who need individual nutrition counseling. You can call the ADA at 800-366-1655 to request the name and contact information of a registered dietitian in your area who has experience with counseling people on vegetarian diets.

The ADA also has a list of a subgroup of dietitians who have a special interest in vegetarian diets. Membership in the Vegetarian Nutrition Dietetic Practice Group (VNDPG) is open to all members of the ADA. However, the practice group's quarterly newsletter is available by subscription to anyone for a nominal fee. The newsletter is appropriate for anyone who needs up-to-date scientific information about vegetarian nutrition. You can contact the ADA at 216 W. Jackson Blvd., Suite 800, Chicago, IL 60606-6995; phone 800-366-1655 or 312-899-0040; Web site www.eatright.org.

The Physicians Committee for Responsible Medicine

The Physicians Committee for Responsible Medicine (PCRM) is a nonprofit organization of physicians and others who work together to advocate for compassionate and effective medical practices, research, and health promotion, including vegetarian diets. The PCRM publishes the quarterly newsletter *Good Medicine*. You can contact PCRM at 5100 Wisconsin Ave., NW, Suite 404, Washington, DC 20016; phone 202-686-2210; Web site www.pcrm.org.

The North American Vegetarian Society

The North American Vegetarian Society (NAVS) may be best known for its annual vegetarian conference, Summerfest, which is usually held in upstate New York in July. This casual, family-oriented conference draws an international crowd of 400 to 600 people with diverse interests. Nonvegetarians are welcome. Summerfest is an excellent opportunity to sample fabulous vegetarian foods, meet other vegetarians, attend lectures, and pick up materials from a variety of vegetarian organizations. The group also publishes *The Vegetarian Voice,* a newsletter for members. You can contact NAVS at PO Box 72, Dolgeville, NY 13329; phone 518-568-7970; e-mail navs@telenet.net, Web site www.}navs-online.org.

Information on Food Ingredients and the Nutritional Content of Foods

The VRG's Web site presents information on food content. Visit www.vrg.org/nutshell/faqingredients.htm for detailed information about the sources of ingredients in foods. This site provides information addressing the most commonly asked questions about hidden animal ingredients, and it defines ingredients listed on food labels.

The U.S. Department of Agriculture (USDA) maintains a comprehensive nutrient database. You can go to www.nal.usda.gov/fnic/cgi-bin/nut_search.pl and look up the nutritional value of most foods.

Vegetarian Cooking

There are literally hundreds of good vegetarian cookbooks. Cookbooks are a matter of personal preference — some people like pretty pictures, some people want simple recipes, some want gourmet food, and others just look for spiral lay-flat bindings. You'll find the full range on this short list. It's an excellent starting point, but you might also want to go to a local library or bookstore and peruse the shelves for others that look appealing to you. The sample listed here is merely a taste of what is out there.

Note that the first two cookbooks contain some high-fat recipes, including recipes made with dairy products and/or eggs. I've included these cookbooks because they're considered classics and sentimental favorites among many vegetarians. However, other books listed here feature recipes that are low in saturated fat and cholesterol and/or are vegan:

- ✔ *The Moosewood Cookbook*. Mollie Katzen. Ten Speed Press, Berkeley, CA, 1977, 1992.

- ✔ *The New Laurel's Kitchen*. Laurel Robertson, Carol Flinders, and Brian Ruppenthal. Ten Speed Press, Berkeley, CA, 1976, 1986.

- ✔ *The Peaceful Palate*. Jennifer Raymond. Heart and Soul Publications, Calistoga, CA, 1996.

- ✔ *Simply Vegan*. Reed Mangels and Debra Wasserman. The Vegetarian Resource Group, Baltimore, MD, 1999.

- ✔ *Soy of Cooking*. Marie Oser. John Wiley & Sons, New York, 1996.

- ✔ *Tofu Cookery,* Revised Edition, Louise Hagler. The Book Publishing Company, Summertown, Tennessee, 1991.

- ✔ *Vegetarian Times Complete Cookbook*. Editors of Vegetarian Times magazine. Macmillan, New York, 1995.

- ✔ *Vegetarian Cooking For Dummies*, Suzanne Havala. Hungry Minds, Inc. Indianapolis, IN, 2001.

Mail Order Sources

If you prefer the convenience of mail order shopping, explore the following sources:

- ✔ The Mail Order Catalog at www.healthy-eating.com/
- ✔ Pangea at www.pangeaveg.com/
- ✔ Whole Foods Market at www.wholefoods.com/

For Traveling Vegetarians

The International Vegetarian Union (IVU) maintains a Web site that gives translations of common vegetarian phrases in virtually any language. Visit the IVU site at www.ivu.org.

Vegetarian Magazines

Recommended vegetarian magazines include *Vegetarian Times* and *The Vegetarian Journal*.

✔ *Vegetarian Times* is a monthly magazine available by subscription or on newsstands. The magazine maintains a Web site at `www.vegetariantimes.com`.

✔ *The Vegetarian Journal* is the bimonthly publication of the VRG. *The Vegetarian Journal* is available on some newsstands and by subscription. For subscription information, contact the VRG at the address or phone number listed at the beginning of this appendix.

Vegetarian Newsletters

The following are two good vegetarian newsletters:

✔ The Loma Linda University School of Public Health publishes the 8-page newsletter *Loma Linda University Vegetarian Nutrition and Health Letter* for consumers ten times a year. For subscription information, contact Loma Linda University School of Public Health, 1711 Nichol Hall, Loma Linda, CA 92350; phone 888-558-8703 or 909-558-8621; e-mail `vegletter'h.llu.edu`; Web site `www.llu.edu/llu/vegetarian/subscribe.htm`.

✔ The Vegetarian Nutrition Dietetic Practice Group of the American Dietetic Association, publishes *Issues in Vegetarian Dietetics* quarterly. The newsletter is primarily for dietitians, but it is available to the general public. The content is generally technical in nature and includes peer-reviewed articles and reviews of current research findings relating to vegetarian nutrition. For contact information, see the section "The American Dietetic Association," earlier in this chapter.

For a listing of vegetarian restaurants in your area, check out *Vegetarian Journal's* "Guide to Natural Foods Restaurants in the U.S. and Canada," available at bookstores or by calling the VRG at 410-366-8343.

Appendix B
Terms and Definitions

• •

amaranth: An ancient grain that was a staple food of the Aztecs of Central America.

amenorrhea: The cessation of regular menstrual cycles in a woman.

amino acids: The building blocks of proteins. Amino acids have other functions in the body as well.

antioxidants: Phytochemicals that are present in abundance in plant products and help rid the body of free radicals.

athlete: For the purposes of this book, anyone who is vigorously physically active most days of the week for extended periods of time.

beta-carotene: A substance found in abundance in deep yellow or deep orange and red fruits and vegetables. It may protect against cancer and coronary artery disease.

cholesterol: A waxy substance that is a major component of the plaques that form in diseased arteries. It is found only in animal products; there is none in foods of plant origin.

complementary proteins: A practice whereby foods were combined in order to optimize their amino acid profiles. Eaten together, the foods formed a "complete protein." This practice is no longer considered necessary.

Creutzfeldt-Jakob Disease: See *mad cow disease*.

cruciferous: Vegetables in the cabbage family, including broccoli, bok choy, brussels sprouts, kale, collard greens, and turnip greens.

cyanocobalamin: The form of vitamin B12 that is physiologically active for humans.

debeaking: The practice of snapping off the end of a chicken's beak with a machine in order to diminish the damage that birds inflict upon each other with their beaks when kept in close quarters with other birds.

desertification: The slow death of the land caused by the overgrazing of cattle. The topsoil erodes and the land dries out, preventing it from supporting the growth of plant life.

empty-calorie foods: Foods that provide little in the way of nutrition in exchange for the calories they contribute to the diet.

essential amino acids: Amino acids that cannot be manufactured by the body and must be obtained from food.

free radicals: Molecules that damage the body's cells.

fruitarian diet: A diet that consists of only fruits, vegetables that are classified as fruits, seeds, and nuts.

gerontology: The study of human aging.

gluten: The protein portion of wheat.

hemochromatosis: A condition in which the body stores excessive amounts of iron.

heme iron: The form of iron found in meat, poultry, and fish. It's more readily absorbed by the body than iron that comes from plant sources.

hydrogenated fats: Fats that are often used in commercial baked goods and other food products. Hydrogenated fats stimulate the body to produce more cholesterol. See *hydrogenation*.

hydrogenation: A process that changes the chemical configuration of a vegetable oil in such a way that the oil is hardened.

iron deficiency anemia: A condition that results when the iron stores in blood are depleted and a person can't get enough oxygen to the cells of the body.

kamut: A type of grain that has been popular in Europe for generations.

lactase: An enzyme produced by infants and very young children. It allows human infants to digest lactose, the form of sugar found in milk. After infancy, lactase production diminishes or stops, except in most people of Northern European descent.

lactose intolerance: A condition in which a person can't digest the milk sugar lactose, since the mature body no longer produces the enzyme lactase. It is the normal condition of most of the adults in the world.

lacto vegetarian: A person whose diet excludes meat, fish, poultry, and eggs but includes dairy products.

lacto ovo vegetarian: A person whose diet excludes meat, fish, and poultry but includes dairy products and eggs.

leavening: An agent that provides lift to baked goods and helps them to be lighter in texture.

legumes: Dried beans and peas such as pinto beans, black beans, kidney beans, garbanzo beans, lentils, and split peas.

Listeria: A type of bacteria found on meats and in other animal products. It can cause severe illness and/or death.

macrobiotic diet: A diet that is sometimes classified as a type of vegetarian diet, even though it may include seafood. With the exception of seafood, a macrobiotic diet excludes all other animal products, as well as refined sugars, tropical fruits, and nightshade vegetables (potatoes, eggplant, and peppers). The diet is based on the Chinese principles of yin and yang.

Mad Cow disease: The popular term for Creutzfeldt-Jakob Disease (CJD). It is characterized by a progressive and fatal deterioration of the brain tissue, literally causing animals or people to lose their minds.

natural foods: Foods that have been minimally processed and are as close to their natural state as possible. This is not a legal definition, but one that is commonly accepted within the natural foods industry.

neural tube defect: A type of birth defect that involves an incomplete closure of the spinal cord. Folic acid, usually in ample supply in well-planned vegetarian diets, has been shown to help prevent neural tube defects.

nonheme iron: The form of iron found in plant foods. Nonheme sources of iron are not as available to the body as are heme sources of iron.

organic food: Food that has been grown without the use of synthetic fertilizers and pesticides, using farming methods that are ecologically sound. To be certified as organic, foods must be grown in soil that has been free of prohibited substances for at least three years. U.S. federal guidelines are pending that will give a legal definition to the term organic.

osteomalacia: A condition in which a lack of vitamin D causes bones to demineralize and soften.

osteoporosis: A condition in which the bones begin to waste away and become porous and brittle. This condition can lead to fractures, often with life-threatening consequences.

oxalates: Substances naturally found in certain plant foods (such as spinach, Swiss chard, and beet greens) that diminish the body's absorption of certain minerals. Also called oxalic acids.

pesco vegetarian: A semi-vegetarian who avoids red meat and poultry but eats seafood occasionally.

phytates: Phytates are substances naturally found in plant foods (such as wheat bran, cereals, and nuts) that diminish the body's ability to absorb certain minerals.

pollo vegetarian: A semi-vegetarian who avoids red meat and seafood but eats poultry occasionally.

protein: A vital part of all living tissues. Proteins are nitrogen-containing compounds that break down into amino acids during digestion.

quinoa: A high-protein grain that was used by the Incas in Peru and is becoming popular again today.

raw foods diet: A diet that consists primarily of uncooked foods.

riboflavin: Also known as vitamin B2. It has multiple functions in the body, many of which are related to enzyme activity. Requirements for riboflavin are related to our energy intake, so the recommended intakes vary according to calorie needs.

rickets: A disease that causes deformity of the bones and is prevalent in children who do not have access to adequate amounts of vitamin D.

Salmonella: A type of bacteria found on meats and in other animal products. *Salmonella* poisoning may be passed off as the "24-hour flu," though some cases can be serious and may result in death.

saturated fat: Fat that raises the body's blood cholesterol level and is found in large amounts in foods of animal origin such as red meats, the skin on poultry, and dairy products.

seitan: An Asian food made from wheat gluten.

semi-vegetarian: A person who is cutting back on his or her intake of meat in general.

spelt: A type of wheat that has been popular in Europe for generations.

strict vegetarian: A person who eats no meat, fish, poultry, eggs, or dairy products, but who doesn't necessarily avoid other animal products, such as wool, silk, leather, or nonfood items made with animal by-products.

teff: One of the oldest cultivated grains, it is used in Ethiopia today to make injera, a traditional bread.

tempeh: A traditional Indonesian soy food made from whole soybeans and sometimes mixed with a grain such as rice. It is fermented and pressed into a flat, rectangular block.

textured vegetable protein (TVP): A food that is made from soy flour that has been denatured by compressing the soy fibers. It's usually sold in granules that resemble ground beef when they are rehydrated. It may also be sold in chunks.

tofu: A traditional Asian soy food that is white, nearly odorless, and bland, and that picks up the flavor of the foods with which it is cooked.

trans fatty acids: Vegetable fats that have had their chemical compositions changed through a method of processing that hardens the vegetable oil. Trans fatty acids are associated with an increased risk of coronary artery disease.

transition foods: Foods that take the place of meat and serve as a crutch or "training wheels" to help people gradually adopt a vegetarian eating style. Examples include veggie burgers and vegetarian hotdogs.

vegan: A person who eats no meat, fish, poultry, eggs, or dairy products and who also avoids the use of other animal products, including wool, silk, leather, and any nonfood items made with animal by-products.

vegetarian: A person who eats no meat, fish, or poultry.

whole foods: Foods that are as close to their natural state as possible, or the least processed as compared to other foods in the same category.

Index

• *H* •

• *I* •

Notes

Notes

FOR DUMMIES®

A world of resources to help you grow

HOME, GARDEN & HOBBIES

Feng Shui
0-7645-5295-3

Gardening
0-7645-5130-2

Guitar
0-7645-5106-X

Also available:

Auto Repair For Dummies
(0-7645-5089-6)

Chess For Dummies
(0-7645-5003-9)

Home Maintenance For
Dummies
(0-7645-5215-5)

Organizing For Dummies
(0-7645-5300-3)

Piano For Dummies
(0-7645-5105-1)

Poker For Dummies
(0-7645-5232-5)

Quilting For Dummies
(0-7645-5118-3)

Rock Guitar For Dummies
(0-7645-5356-9)

Roses For Dummies
(0-7645-5202-3)

Sewing For Dummies
(0-7645-5137-X)

FOOD & WINE

Cooking
0-7645-5250-3

Cookies
0-7645-5390-9

Wine
0-7645-5114-0

Also available:

Bartending For Dummies
(0-7645-5051-9)

Chinese Cooking For
Dummies
(0-7645-5247-3)

Christmas Cooking For
Dummies
(0-7645-5407-7)

Diabetes Cookbook For
Dummies
(0-7645-5230-9)

Grilling For Dummies
(0-7645-5076-4)

Low-Fat Cooking For
Dummies
(0-7645-5035-7)

Slow Cookers For Dummie
(0-7645-5240-6)

TRAVEL

Italy
0-7645-5453-0

Hawaii
0-7645-5438-7

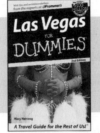

Las Vegas
0-7645-5448-4

Also available:

America's National Parks For
Dummies
(0-7645-6204-5)

Caribbean For Dummies
(0-7645-5445-X)

Cruise Vacations For
Dummies 2003
(0-7645-5459-X)

Europe For Dummies
(0-7645-5456-5)

Ireland For Dummies
(0-7645-6199-5)

France For Dummies
(0-7645-6292-4)

London For Dummies
(0-7645-5416-6)

Mexico's Beach Resorts Fo
Dummies
(0-7645-6262-2)

Paris For Dummies
(0-7645-5494-8)

RV Vacations For Dummie
(0-7645-5443-3)

Walt Disney World & Orlar
For Dummies
(0-7645-5444-1)

Available wherever books are sold. Go to www.dummies.com or call 1-877-762-2974 to order direct.

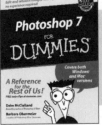

FOR DUMMIES®

The advice and explanations you need to succeed

SELF-HELP, SPIRITUALITY & RELIGION

Sex FOR DUMMIES
A Reference for the Rest of Us!
0-7645-5302-X

Parenting FOR DUMMIES
A Reference for the Rest of Us!
0-7645-5418-2

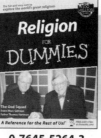

Religion FOR DUMMIES
A Reference for the Rest of Us!
0-7645-5264-3

Also available:

The Bible For Dummies
(0-7645-5296-1)

Buddhism For Dummies
(0-7645-5359-3)

Christian Prayer For Dummies
(0-7645-5500-6)

Dating For Dummies
(0-7645-5072-1)

Judaism For Dummies
(0-7645-5299-6)

Potty Training For Dummies
(0-7645-5417-4)

Pregnancy For Dummies
(0-7645-5074-8)

Rekindling Romance For Dummies
(0-7645-5303-8)

Spirituality For Dummies
(0-7645-5298-8)

Weddings For Dummies
(0-7645-5055-1)

PETS

Puppies FOR DUMMIES
A Reference for the Rest of Us!
0-7645-5255-4

Dog Training FOR DUMMIES
A Reference for the Rest of Us!
0-7645-5286-4

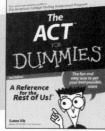

Cats FOR DUMMIES
A Reference for the Rest of Us!
0-7645-5275-9

Also available:

Labrador Retrievers For Dummies
(0-7645-5281-3)

Aquariums For Dummies
(0-7645-5156-6)

Birds For Dummies
(0-7645-5139-6)

Dogs For Dummies
(0-7645-5274-0)

Ferrets For Dummies
(0-7645-5259-7)

German Shepherds For Dummies
(0-7645-5280-5)

Golden Retrievers For Dummies
(0-7645-5267-8)

Horses For Dummies
(0-7645-5138-8)

Jack Russell Terriers For Dummies
(0-7645-5268-6)

Puppies Raising & Training Diary For Dummies
(0-7645-0876-8)

EDUCATION & TEST PREPARATION

Spanish FOR DUMMIES
A Reference for the Rest of Us!
0-7645-5194-9

Algebra FOR DUMMIES
A Reference for the Rest of Us!
0-7645-5325-9

The ACT FOR DUMMIES
A Reference for the Rest of Us!
0-7645-5210-4

Also available:

Chemistry For Dummies
(0-7645-5430-1)

English Grammar For Dummies
(0-7645-5322-4)

French For Dummies
(0-7645-5193-0)

The GMAT For Dummies
(0-7645-5251-1)

Inglés Para Dummies
(0-7645-5427-1)

Italian For Dummies
(0-7645-5196-5)

Research Papers For Dummies
(0-7645-5426-3)

The SAT I For Dummies
(0-7645-5472-7)

U.S. History For Dummies
(0-7645-5249-X)

World History For Dummies
(0-7645-5242-2)

Available wherever books are sold. Go to www.dummies.com or call 1-877-762-2974 to order direct.

FOR DUMMIES

We take the mystery out of complicated subjects